W9-BDU-193

Names: Feld, Brad, 1965– author. | Mendelson, Jason, 1971– author.
Title: Venture deals : be smarter than your lawyer and venture capitalist /
Brad Feld, Jason Mendelson.
Description: Fourth edition. | Hoboken, New Jersey : Wiley, [2019] | Includes
bibliographical references and index. |
Identifiers: LCCN 2019005878 (print) | LCCN 2019007456 (ebook) | ISBN
978-1-119-59485-7 (Adobe PDF) | ISBN 978-1-119-59484-0 (ePub) | ISBN 978-1-119-59482-6
(hardcover) | ISBN 978-1-119-59485-7 (ePDF)
Subjects: LCSH: Venture capital. | New business enterprises—Finance. |
BISAC: BUSINESS & ECONOMICS / General.
Classification: LCC HG4751 (ebook) | LCC HG4751 .F45 2019 (print) | DDC
658.15/224—dc23
LC record available at https://lccn.loc.gov/2019005878

Printed in the United States of America.

V10028724_080421

Venture Deals

BE SMARTER THAN YOUR LAWYER AND VENTURE CAPITALIST

Fourth Edition

Brad Feld

Jason Mendelson

Contents

Foreword by Fred Wilson (3rd Edition)

I remember the first week of my career as a VC. I was 25 years old, it was 1986, and I had just landed a summer job in a venture capital firm. I was working for three experienced venture capitalists in a small firm called Euclid Partners, where I ended up spending the first 10 years of my VC career. One of those three partners, Bliss McCrum, poked his head into my office (yes, I had an office in Rockefeller Center at age 25) and said to me, "Can you model out a financing for XYZ Company at $9 million pre-money, raising $3 million, with an unissued option pool of 10%?" and then went back to the big office in the rear he shared with the other founding partner, Milton Pappas.

I sat at my desk and started thinking about the request. I understood the "raising $3 million" bit. I thought I could figure out the "unissued option pool of 10%" bit. But what the hell was "pre-money"? I had never heard that term. This was almost a decade before Netscape and Internet search and so that wasn't an option. So, after spending about 10 minutes getting up the courage, I walked back to that big office, poked my head in, and said to Bliss, "Can you explain pre-money to me?"

Thus, began my 31-year education in venture capital that is still going on as I write this.

The venture capital business was a cottage industry back in 1985, with club deals and a language all of its own. A cynic would say it was designed this way to be opaque to everyone other than the VCs so that they would have all the leverage in negotiations with entrepreneurs. I don't entirely buy that narrative. I think the VC business grew up in a few small offices in Boston, New York, and San Francisco, and the dozens—maybe as many as a hundred—of main participants, along with their lawyers, came up with structures that made sense to them. They then developed a shorthand so that they could communicate among themselves.

But whatever the genesis story was, the language of venture deals is foreign to many and remains opaque and confusing to this day. This works to the advantage of industry insiders and to the disadvantage of those who are new to startups and venture capital.

In the early 2000s, after I wound down my first venture capital firm, Flatiron Partners, and before we started Union Square Ventures, I started blogging. One of my goals with my AVC blog (at www.avc.com) was to bring transparency to this opaque world that I had been inhabiting for almost 20 years. I was joined in this blogging thing by a friend and frequent co-investor, Brad Feld. Club investing has not gone away and that's a good thing. By reading AVC and Feld Thoughts regularly, an entrepreneur could get up to speed on startups and venture capital. Brad and I got a tremendous amount of positive feedback on our efforts to bring transparency to the venture capital business, so we kept doing it, and now if you search for something like "participating preferred" you will find posts written by both me and Brad on that first search results page.

Brad and his partner Jason Mendelson (a recovering startup lawyer turned VC) took things a step further and wrote a book called *Venture Deals* back in 2011. It has turned into a classic and is now on its third edition. If *Venture Deals* had been around in 1985, I would not have had to admit to Bliss that I had no idea what pre-money meant.

If there is a guidebook to navigating the mysterious and confusing language of venture capital and venture capital financing structures, it is *Venture Deals*. Anyone interested in startups, entrepreneurship, angel, and venture capital financings should do themselves a favor and read it.

Fred Wilson
USV Partner
July 2016

Foreword by James Park (3rd Edition)

I remember the first time I saw the exit sign for Sand Hill Road off of Highway 280. It was 1999. I was 22 years old, had just dropped out of Harvard, and was the cofounder and CTO of a startup based in Boston. My cofounder and I decided to cast the net wide in our search for money and flew out to Silicon Valley to meet with VCs. As I saw the exit for Sand Hill Road, I started to feel incredibly nervous and unwell. I immediately noticed the telltale signs of a distinct lack of preparation and knowledge. I felt this way if I hadn't studied thoroughly for a test in school. In high school, right before a cross-country race, I felt this way if I hadn't put in enough miles of running in practice. By this time, hadn't I learned my lesson about preparation and its effect on my digestive system? Why did I show up to such important meetings so uninformed about the people and the industry from whom I was trying to raise money? Well, in 1999, it wasn't so easy for a 22-year-old first-time entrepreneur to figure all of this out.

We did succeed in raising money for that startup, but due to our own mistakes and the tough environment at the time, we ended up closing our doors a couple of years later. However, I made a couple great friends, Eric and Gokhan, from that startup, and we picked ourselves up and immediately started another company called Windup Labs. After four years of incredibly hard work, we sold Windup to CNET Networks (now part of CBS Interactive) in 2005, and as part of the acquisition, we all moved to San Francisco.

In 2007, Eric and I left CNET to start Fitbit. Honestly, Eric and I started off with fairly modest ambitions for the company, but as the years passed, our ambitions grew. From 2007 to today, the company grew to over 1,500 employees, and our most recent guidance to investors called for approximately $2.5 billion in revenue in 2016.

We raised over $66 million in private capital from VCs, including Brad and Jason at Foundry Group. In 2015, Fitbit went public, raising over $800 million in the biggest-ever consumer electronics initial public offering (IPO) in history. I've remained its CEO from founding to today.

As I read this book, I was amazed at how succinctly it captured the sum of my 16 years of experience raising money and dealing and working with VCs and corporate lawyers. I wish I could travel back in time and hand this book off to my nervous and ill 22-year-old self (along with an iPhone and the idea for Facebook).

You, the reader, have gotten a huge bargain. After finishing this book, you will have skipped years of painful experience, trial and error, and learning on the clock from expensive lawyers. This is literally the business book equivalent of Neo jacking in and learning kung fu in an instant in *The Matrix*. As you find yourself driving down 280 (or depending on how long this foreword lasts, being whisked in your autonomous electric car) and the sign for Sand Hill Road comes into view, feel confident that you've been prepared the best you can with advice from some of the best VCs I know.

James Park
Fitbit Cofounder and CEO
July 2016

Foreword by Dick Costolo
(1st and 2nd Editions)

I wish I'd had this book when I started my first company. At the time, I didn't know preferred stock from chicken stock and thought a right of first refusal was something that applied to the NFL waiver wire.

Today, as the CEO of Twitter and the founder of three previous companies, the latter two acquired by public companies and the first acquired by a private company, I've learned many of the concepts and lessons in this book the hard way. While I had some great investors and advisers along the way, I still had to figure out all the tricks, traps, and nuances on my own.

My partners and I in our first company, Burning Door Networked Media, were novices, so we made a lot of mistakes, but we managed to sell the company in 1996 for enough money to keep ourselves knee-deep in Starbucks tall coffees every morning for a year.

Several years later, my partners at Burning Door and I started a new company called Spyonit. This company did better and was sold to a public company called 724 Solutions in September 2000. Our stock was tied up for a year (we weren't that tuned in to registration rights at the time) and when we got our hands on the stock in mid-September 2001, the collapse of the Internet bubble and the financial aftermath of 9/11 had caused our stock to decline to the point that it was worth enough money to keep us knee-deep in tall skim lattes at Starbucks every morning for a year.

So, like all good entrepreneurs, we tried again. This time, armed with a lot more knowledge and humility, we started FeedBurner in 2004. We raised several rounds of venture capital, including a seed round from DFJ Portage, a Series A round from Mobius Venture Capital (the firm Brad Feld and Jason Mendelson were part of at the time) and Sutter Hill, and a Series B round from Union Square Ventures. FeedBurner grew quickly, and before we knew it we had attracted acquisition interest from several companies, including Google, which purchased us in 2007 and allowed me to stop using coffee-purchase analogies to quantify the payout.

After spending several years at Google, I was recruited to join Twitter, where I now am the CEO. During my tenure with the company, Twitter has grown dramatically, from 50 people to more than 430 people, and has completed two major rounds of financing, having raised over $250 million.

When I reflect back on what I now know about VC deals, acquisitions, how VCs work, and how to negotiate, it's very satisfying to see how far I've come from that day back in the early 1990s when I co-founded Burning Door Networked Media. When I read through this book, I kept thinking over and over, "Where were you when I started out?" as the knowledge contained between these covers would have saved me a remarkable amount of time and money on my journey.

Brad and Jason have written a book that is hugely important for any aspiring entrepreneurs, students, and first-time entrepreneurs. But it's not just limited to them—as I read through it I found new pearls of wisdom that even with all the experience I have today I can put to good use. And if you are a VC or aspire to be a VC, get in the front of the line to read this to make sure you are armed with a full range of understanding of the dynamics of your business. Finally, if you are a lawyer who does these deals for a living, do yourself a favor and read this also, if only to be armed with things to use to torture your adversaries.

Dick Costolo
Twitter CEO
March 2011

Preface

One of the ways to finance a company is to raise venture capital. While only a small percentage of companies raise venture capital, many of the great technology companies that have been created, including Google, Apple, Cisco Systems, Yahoo!, Netscape, Sun Microsystems, Compaq, Digital Equipment Corporation, and America Online, raised venture capital early in their lives. Some of today's most significant entrepreneurial companies, such as Facebook, Twitter, Airbnb, LinkedIn, and Uber were also recipients of venture capital.

Over the past 25 years we've been involved in hundreds of venture capital financings. About 15 years ago, after a particularly challenging financing, we decided to write a series of blog posts to demystify the venture capital financing process. The result was the Term Sheet Series on Brad's blog (www.feld.com/archives/category/term-sheet), which was the inspiration for this book.

As each new generation of entrepreneurs emerges, there is a renewed interest in how venture capital deals come together. We encounter many of these first-time entrepreneurs through our activities as venture capitalists at our firm, Foundry Group (www.foundrygroup.com), as well as our involvement in Techstars (www.techstars.com). We were regularly reminded that there was no definitive guide to venture capital deals and decided to create one.

In addition to describing venture capital deals in depth, we have tried to create context around the players, the deal dynamics, and how venture capital funds work. We have tossed in a section on negotiation, if only to provide another viewpoint into how venture capitalists (at least the two of us) might think about negotiation.

We also took on the task of explaining the other term sheet that fortunate entrepreneurs will encounter—namely, the letter of intent to acquire your company.

With each subsequent edition of the book, we have added sections on alternative forms of financing, including convertible notes, crowdfunding, and initial coin offerings. Most recently, we've added sections on hiring a lawyer and an investment banker, as well as a detailed section on raising venture debt.

We have tried to take a balanced view between the entrepreneurs' perspective and the venture capitalists' perspective. As early stage investors, we know we are biased toward an early stage perspective, but we try to provide context that will apply to any financing stage. We also try to make fun of lawyers any chance we get.

We hope you find this book useful in your quest to create a great company.

Audience

When we first conceived this book, we planned to aim it at first-time entrepreneurs. We both have a long history of funding and working with first-time entrepreneurs and often learn more from them than they learn from us. Through our involvement in Techstars, we have heard a wide range of questions about financings and venture capital from first-time entrepreneurs. We have tried to do a comprehensive job of addressing those questions in this book.

As we wrote the book, we realized it was also useful for experienced entrepreneurs. A number of the entrepreneurs who read early drafts or heard about what we were writing gave us the feedback that they wished a book like this had existed when they were starting their first company. When we asked the question "Would this be useful for you today?" many said, "Yes, absolutely." Several sections, including those on negotiation and how venture capital funds work, were inspired by long dinner conversations with experienced entrepreneurs who told us that we had to write this stuff down, either on our blog or in a book. Well, here it is!

Before one becomes a first-time entrepreneur, one is often an aspiring entrepreneur. This book is equally relevant for the aspiring entrepreneur of any age. If you are in school and interested in entrepreneurship—whether in business school, law school, an undergraduate program, high school, or an advanced degree program—you will benefit from this book. We have each taught many classes on various topics covered in this book and hope it becomes standard reading for any class on entrepreneurship.

We were once inexperienced investors. We learned mostly by paying attention to more experienced investors, as well as actively engaging in deals. We hope this book becomes another tool in the tool chest for any aspiring investor, whether an angel investor or venture capitalist.

While we have aimed this book at entrepreneurs and investors, we hope that even lawyers will benefit from us putting these thoughts down in one place. At the minimum, we hope they recommend the book to their less experienced colleagues so that we can all speak a similar language around venture deals.

Finally, unintended beneficiaries of this book are the significant others of investors, lawyers, and entrepreneurs, especially those entrepreneurs actively involved in a deal. While our wives are quick to say, "Everything I've learned about venture came from overhearing your phone calls," we hope your life partner can dip into this book every now and then. This can be especially useful when an entrepreneur needs some spousal empathy while complaining about how a venture capitalist is forcing a participating preferred upon them.

Overview of the Contents

We begin with a brief history of the venture capital term sheet and a discussion of the different parties who participate in venture capital transactions. Following this is a section on preparing for fundraising and choosing the right lawyer.

We then discuss how to raise money from a venture capitalist, including determining how much money an entrepreneur should raise. This includes a section on how to properly prepare your company for fundraising and discusses the materials you will need before hitting the fundraising trail. As part of this, we explore the process that many venture capitalists follow to decide which companies to fund.

We then dive deeply into the particular terms that are included in venture capital term sheets. We have separated this topic into three chapters: terms related to economics, terms related to control, and all of the other terms. We strive to give a balanced view of the particular terms along with strategies for getting to a fair deal.

Following the chapters on terms, we discuss how convertible debt works and the pros and cons versus raising equity.

We next cover several alternative forms of fundraising, including product, equity, and token crowdfunding and how they differ from traditional venture capital deals. This is followed by a detailed section on venture debt.

We then go into a frank discussion about how venture capital firms operate, including how venture capitalists are motivated and compensated. We discuss how these structural realities can impact a company's chance of getting funded or could impact the relationship between the venture capitalist, her firm, and the entrepreneur after the investment is made.

Since the process of funding involves a lot of negotiation, the book contains a primer on negotiating and how particular strategies may work better or worse in the venture capital world. We attempt to help the entrepreneur learn ways to consummate a transaction in a venture capital financing while avoiding common mistakes and pitfalls.

Since there is no such thing as a standard venture capital financing, we cover different issues to consider that depend on the stage of financing a company is raising. We discuss some of the theories behind why any of these documents even exist so that you can understand the hidden incentives in the process.

As a bonus, we've tossed in a chapter about the other important term sheet that entrepreneurs need to know about: the letter of intent to acquire your company. We include a section on how and when to hire an investment banker to help you sell your company.

Finally, we end with a section on why term sheets even exist in the first place, along with tips concerning several common legal issues that many startups face. While it's not a dissertation on everything an entrepreneur needs to know, we've tried to include a few important things that we think entrepreneurs should pay attention to.

Whenever we introduce a new term, we italicize it. There is a glossary in the back of the book with short definitions for each of these italicized terms. Throughout the book we've enlisted a close friend and longtime entrepreneur, Matt Blumberg, the CEO of

Return Path, to add his perspective. Whenever you see a sidebar titled "The Entrepreneur's Perspective," these are comments from Matt on the previous section.

Additional Materials

Along with this book, we have created some additional materials that you may want to review, including resources for use of this book in a classroom. These materials are all on the Venture Deals website at www.venturedeals.com (referred to in previous editions as the AsktheVC website at www.askthevc.com). And no, the venturedeals .com domain wasn't very expensive.

Venturedeals.com started out several years ago as a question-and-answer site that we managed. We've recently added a new section called "Resources," where the reader can find many standard forms of documents that are used in venture financings. They include the term sheet as well as all of the documents that are generated from the term sheet as part of a venture financing.

We have provided the standard forms that we use at Foundry Group (yes, you can use these if we ever finance your company). We also included links for the most popular standard documents that are used in the industry today, along with commentary about some of the advantages and disadvantages of using them.

If you use our book in an online course or at a university, you will now find an extensive "Teaching" section on the website, along with several example syllabi.

As we complete the fourth edition of this book, we humbly appreciate all the support we have received and people we have met through our writing. Thank you all very much for allowing us to do what we do.

Jason Mendelson and Brad Feld
May 2019

Acknowledgments

We wouldn't have been able to write this book without the capable assistance of many people.

Huge thanks go to Matt Blumberg, CEO of Return Path, for all of his insightful and entrepreneur-focused comments. Matt provided all of the sidebars for "The Entrepreneur's Perspective" throughout the book, and his comments helped focus us (and hopefully you) on the key issues from an entrepreneur's perspective.

Our Foundry Group partners Lindel Eakman, Seth Levine, Ryan McIntyre, and Chris Moody put up with us whenever Brad said, "I'm working on Jason's book again," and whenever Jason said, "I'm working on Brad's book again." We couldn't do any of this without our amazing colleagues at Foundry Group, including our assistants, Jill Spruiell and Annie Heissenbuttel.

In this edition of the book, we appreciate the efforts of Cooley LLP (Eric Jensen, Sepideh Mousakhani, and Bill Galliani), Silicon Valley Bank (General Counsel Michael Zuckert, former Credit Research & Development Officer Derek Ridgley, and the SVB Legal and Marketing teams), and Rex Golding to help us craft chapters where their expertise was essential to us getting it right. Thanks for being great partners in our ecosystem.

A number of friends, colleagues, and mentors reviewed early drafts of the book and gave us extensive feedback. Thanks to the following for taking the time to meaningfully improve this book: Amy Batchelor, Raj Bhargava, Jeff Clavier, Greg Gottesman, Brian Grayson, Douglas Horch, David Jilk, T.A. McCann, George Mulhern, Wiley Nelson, Heidi Roizen, Ken Tucker, and Jud Valeski.

Jack Tankersley, one of the fathers of the Colorado venture capital industry, provided a number of his early deal books from his time at Centennial Funds. In addition to being fascinating history on some legendary early venture capital deals, they confirmed that the term sheet hasn't evolved much over the past 30 years. We'd also like to thank Jack for the detailed comments he made on an early draft of the book.

Thanks to Bill Aulet and Patricia Fuligni of the MIT Entrepreneurship Center for helping track down the original Digital Equipment Corporation correspondence between Ken Olson and Georges Doriot.

Our VC colleagues, whether they realize it or not, have had a huge impact on this book. The ones we've learned from—both good and bad—are too numerous to list. But we want to thank them all for participating with us on our journey to help create amazing companies. We can't think of anything we'd rather be doing professionally, and we learn something new from you every day.

We've worked with many lawyers over the years, some of whom have taken us to school on various topics in this book. We thank you for all of your help, advice, education, and entertainment. We'd especially like to thank our friends Eric Jensen and Mike Platt at Cooley LLP, who have consistently helped us during the fog of a negotiation. Eric was Jason's mentor, boss, and friend while at Cooley and originally taught Jason how all of this worked.

We'd like to thank one of Brad's original mentors, Len Fassler, for creating the spark that initiated this book. Len's introduction to Matthew Kissner, a board member at John Wiley & Sons, resulted in a two-book contract with Wiley, which included *Do More Faster: TechStars Lessons to Accelerate Your Startup* by Brad and David Cohen. Although *Do More Faster* was published first, the idea for this book was the one that originally captured the attention of several people at Wiley.

Brad would like to thank Pink Floyd for *The Dark Side of the Moon* and *Wish You Were Here*, two albums that kept him going throughout the seemingly endless "read through and edit this just one more time" cycle. He'd also like to thank the great staff at Canyon Ranch in Tucson for giving him a quiet place to work for the last week before the "final final draft of the first edition" was due.

Jason would like to thank the University of Colorado Law School and especially Brad Bernthal and Phil Weiser for letting him inflict himself on both law and business students while teaching many of the subjects contained in this book. Special thanks to Supreme

Beings of Leisure for providing the background music while Jason worked on this book.

A number of friends and colleagues found errors in previous editions, which we have corrected in this edition. Special thanks go to David Cohen, Anurag Mehta, Tom Godin, Philip Lee, Tal Adler, Jason Seats, and Jeff Thomas, who were the first to identify various errors. Thanks to Ian Herrick for all of his grammatical and spelling help with the fourth edition.

We thank all of the entrepreneurs we have ever had the chance to work with. Without you, we would have nothing to do. Hopefully we have made you proud in our attempt to amalgamate in this book all of the collective wisdom we gained from working with you.

Finally, we thank our wives, Amy Batchelor and Jennifer Mendelson, for putting up with us and making our lives so much more fulfilling.

Introduction: The Art of the Term Sheet

One of the first famous venture capital investments was Digital Equipment Corporation (DEC). In 1957 American Research and Development Corporation (AR&D), one of the first venture capital firms, invested $70,000 in DEC. When DEC went public in 1968, this investment was worth over $355 million, or a return of over 5,000 times the invested capital. AR&D's investment in DEC was one of the original venture capital home runs.

In 1957 the venture capital industry was just being created. At the time, the investor community in the United States was uninterested in investing in computer companies, as the last wave of computer-related startups had performed poorly and even large companies were having difficulty making money in the computer business. We can envision the frustration of DEC's cofounders, Ken Olson and Harlan Anderson, as the investors they talked to rejected them and their fledgling idea for a business. We can also imagine their joy when Georges Doriot, the founder of American Research and Development Corporation, offered to fund them. After a number of conversations and meetings, Doriot sent Olson and Anderson a letter expressing his interest in investing, along with his proposed terms. Today, this document is called the *term sheet*.

Now, imagine what that term sheet looked like. There are three different possibilities. The first is that it was a typed one-page letter that said, "We would like to invest $70,000 in your company and buy 78 percent of it." The next is that it was two pages of legal terms that basically said, "We would like to invest $70,000 in your company and buy 78 percent of it." Or it could have been an eight-page typed document that had all kinds of protective provisions, vesting arrangements, drag-along rights, and Securities and Exchange Commission (SEC) registration rights.

1

Our guess is that it was not the third option. Over the past 50 years, the art of the term sheet has evolved and expanded, reaching its current eight (or so) page literary masterpiece. These eight pages contain a lot more than "We'd like to invest $X in your company and get Y% of it," but, as you'll learn, there really are only two key things that matter in the actual term sheet negotiation—economics and control.

In DEC's case, by owning 78% of the company, AR&D effectively had control of the company. And the price was clearly defined—$70,000 bought 78% of the company, resulting in a $90,000 post-money valuation.

Today's venture capital investments have many more nuances. Individual venture capitalists (VCs) usually end up owning less than 50% of the company, so they don't have effective voting control but often negotiate provisions that give them control over major decisions by the company. Many companies end up with multiple VCs who invest in the company at different points in time, resulting in different ownership percentages, varying rights, and diverging motivations. Founders don't always stay with the company through the exit and, in some cases, they end up leaving relatively early in the life of a company for a variety of reasons. Companies fail, and venture capitalists have gotten much more focused on protecting themselves for the downside as well as participating in the upside. Governance issues are always complex, especially when you have a lot of people sitting around the negotiation table.

While it would be desirable to do venture capital deals with a simple agreement on price, a handshake, and a short legal agreement, this rarely happens. And while there have been plenty of attempts to standardize the term sheet over the years, the proliferation of lawyers, venture capitalists, and entrepreneurs, along with a steadily increasing number of investments, has prevented this from happening. Ironically, the actual definitive documents have become more standard over time. Whether it is the Internet age that has spread information across the ecosystem or clients growing tired of paying legal bills, there are more similarities in the documents today than ever before. As a result, we can lend you our experience in how venture financings are usually done. The good news is once you've negotiated the term sheet, you are done with the hard part. As a result, that's where we are going to focus our energy in this book.

Throughout this book we will cover not only the what and how of venture capital financings, but also why things work as they do. Let's begin our exploration by discussing the various players involved.

CHAPTER 1

The Players

While it might seem like there are only two players in the financing dance—the entrepreneur and the venture capitalist—there are often others, including angel investors, lawyers, accountants, and mentors. Any entrepreneur who has created a company that has gone through multiple financings knows that the number of people involved can quickly spiral out of control. This is especially true if you aren't sure who is actually making the decisions at each step along the way.

The experience, motivation, and relative power of each participant in a financing can be complex, and the implications are often mysterious. Let's begin our journey to understanding venture capital financings by making sure we understand each player and the dynamics surrounding the participants.

The Entrepreneur

Not all investors, bankers, and lawyers realize it, but the entrepreneur is the center of the entrepreneurial universe. Without entrepreneurs there would be no term sheets and no startup ecosystem.

Throughout this book we use the terms *entrepreneur* and *founder* interchangeably. While some companies have only one founder, many have two, three, or even more. Sometimes these cofounders are equals; other times they aren't. Regardless of the number, they each have a key role in the formation of the company and any financing that occurs.

The founders can't and shouldn't outsource their involvement in a financing to their lawyers. There are many issues in a financing negotiation that only the entrepreneurs can resolve. Even if you hire a fantastic lawyer who knows everything, don't forget that if your lawyer and your future investors don't get along, you will have larger issues to deal with, since the way your lawyer represents themselves will directly reflect on you. If you are the entrepreneur, make sure you direct and control the process.

The relationship between cofounders at the beginning of the life of a company is almost always good. If it's not, the term sheet and corresponding financing are probably the least of the founders' worries. However, as time passes, the relationship between cofounders often frays. This could be due to many different factors: the stress of the business, competence, personality, or even changing life priorities like a new spouse or children.

When this happens, one or more founders will often leave the business. This can happen on good terms or not, and experienced investors know that it's best to anticipate these kinds of issues up front and will try to structure terms that predefine how things will work in these situations. The investors are often trying to protect the founders from each other by making sure things can be cleanly resolved without disrupting the company more than the departure of a founder already does.

We cover this dynamic in terms like *vesting, drag-along* rights, and *co-sale* rights. When we do, we discuss both the investor perspective and the entrepreneur perspective. You'll see throughout the book that we've walked in both the investor's and the entrepreneur's shoes, and we try hard to take a balanced approach to our commentary. We have witnessed a lot of bad behavior on both sides of the table and will try to be clear about these difficult issues.

The Venture Capitalist

The *venture capitalist* (VC) is the next character in the term sheet play. VCs come in many shapes, sizes, and experience levels. While most (but not all) profess to be entrepreneur friendly, many fall far short of their aspirations and marketing campaigns. The first sign of this often appears during the term sheet negotiation.

Venture capital firms have their own hierarchies that are important for an entrepreneur to understand. Later in the book we'll dive into all the deep, dark secrets about how VCs are motivated, how they are paid, and what their incentives can be. For now, we'll consider VCs as humans and talk about the people.

The most senior person in the firm is usually called a *managing director* (MD) or a *general partner* (GP). In some cases, these titles have an additional prefix such as *executive managing director* or *founding general partner* to signify even more seniority over the other managing directors or general partners. These VCs make the final investment decisions and sit on the boards of directors of the companies they invest in.

Partners can be but often are not what their title says they are. Many VCs these days carry business cards with a "partner" title but are not actually partners in the firm. Instead, they are often junior deal professionals (also referred to as *principals* or *directors*) or are involved in specific aspects of the investing process, such as deal sourcing or due diligence. In some firms, which are described as *full-stack VC firms*, these partners help companies across a variety of dimensions, including recruiting, operations, technology, sales, and marketing, but are not decision makers in the investment process. Some firms give everyone a "partner" title regardless of whether they have decision-making authority. This is an old investment-banking trick (where everyone is at least a vice president) to try to blur the lines between GPs and non-GPs so that entrepreneurs don't really know the seniority level of the person they are interacting with. In the case of our firm, Foundry Group, we got tired of the pomp and circumstance of the MD and GP designations and now simply call each of the decision makers "partner."

Clear as mud? Good. As a founder, you should do your own due diligence into whom you are speaking to at any given firm. Figure out if the people you are spending time with have the authority to actually get your company the investment you are seeking. And, while we generally use the terms "managing director" and "general partner" throughout this book as the most senior partners in a firm, understand that their titles in real life could be as simple as partner. Or not.

Principals, or *directors,* are usually next in line. These are junior deal professionals working their way up the ladder to managing director. Principals usually have some deal responsibility, but they almost always require support from a managing director to move a deal through the VC firm. While a principal has some power, she probably can't make a final decision.

Associates are typically not deal partners, those who can lead an investment process inside a venture fund and effectively get a company funded. Instead, associates work directly for one or more deal partners, usually a managing director. Associates do a wide variety of things, including scouting for new deals, helping with due diligence on existing deals, and writing up endless internal memos about prospective investments. They are also likely to be the person in the firm who spends the most time with the *capitalization table* (also known as a *cap table*), which is the spreadsheet that defines the economics of the deal. Many firms have an associate program, usually lasting two years, after which time the associate leaves the firm to work for a portfolio company, attend business school, or start their own company. Occasionally, star associates become principals.

Analysts are at the bottom of the ladder. These are very junior people, usually recently graduated from college, who sit in a room with no windows down the hall from everyone else, crunch numbers, and write memos. In some firms, analysts and associates play similar roles and have similar functions; in others, the associates are more deal-centric. Regardless, analysts are generally smart people who are usually very limited in power and responsibility.

Some firms, especially larger ones, have a variety of *venture partners* or *operating partners*. These are usually experienced entrepreneurs who have a part-time relationship with the VC firm. While they have the ability to advocate for a deal, they often need explicit support of one of the MDs, just as a principal would, in order to get a deal done. In some firms, operating partners don't sponsor deals, but take an active role in managing the investment as a chairman or board member.

Entrepreneurs in residence (EIRs) are another type of part-time member of the VC firm. EIRs are experienced entrepreneurs who park themselves at a VC firm, usually for up to a year, while they are working on figuring out their next company. They often help the VC with introductions, due diligence, and networking during the period that they are an EIR. Some VCs pay their EIRs; others simply provide them with free office space and an implicit agreement to invest in their next company.

In small firms, you might be dealing with only MDs. For example, in our firm, Foundry Group, we have a total of six partners (previously called managing directors), each of whom has the same responsibility, authority, and power. In large firms, you'll be dealing with a wide array of MDs, principals, associates, analysts, venture partners, operating partners, EIRs, and other titles. Since we wrote the first edition of this book in 2011, there has been a huge amount of title inflation among VC firms: a person who was called an associate back then might now be referred to as a partner.

Entrepreneurs should do their research on the firms they are negotiating with, in order to understand who they are talking to, what decision-making power that person has, and what process they have to go through to get an investment approved. The best source for this kind of information is other entrepreneurs who have worked with the VC firm in the past, although you'd also be surprised how much of this you can piece together just by looking at how the VC firm presents itself on its website. If all else fails, you can always ask the VC how things work, although the further down the hierarchy of the firm the person is, the less likely you are to get completely accurate information.

The Entrepreneur's Perspective

Managing directors or general partners have the mojo inside venture capital firms. If you have anyone else prospecting you or working on the deal with you (associate, senior associate, principal, venture partner, or EIR), treat her with an enormous amount of respect, but insist on developing a direct relationship with an MD or a GP as well. Anyone other than an MD or a GP is unlikely to be at the firm for the long haul. The MDs and GPs are the ones who matter and who will make decisions about your company.

Financing Round Nomenclature

Aside from the humans who work at a venture firm, there are also different types of venture firms. Understanding the different types of firms will help you target the right ones as you go fundraising.

Most firms define themselves by the stage of financing they invest in. You've probably heard of different letters associated with financing rounds: Series A, Series B, Series B Prime, Series G, Series Seed, and even Series Pre-Seed. You'll hear about Series B-2 rounds and Series D-3 rounds. Venture capital is defined by constantly changing funding cycles. What is hot today may not be tomorrow. As the market changes, you'll hear about things like "The Series A Crunch" or "The Series B Crunch," or even the notion that "The Series A is the new Series B." What does this all mean? Since many things around entrepreneurship are dynamic, do a Google search (or Bing, if you really insist). Recognize simply that as times change, the nomenclature does also.

There is no magic or legal definition in naming rounds. We'd prefer to name them after different hiking trails in Boulder, but we'd confuse too many people, so we stick to letters. It used to be that the Series A round was the first financing, the Series B was the next round, and the Series C was the next round. After the Series C often came the Series D. You get the picture.

At some point, investors who were making very early stage investments, also referred to as *seed rounds,* decided that there must be a letter before "A." Since there is no letter before A, people started to call those deals Series Seed. While we have always felt it was perfectly reasonable to call these seed rounds a Series A, this emerged around the time that there was a new wave of VC firms making seed investments. At the same time, many of the firms who previously considered themselves Series A (or first round) investors were letting these new firms make the first investments. The other firms still liked to refer to themselves as early stage investors, so the old Series A became the Series Seed and the old Series B started to be called Series A. Today, you'll even hear of a *Pre-Seed Round,* which is simply an effort to label an earlier round that occurs before the seed round.

Note also that companies don't want to have letters for financing rounds that extend too far into the alphabet. When you are doing your Series K round, the first thing a VC wonders is what is wrong with you? Since an increasing number of rounds inherit the same terms, but with a different price from the preceding round, numerical round extensions appeared. When the same investors who invested $10 million in a Series B added on another $5 million to the company on the same terms but at a different price, this became the Series B-1. If another $5 million was invested in the company on the same terms and again at a different price, this became the Series B-2. When a new investor led the next $22 million financing, this finally became the Series C, instead of the Series E, which is what it would have been if the B-1 was the C round and the B-2 was the D round.

While the labeling of rounds can be complicated, what is important is that there is a language to discuss how early or late stage a company is. This is important when determining what VC might be right for it. Generally, Pre-Seed, Seed, and Series A are early stage companies, Series B, C, and D are mid stage companies, and Series E or later is a late stage company. That said, the lines are often blurry.

Types of Venture Capital Firms

Now that we've got the nomenclature of rounds down, we can talk about which types of firms invest in which rounds.

A *micro VC fund* is a small venture firm that often has only one general partner. Many of these folks started out as *angel investors,* which we will talk about in the next section, and, after some success, created a fund to invest other people's money alongside their own. Sizes of these funds can vary but are usually less than $15 million in total capital per fund. These firms almost exclusively invest at the seed and early stage, often alongside other micro VC firms, angel investors, and friends and family investors.

Seed stage funds are generally bigger than a micro VC and can scale up to $150 million per fund. Seed funds focus on being the first institutional money into a company and rarely invest in later rounds past a Series A. Seed stage firms often provide your first non-company board member, so be thoughtful as this relationship goes well beyond just the investment.

Next up are the *early stage funds.* These are the funds that are generally $100 million to $300 million in size and invest in seed stage and Series A companies but occasionally lead a Series B round. These firms also often continue to invest later in the life of a company, often taking their *pro rata* in subsequent rounds, which we'll explain later in this book.

Mid stage funds are those that generally invest in Series B and later rounds. The funds are often called *growth investors,* as their first investment in a company is at a point where a company is clearly working, but now needs capital to accelerate, or continue, its growth. These funds usually range from $200 million to $1 billion in size.

Late stage funds enter the picture when the company is now a successful stand-alone business, typically doing its last financing before a prospective initial public offering (IPO). These include specific late stage VC funds, but also can be hedge funds, crossover investors that invest primarily in the public markets, funds associated with large banks, or sovereign wealth funds.

Like all things in the VC world, you can't categorize each firm tightly. Some firms with billion-dollar funds have early stage programs that invest in young companies. Some firms have multiple funds that invest in different stages of a company. At Foundry Group, we have traditionally raised early stage funds that invested in the early stages (seed, A, and occasionally B) and separate later stage funds that invested in growth rounds, similar to what a mid stage firm would do. These days, we raise just one fund that invests across each of these stages.

Some firms have dedicated programs or partners for different investment stages while others invest along the company life cycle with no special delineations. A few, like ours, have all the partners work on everything together.

It's essential to make sure that you are targeting the types of firms that invest in your stage of company. One of the most common mistakes entrepreneurs make is focusing on firms that are irrelevant for them at their current stage. Try to avoid the common mistake of putting energy into raising money from a firm that doesn't invest in companies at your stage of growth.

The Angel Investor

In addition to VCs, your investor group may include individual investors, usually referred to as *angel investors* (or *angels* for short). These angels are often a key source of seed and early stage investment and are very active in the first round of investment. Angels can be professional investors, successful entrepreneurs, friends, or family members.

Many VCs are very comfortable investing alongside angels and often encourage their active involvement early in the life of a company. As a result, the angels are an important part of any financing dance. However, not all angels are created equal, nor do all VCs share the same view of angels.

While angels will invest at various points in time, they usually invest in the early rounds and often don't participate in future rounds. In cases where everything is going well, this is rarely an issue. However, if the company hits some speed bumps and has a difficult financing, the angels' participation in future rounds may come into question. Some of the terms we discuss in the book, such as *pay-to-play* and drag-along rights, are specifically designed to help the VCs force a certain type of behavior on the angels (and other VC investors) in these difficult financing rounds.

While angel investors are usually high-net-worth individuals, they aren't always. There are specific Securities and Exchange Commission (SEC) rules around *accredited investors,* and you should make sure that each of your angel investors qualifies as an accredited investor or has an appropriate exemption. This has become more complicated with the passage of the JOBS Act in 2012, which we discuss further in Chapter 10, "Crowdfunding." The best way to ensure you are following the rules correctly is to ask your lawyer for help.

Some angel investors make a lot of small investments. These very active, or promiscuous, angels are called *super angels.* These super angels are often experienced entrepreneurs who have had one or more exits and have decided to invest their own money in new startups. In most cases, super angels are well known in entrepreneurial circles and are often a huge help to early stage companies.

As super angels make more investments, they often decide to raise capital from their friends, other entrepreneurs, or institutions. At this point the super angel raises a fund similar to a *VC fund* and becomes a micro VC. While these micro VCs often want to be thought of as angels instead of VCs, once they've raised money from other people, they have the same fiduciary responsibility to their investors that a VC has, and as a result they are really just VCs.

It's important to remember that just like founders and VCs, there isn't a generic angel investor archetype. Lumping them together and referring to them as a single group can be dangerous. Never assume any of these people are like one another. They will all have their own incentives, pressures, experiences, and sophistication levels. Their individual characteristics will often define your working relationship with them well beyond any terms that you negotiate.

The Entrepreneur's Perspective

Don't put yourself in a position where you can be held hostage by angels. They are important, but they are rarely in a position to determine the company's direction. If your angel group is a small, diffuse list of friends and family, consider setting up a special-purpose limited partnership controlled by one of them as a vehicle for them to invest. Chasing down 75 signatures when you want to do a financing or sell the company is not fun.

Also, true friends and family need special care. Make sure they understand up front that (1) they should think of their investment as a lottery ticket, and (2) every holiday or birthday party is not an investor relations meeting.

The Syndicate

While some VCs invest alone, many invest with other VCs. A collection of investors is called a *syndicate.*

When VCs refer to the syndicate, they are often talking about the major participants in the financing round, who are usually, but not always, VCs. The syndicate includes any investor, whether a VC, angel, super angel, strategic investor, corporation, law firm, or anyone else that ends up purchasing equity in a financing.

Most syndicates have a *lead investor,* who is typically one of the VC investors. Two VCs will often co-lead a syndicate, and occasionally you'll see three co-leads.

While there is nothing magical about who the lead investor is, having one often makes it easier for the entrepreneurs to focus their energy around the negotiation. Rather than having one-off negotiations with each investor, the lead in the syndicate will often take the role of negotiating terms for the entire syndicate.

Regardless of the lead investor or the structure of the syndicate, it is the entrepreneurs' responsibility to make sure they are communicating with each of the investors in the syndicate. Even though the lead investor may help corral the other investors through the process, don't assume that you don't need to communicate with each of the investors—you do!

Be careful of too many cooks in the kitchen. In the past few years, the idea of a *party round,* where many investors make relatively small investments at the early stage, has become popular. It isn't unusual to see a $2 million seed round with 10 VCs and 20 angel investors in the round. While it might seem nice to have all these fancy names in a press release, the entrepreneurs get very little attention from any of the investors since their investments were all tiny relative to what the VCs normally invest. As companies raise their next round, they realize they have the worst of all possible worlds, which is having a lot of VCs as investors, but none who are committed in a meaningful way.

The Entrepreneur's Perspective

While you should communicate with all investors, you should insist that investors agree (at least verbally) that the lead investor can speak for the whole syndicate when it comes to investment terms. You should not let yourself be in a position where you have to negotiate the same deal multiple times. If there is dissension in the ranks, ask the lead investor for help.

The Lawyer

Ah, the lawyers—I bet you thought we'd never get to them. In deals, a great lawyer can be a huge help and a bad lawyer can be a disaster.

For the entrepreneur, an experienced lawyer who understands VC financings is invaluable. VCs make investments all the time while entrepreneurs raise money occasionally. Even an experienced entrepreneur runs the risk of getting hung up on a nuance that a VC has thought through many times.

In addition to helping negotiate, a great lawyer can focus the entrepreneur on what really matters. While this book will cover all the terms that typically come up in a VC financing, we'll repeat a simple mantra that the only real terms that matter are *economics* and *control*. Yes, annoying VCs will inevitably spend time negotiating unimportant terms even though the chance these terms will ever matter is very slight. This is just life in a negotiation where there are always endless tussles over unimportant points, sometimes due to silly reasons, but they are often used as a negotiating strategy to distract you from the main show. VCs are experts at this; a great lawyer can keep you from falling into these traps.

A bad lawyer, or one inexperienced in VC financings, can do you a world of harm. In addition to getting out-negotiated, the inexperienced lawyer will focus on the wrong issues, fight hard on things that don't matter, and run up the bill on both sides. Whenever entrepreneurs want to use their cousin who is a divorce lawyer, we take an aggressive position before we start negotiating that the entrepreneur needs a lawyer who has a clue.

Never forget that your lawyer is a reflection on you. Your reputation in the startup ecosystem is important, and a bad or inexperienced lawyer will tarnish it. Furthermore, once the deal is done, you'll be partners with your investors, so you don't want a bad or inexperienced lawyer creating unnecessary tension in the financing negotiation that will carry over once you are partners with your investors. If you are a lawyer, think twice before you act unreasonably toward a future board member of the company you represent. While you are responsible to the company in the current negotiation, the investor you are negotiating with will be a future owner in the company. Be thoughtful and play a multiturn game, as it is likely that the company's future investor will know other lawyers whom they are comfortable with and may push to make a switch post financing if they think you are an irrational or unhelpful negotiator.

The Entrepreneur's Perspective

At the same time that you don't want an inexperienced lawyer creating unnecessary tension in the negotiation, don't let a VC talk you out of using your lawyer of choice just because that lawyer isn't from a nationally known firm or the lawyer rubs the VC the wrong way. This is your lawyer, not your VC's lawyer. That said, to do this well, you need to be close enough to the communication to make sure your lawyer is being reasonable and communicating clearly and in a friendly manner.

While lawyers usually bill by the hour, many lawyers experienced with VC investments will cap their fees in advance of the deal. As of this writing in 2019, a very early stage financing can be done for between $5,000 and $20,000 and a typical financing can be completed for between $20,000 and $40,000. Lawyers in large cities tend to charge more, and if your company has any items to clean up from your past, your costs will increase.

If your lawyers and the VC's lawyers don't get along, your bill can skyrocket if you don't stay involved in the process. If the lawyers are unwilling to agree to a modest fee cap, you should question whether they know what they are doing.

Interestingly, these numbers are virtually unchanged from a decade ago while billable rates have more than doubled in the same time. While some document standardization has occurred, the average lawyer spends less time per deal than in ancient times (the 1990s). Ultimately, the entrepreneur must take responsibility for the final results.

The Entrepreneur's Perspective

Don't be shy about insisting that your lawyer cap their fee at a modest number or even that the lawyer will only get paid out of the proceeds of a deal. There's no reason, if you are a solid entrepreneur with a good business, that even a top-tier law firm won't take your unpaid deal to its executive committee as a flier to be paid on closing.

The Accountant

In early stage financings, accountants are rarely seen unless there are cross-border issues, or the company is restructuring from an LLC or other pass-through tax entity to a C corporation. However, if you have any concerns about tax treatment resulting from a financing, engage an accountant to assist your lawyer. As companies raise money in later rounds, accounting issues surrounding stock option pricing, tax filings, and tax credits become more prevalent. While the traditional approach was to use a Big 8 accounting firm (which are now the Big 4), we encourage you to explore mid-size and smaller local firms who are used to working with startups.

The Banker

Investment bankers are rarely seen in early stage financings but can be the ones running the show on behalf of the company for later rounds that raise $50 million or more of capital. We are always perplexed when we receive a funding inquiry from an investment banker representing an early stage company. We know that the banker is going to charge the company a substantial amount of its funding capital to do the work. Many angels and early stage VCs don't respond well to bankers in early rounds. Most importantly, we wonder why the entrepreneur didn't just contact us directly.

We have generally observed that if an early stage company has hired a banker to help with fundraising, either it has been unsuccessful in its attempt to raise money and is hoping the banker can help it in a last-ditch effort or it is getting bad advice from its advisers. Either way, most of the early stage inquiries we get from investment bankers end up being filed in the circular file.

There is a role for a banker in a later stage financing, especially one aimed at strategic or nontraditional investors. Bankers can be especially useful for deals that include a partial recapitalization by a financial sponsor, such as a private-equity firm.

The Mentor

Every entrepreneur should have a stable of experienced *mentors*. These mentors can be hugely useful in any financing, especially if they know the VCs involved.

We like to refer to these folks as mentors instead of advisers, since the term *adviser* often implies that there is some sort of fee agreement with the company. It's unusual for a company, especially an early stage one, to have a fee arrangement with an adviser around a financing. Nonetheless, there are advisers who prey on entrepreneurs by showing up, offering to help raise money, and then asking for compensation by taking a cut of the deal. There are even some bold advisers who ask for a retainer relationship to help out. We encourage early stage entrepreneurs to stay away from these advisers.

In contrast, mentors help the entrepreneurs, especially early stage ones, because someone once helped them. Many mentors end up being early angel investors in companies or get a small equity grant for serving on the board of directors or board of advisers, but they rarely ask for anything up front.

While having mentors is never required, we strongly encourage entrepreneurs to find them, work with them, and build long-term relationships with them. The benefits are enormous and often surprising. Most great mentors we know do it because they enjoy it. When this is the motivation, you often see some important and lasting relationships develop.

The Entrepreneur's Perspective

Mentors are great. There's no reason not to give someone a small success fee if they truly help you raise money (random email introductions to a VC they met once at a cocktail party don't count). Sometimes it will make sense to compensate mentors with options as long as you have some control over the vesting of the options based on your satisfaction with the mentor's performance as an ongoing adviser.

CHAPTER

Preparing for Fundraising

While it's tempting to jump right in to fundraising, huge issues can be avoided simply by being a good Boy (or Girl) Scout and being prepared. A capable lawyer, who knows how to do venture deals, is a key part of this. Our friends at Cooley LLP (where Jason was an associate two decades ago) were kind enough to provide some of the content to help us help you be prepared.

Choosing the Right Lawyer

A startup's legal adviser is an integral partner who will guide a company through its corporate lifecycle from incorporation to acquisition or initial public offering (IPO), and act as trusted adviser and connector to investors and other resources. In selecting an attorney, entrepreneurs have a variety of options to choose from, ranging from solo practitioners to multinational firms. Evaluating these options to find the right fit requires a management team to expend time and energy. This up-front investment can ensure the company avoids common legal pitfalls that can derail startups.

When evaluating candidates for corporate counsel, entrepreneurs should consider a short list of factors, including experience level, cost, and comfort with an attorney's communication style. For early stage companies, partnering with an attorney or law firm with a proven track record of representing startups can be especially valuable since experienced startup attorneys have an appreciation for the types of legal hurdles emerging companies may face. In addition, they are often well-connected to early stage investors, accelerators, and other resources that are critical to a startup's success.

We highly recommend that you find a lawyer with whom you have a personal connection. Your most intimate business details will be shared with the person and firm that you choose, and you deserve an attorney whom you trust completely and with whom you enjoy working. In addition, whoever represents you will impact your reputation, because they will be a representative of your company. Do your research, get references from trusted advisers, friends, and colleagues, and spend time with your prospective lawyer before making a choice.

Although it's natural and appropriate to focus on cost, don't obsess on the hourly rate. While the bill you receive is made up of the hourly rate times the hours spent, the efficiency of a lawyer is always the biggest factor in a bill. A competent lawyer who knows her way around startups is worth much more than someone who specializes in estate planning but charges half the rate per hour.

Proactive versus Reactive

The cliché "the best defense is a good offense" is as relevant for a company preparing for a venture financing as for a sports team on its way to a championship game. Any entrepreneur who has lived through pitching, negotiating, and closing a venture round can confirm that navigating a venture financing is a demanding process that involves unexpected challenges. There are several proactive steps that a startup's management team can take in advance of receiving its first term sheet to ensure that their company is set up for success.

Begin by preparing your company to meet investors' expectations. Among these expectations is that any company that will receive venture funding be structured as a C Corporation registered in Delaware. Startups that are structured as LLCs or other corporate forms should consult counsel to convert into C Corp status in advance of approaching investors. VCs don't like to, and often can't invest in pass-through tax entities (such as LLCs and S Corps) and therefore the C Corp status is a must. As for Delaware, there isn't a single investor that we've met who has rejected this state of incorporation. Yes, we've seen some accept California, New York, and a few other states, but you simply can't go wrong in picking Delaware.

Investors will expect a startup to be qualified to do business in every state in which the company is operating and be able to provide legal documentation to confirm their registrations in each state. You should work with counsel to verify that the company is qualified as a foreign corporation to do business in every state in which it has operations requiring such qualification.

The due diligence process is a key component of any venture financing. During due diligence, your legal and financial records will be reviewed by your potential investor to identify any issues that could prevent a deal's closing. To prepare for this, you should establish a data site and work with counsel to organize the company's legal and financial records to make them easy for investors to review. A data site can be an enterprise-grade, high-cost data site that one would use in a larger acquisition deal, or better yet, a Dropbox, Box, Google, or Carta folder that is cheap and easy to share.

Investors will expect a startup to provide copies of its original organizational documents, including the company's Certificate of Incorporation, Bylaws, and all of its board and shareholder actions and minutes. In addition, a startup should be prepared to grant access to any documentation related to its capital stock, including a detailed list of every person or entity who owns or has rights to any of the company's securities, as well as any agreements that grant stockholders preemptive or preferential rights.

Among these records, entrepreneurs should pay close attention to a company's capitalization table ("cap table"). A cap table is a complete list of all of a company's securities and their ownership organized in a spreadsheet. Corporate counsel can assist a company in preparing and updating a cap table, but you should be well versed in the contents of this document to prepare for conversations with potential investors.

Investors will also expect a company to include copies of its financial records, budgets, major customer lists, and employment agreements in its data site. While preparing a data site, a company's team should take the time to review these documents and ensure they are properly executed. Performing this review will allow a company to address any problems with signatures and other issues in advance, rather than having to address them in the midst of negotiating the terms of a financing.

Intellectual Property

For many investors, what distinguishes a company from its competitors as a compelling investment opportunity is the value of its intellectual property (IP). While some entrepreneurs and investors think the phrase "intellectual property" refers to patents, we are referring to patents, copyrights (to the code), trademarks (of the brand), and trade secrets (almost anything).

It is critical that in preparing for a financing, a startup be ready to demonstrate a clear, documented chain of title for all of its intellectual property. A founding team should ensure that anyone who has had contact with their company's intellectual property has signed agreements with confidentiality and IP assignment provisions. In addition, you should work with your corporate counsel to plan, and when appropriate, execute an intellectual property protection strategy to ensure your company's most valuable assets are properly safeguarded prior to a financing. This is especially important if you had a cofounder, prior to the financing, who is no longer with the company.

Given the importance of a company's intellectual property, you should be rigorous in ensuring that every person who comes in contact with your company's intellectual property signs confidentiality and assignment agreements. At a minimum, these agreements should identify the parties, the intellectual property in question, and any consideration associated with the IP assignment. We've seen venture deals fail to close because something as simple as one IP assignment agreement was missing.

A common source of intellectual property issues for startups is when founders of a company begin working on their new venture while still employed by another company. The Proprietary Information and Inventions Agreement a founder entered into with her primary employer can have significant implications for her new startup. The majority of such agreements specify that any intellectual property an employee creates that is connected with their primary employer's existing or reasonably anticipated business will be owned by the primary employer. This is the case even when an employee created the intellectual property independent of the primary employer's materials and on the employee's personal time. For investors, it is essential that entrepreneurs make a clean break from previous employers to be able to avoid any related intellectual property ownership issues. Where possible, it is preferable for founders to get a signed agreement from their recent employer to eliminate the potential for subsequent controversies over IP ownership. Where a signed agreement is not feasible, founders should leave their employer as soon as possible.

Every employee of a startup, including founders and each of the company's executives, must sign a Proprietary Inventions and Assignment Agreement to protect the startup's rights to its intellectual property. Ideally a Proprietary Inventions and Assignment Agreement should be included with every employment offer.

It is also important for a startup to ensure all of its service providers sign some form of agreement that clearly assigns any intellectual property that is created from their relationship to the company. While the provisions for employees are included in a Proprietary Inventions and Assignment Agreement, for contractors the IP provisions can be included in the independent contractor agreement.

In their early stages, startups often look to external advisers to guide them through the complexities of developing and launching a product. Given that these advisers have access to a startup's intellectual property, they should also sign agreements to maintain the confidentiality of a company's IP and ensure that the IP is owned exclusively by the company. When advisers do not assign their IP rights, issues can arise where an adviser may be categorized as a co-inventor or joint inventor of a company's IP. While you may trust your advisers, we've seen egregious situations, such as an adviser stealing the IP and filing his own patent unbeknownst to the company. Advisers may at times express concerns regarding agreeing to the same IP assignment terms as used with employees or contractors. In these cases, an entrepreneur should work with corporate counsel to craft an agreement with which the adviser is comfortable but leaves no ambiguity regarding the IP ownership. If you are enthralled by intellectual property issues, we will dive deeper into some legal issues in Chapter 19.

How to Raise Money

Your goal when you are raising a round of financing should be to get several term sheets since competition drives better terms for the entrepreneur. While we have plenty of suggestions on how to do this, there is no single magic trick. Financings come together in lots of different ways and result from an outstanding strategy to plain old good luck. Venture capitalists are not a homogeneous group; what might impress one VC might turn off another. Although we know what works for us, every venture capital firm is different, so make sure you know who you are dealing with, what their approach is, and what kind of material they need during the fundraising process. Following are some fundamental, but by no means complete, rules of the road, along with some things that you shouldn't do.

"Do. Or Do Not. There Is No Try."

In addition to being a small, green, hairy puppet with big hairy ears, Yoda was a wise being. We believe every entrepreneur should internalize his advice to young Luke Skywalker before hitting the fundraising trail: "Do. Or do not. There is no try." You must have the mind-set that you will succeed on your quest.

When we meet founders who say they are "trying to raise money," "testing the waters," or "exploring different options," this turns us off and signals that they haven't had much success. Instead, you should start with an attitude of presuming success. If you don't, investors will smell this uncertainty on you if it permeates your words and actions.

Not all entrepreneurs will succeed when they go out to raise a financing. Failure is a key part of entrepreneurship, but, as with many things in life, attitude impacts outcome.

Note that this advice does not pertain to informal meetings with investors about what you are doing. We meet with plenty of entrepreneurs who aren't raising money, just to get to know them. However, as soon as the switch flips to an active fundraising process, you must be all in.

Determine How Much You Are Raising

One of the common mistakes entrepreneurs make when raising money is targeting the wrong potential investors. Before you hit the road, figure out how much money you are going to raise since this impacts the choice of who you speak to in the process. For instance, if you are raising a $500,000 seed round, you'll talk to angel investors, seed stage VCs, super angels, micro VCs, and early stage investors, including ones from very large VC funds. However, if you are going out to raise $10 million, you should start with larger VC firms since you'll need a lead investor who can write at least a $5 million check.

While you can create complex financial models that determine how much money you need down to the penny, we know one thing with complete certainty: these models will be wrong. Instead, focus on the length of time you want to fund your company to get to the next meaningful milestone. If you are just starting out, how long will it take you to ship your first product? If you have a product in the market, how long will it take to get to a certain number of users or a specific revenue amount? Then, assuming no revenue growth, what is the monthly spend (also known as *burn rate*) that you need to get to that point? For example, if you are starting out and think it will take six months to get a product to market with a team of eight people, you can quickly estimate that you will spend around $100,000 per month for six months. Give yourself some time cushion (say, a year) and raise $1 million, since it'll take you a few months to hire people and ramp up spending to a $100,000-per-month burn rate.

The length of time you need varies dramatically by the type of business. In a seed stage software company, you should be able to make real progress in around a year. If you are trying to get a drug approved by the Food and Drug Administration, you will need at least several years. Don't obsess about getting this exactly right. As with your financial model, it's likely wrong, or approximate at best. Just make sure you have enough cash to get to a clear point of demonstrable success while being careful not to overspecify the milestones that you are going to achieve. You don't want them showing up in your financing documents as specific milestones that you have to attain.

Be careful not to go out asking for an amount of money that is significantly larger than you need. One of the worst positions you can be in during a financing is to have investors interested but you are far short of your total fundraising goal. For example, assume you are a seed stage company that needs $500,000 but you go out looking for $1 million. One of the questions that the VCs and angels you meet with will probably ask you is: "How much money do you have committed to the round?" If you answer "I have $250,000 committed," a typical angel may feel you are never going to get there and will hold back on engaging, based simply on the status of your financing. However, being able to say "I'm at $400,000 on a $500,000 raise and we've got room for one or two more investors" is a powerful statement to a prospective angel since most investors love to be part of an oversubscribed round.

Finally, we don't believe in ranges in the fundraising process. When someone says they are raising $5 million to $7 million, our first question is: "Is it $5 million or $7 million?" Though it might feel comfortable to offer up a range in case you can't get to the high end of it, presumably you want to raise at least the low number. The range makes it appear like you are hedging your bets or that you haven't thought hard about how much money you actually need to raise. Instead, we always recommend stating that you are raising a specific number. If you end up with more investor demand than you anticipated, you can always raise a larger amount of money.

Also keep in mind that while the difference between $5 million and $7 million might not sound like much to you, it could make all the difference in the world to a VC. If the largest first check a VC writes is $3 million, a $5 million round means they can be the lead investor. However, in a $7 million round, they can only be a co-lead or a follower. While you should never change the amount of money you are raising to entice a VC, keep in mind that having a range makes your targeting and conversations murkier.

Fundraising Materials

While the exact fundraising materials you need varies widely by VC, there are a few basic things that you should create before you hit the fundraising trail. At the minimum, you need a short description of your business, an *executive summary*, and a presentation that is often not so fondly referred to as "a PowerPoint" despite the fact many of us are using Google Docs these days (and no, we don't know anyone who actually uses Keynote). Some investors will ask for a business plan or a *private placement memorandum* (PPM). While this is rarely requested in early stage investments, it's common in later-stage investments.

Once upon a time, physical form seemed to matter. In the 1980s, elaborate business plans were professionally printed at the corner copy shop and mailed out. Today, virtually all materials are sent via email. Quality still matters a lot, but don't overdesign your information. We can't tell you the number of times we've received a highly stylized executive summary that was organized in such a way as to be visually appealing, yet was completely lacking in substance. Focus on the content while making the presentation solid and able to stand on its own.

Whatever you send an investor should be clear, concise, interesting, and easy to process alone early in the morning in the darkness of a home office. If you need to talk the investor through it, you have lost the battle before you've started. Do not make the common mistake of thinking that you'll send out a teaser and then get to talk through the details at a meeting. Realize that whatever you send a VC is often both your first and last impression, so make it count.

Finally, while it's never required, many investors (such as us) respond to things we can play with, so even if you are a very early stage company, a prototype or demo is desirable.

Short Description of Your Business

You'll need a summary that you can email, often called the *elevator pitch*, meaning you should be able to present it during the length of time it takes for an elevator to go from the first floor to your prospective investor's office. Don't confuse this with the *executive summary*, which we discuss next; rather, this is one to three paragraphs that describe the product, the team, and the business very directly. It doesn't need to be a separate document that you attach to an email; rather, this is the bulk of the email. Often it is wrapped with an introductory paragraph, especially if you know the investor or are being referred to the person, and a concluding paragraph with a very clear request for whatever next step you want.

Executive Summary

The executive summary is a short, concise, well-written description of your idea, product, team, and business. It is the first substantive document and interaction you will likely have with a prospective investor with whom you don't have a preexisting relationship. Think of the executive summary as the basis for your first impression and expect it to be passed around within a VC firm if there is any interest in what you are doing.

Work hard on the executive summary. The more substance you can pack into this short (up to three-page) document, the more a VC will believe that you have thought critically about your business. The executive summary is also a direct indication of your communication skills. A poorly written summary that leaves out key pieces of information will cause a VC to assume that you haven't thought deeply about some important issues or that you are trying to hide bad facts about the business. Our inner grammar nerds suggest you have someone not involved in your company proofread your materials.

In the executive summary, include the problem you are solving and why it's important to solve. Explain why your product is awesome, why it's better than what currently exists, and why your team is the right one to pursue it. End with some high-level financial data to show that you have aggressive but sensible expectations about how your business will perform over time.

Your first communication with a VC is often an introductory email, either from you or from someone referring you to the VC, that is a combination of the short description of your business along with the executive summary attached to the email. If your first interaction was a face-to-face meeting at a conference, at a coffee shop, or in an elevator, an interested VC will often say something like "Can you send me an executive summary?" Do this the same day that it is requested of you to start to build momentum to the next step in the process.

Presentation

Once you have engaged with a VC firm, you will quickly be asked to either give or email them a presentation. This is usually a 10- to 20-page PowerPoint presentation consisting of a substantive overview of your business. There are many different presentation styles and approaches, and what you need will depend on the audience (one person, a VC partnership, or 500 people at an investor-day event). Your goal with the presentation is to communicate the same information from the executive summary, often with more examples, but using a visual presentation.

Over time, a number of different presentation styles have emerged. A three-minute presentation at a local pitch event is as different from an eight-minute presentation at an *accelerator's* investor day as it is from a 30-minute presentation to a VC partnership. Recognize your audience and tune your presentation to them. The deck you email as an overview can be different from the one you present, even if you are covering similar material.

Work hard on the presentation flow and format. In this situation, form matters a great deal. It's amazing how much more positive a response is to well-designed and well-organized slides, especially if you have a consumer-facing product where user experience will matter for its success. If you don't have a good designer on your team, find a friend who is a freelance designer to help you turn your presentation into something visually appealing. Put some extra effort into this as it will pay off many times over.

The Entrepreneur's Perspective

"Less is more" when it comes to an investor presentation. There are only a few key things most VCs look at to understand and get excited about a deal: the problem you are solving, the size of the opportunity, the strength of the team, the level of competition or competitive advantage that you have, your plan of attack, and current status. Summary financials, use of proceeds, and milestones are also important. Most good investor presentations can be done in 10 slides or fewer.

Business Plan

We haven't read a business plan in over 25 years. Sure, we still get plenty of them, but it is not something we care about since we invest in areas we know well. Instead, we much prefer demos and live interactions. Fortunately, most business plans arrive in email these days, so they are easy enough to ignore since one doesn't have to physically touch them. However, some VCs care a lot about seeing a business plan, regardless of the current view by many people that a business plan is an obsolete document.

The business plan is usually a 30-plus-page document that has all sorts of sections and is something you would learn to write if you went to business school. It goes into great detail about all facets of the business, expanding on the executive summary to have comprehensive sections about the market, product, target customer, go-to market strategy, team, and financials.

While we think business plans prepared specifically for fundraising are a waste of time, we still believe that they are a valuable document for entrepreneurs to write while they are formulating their business. There are lots of different approaches today, including many that are user- or customer-centric, but the discipline of writing down what you are thinking, your hypotheses about your business, and what you believe will happen is still very useful. In addition, you will have a written record to help keep you and your team accountable down the road.

Now, we still aren't talking about a conventional business plan, although this can be a useful approach. Rather, if you are a software company, consider some variant of the *Lean Startup methodology* that includes the creation, launch, and testing of a minimum viable product as a starting point. Or, rather than writing an extensive document, use PowerPoint to organize your thoughts into clear sections, but also recognize that this is very different from the presentation you are going to give potential investors.

You will occasionally be asked for a business plan. Be prepared for this and know how you plan to respond, along with what you will provide, if and when this comes up.

Private Placement Memorandum

A private placement memorandum (PPM) is essentially a traditional business plan wrapped in legal disclaimers that are often as long as the plan itself. It's time consuming and expensive to prepare, and you get the privilege of paying lawyers thousands of dollars to proofread the document and provide a bunch of legal boilerplate to ensure you don't say anything that you could get sued for later.

Normally, PPMs are generated only when investment bankers are involved and are fundraising from large investors that demand a PPM. In the past few years, bankers have often shifted to PowerPoint-type presentations with endless bullet points, instead of prose, because they are easier to create and likely easier to consume.

We've seen plenty of early stage companies hire bankers and draft PPMs. To us, this is a waste of money and time. When we see an email from a banker sending us a PPM for an early stage company, we automatically know that investment opportunity isn't for us and almost always toss it in the circular file.

Detailed Financial Model

The only thing that we know about financial predictions of startups is that 100 percent of them are wrong. If you can predict the future accurately, we have a few suggestions for other things you could be doing besides starting a risky early stage company. Furthermore, the earlier the stage of the startup, the less accurate any predications will be. While we know you can't predict your revenue with any degree of accuracy (although we are always pleased in that rare case where revenue starts earlier and grows faster than expected), the expense side of your financial plan is very instructive as to how you think about the business.

While you can't predict your revenue with any level of precision, you should be able to manage your expenses closely to plan. Your financials will mean different things to different investors. In our case, we focus on two things: (1) the assumptions underlying the revenue forecast (which we don't need a spreadsheet for—we'd rather just talk about them) and (2) the monthly burn rate or cash consumption of the business. Since your revenue forecast will be wrong, your cash flow forecast will be wrong. However, if you are an effective manager, you'll know how to budget for this by focusing on lagging your increase in cash spend behind your expected growth in revenue.

Some VCs are very spreadsheet driven. Some firms (usually those with associates) may go so far as to perform discounted cash flow analysis to determine the value of your business. Some will look at every line item and study it in detail. Others will focus much less on all the details but focus on certain things that matter to them. For instance, what is your headcount over the next few quarters, and how fast do you expect to acquire users or customers? Although none of us know your business better than you, VCs will apply their experience and frame of reference to your financial model as they evaluate how well you understand the financial dynamics of your business.

In later financing rounds, your company's historical financial performance, underlying unit economics, cost structure, key metrics, and future financial plan will matter a lot more to your prospective VCs. At that point, you have been in business for a while. You will be raising money against your track record and the extrapolation of that into the future, rather than just an idea, a dream, and a startup fantasy.

The Demo

Most VCs love demos. In the short time before we wrote this section, we got to play with an industrial robot, wear a device that tracked our body temperatures and anxiety levels, interact with software that measured the number of times we smiled while we watched a video, saw a projection system that worked on curved walls with incredible fidelity, gave real blood out of our arms for a new analysis technology, and played around with a Web service that predicted what we were going to do before we actually did it. We learned more from these demos, especially about our emotional interest in the products we played with, than any document could communicate. Each of these demos also gave us a chance to talk directly to the entrepreneurs about how they thought about their current and future products, and we got a clear view of the enthusiasm and obsession of the entrepreneurs for what they are working on.

We believe the demo or a prototype (often called an *alpha*) is far more important than a business plan or financial model for a very early stage company. The demo shows us your vision in a way we can interact with. More importantly, it shows us that you can build something and then show it off. We expect demos to be underfeatured, to be rough around the edges, and to crash. We know that you'll probably throw away the demo on the way to a final product and what we are investing in will evolve a lot. But like most 14-year-olds, we just want to play.

Demos are just as important in existing companies. If you have a complex product, figure out a way to show it off in a short period of time. We don't need to see every feature; use your demo to tell us a story about the problem your product addresses. We want to play with the demo, not just be passive observers, so give us the steering wheel. While we are playing, watch us carefully because you'll learn an enormous amount about us in that brief period of time while you see how comfortable we are, whether our eyes light up, and whether we really understand what you are pursuing.

Due Diligence Materials

VCs will ask for additional information as you go further down the financing path. If a VC offers you a term sheet, expect their lawyers to ask you for a bunch of stuff such as capitalization tables, material customer agreements, employment agreements, and board meeting minutes. The list of documents requested during the formal due diligence process (usually after signing of the term sheet, but not always) can be long. For an example, see the "Resources" page at www.venturedeals.com. The number of documents you will actually have depends on how long you have been in business. Even if you are a young company just starting up, we recommend that you organize all of these documents for quick delivery before going out to raise money, so you don't slow down the process when an investor asks for them.

You should never try to hide anything with any of these fundraising materials. Although you are trying to present your company in the best light possible, you want to make sure any issues you have are clearly disclosed. Deal with any messy stuff up front. If a VC forgets to ask for something early on, assume you will be asked for it before the deal is done. If you happen to get something past a VC and get funded, it will eventually come out that you weren't completely transparent, and your relationship will suffer. A good VC will respect full disclosure early on and, if they are interested in working with you, will actively engage to help you get through any challenges you have, or at least give you feedback on why there are showstoppers that you have to clear up before you raise money.

Finding the Right VC

The best way to find the perfect VC is to ask your friends and other entrepreneurs. They can give you unfiltered data about which VCs they've enjoyed working with and who have helped them build their businesses. It's also the most efficient approach, since an introduction to a VC from an entrepreneur who knows both you and the VC is always more effective than sending a cold email to vcname@vcfirm.com.

But what should you do if you don't have a large network for this? Back in the early days of venture capital, it was very hard to locate even the contact information for a VC, and you rarely found them in the yellow pages, not even next to the folks who gave payday loans. Today, VCs have websites and blogs, tweet endlessly, and even list their email addresses on their websites.

Entrepreneurs can discover a lot of information about their potential future VC partner well beyond the mundane contact information. You will be able to discover what types of companies they invest in, what stages they prefer to invest in, past successes, failures, approaches, strategies, and bios on the key personnel at the firm. If the VC has a social media presence, you will be able to take all of that information and infer things like their hobbies, theories on investing, beer they drink, food they eat, instruments they play, and type of building or facility—such as a bathroom—they like to endow at their local universities. Recognize that some VCs spend a lot of money and time on marketing to shape the impression you will have of them, so your personal network and stories from founders who have worked with them is often the most valuable information.

While it may seem obvious, engaging a VC who you don't know via social media can be useful as a starting point to develop a relationship. Besides adding to the VC's ego gratification of having a lot of Twitter followers (hint: now is the time to follow @jasonmendelson and @bfeld if you aren't already), you will develop an impression and, more importantly, a relationship, if you comment thoughtfully on blog posts the VC writes. Engage at a personal level. It doesn't have to be all business. Offer suggestions, interact, and follow the best rule of developing relationships: "give more than you get." Never forget the simple idea that if you want money, ask for advice. Try to develop a relationship that evolves over time, instead of viewing fundraising as a single, transactional experience. And, for the avoidance of doubt, building an email list and sending out a mass mailing to everyone whose email address you can find is not what we are talking about.

Do your homework. When we get business plans from medical technology companies or somebody insisting we sign a nondisclosure agreement before we review a business plan, we know that they did absolutely zero research on us or our firm before they sent us the information. At best, the submission doesn't rise to the top compared to more thoughtful correspondences, and at worst it doesn't even elicit a response from us.

A typical VC gets thousands of inquiries a year. The vast majority of these requests are from people whom the VC has never met and with whom the VC has no relationship. Improve your chances of having VCs respond to you by researching them, getting a referral to them, and engaging with them in whatever way they seem to be interested in.

Finally, don't forget this works both ways. You may have a super-hot deal and as a result have your pick of VCs to fund your company. Do your homework and find out who will be most helpful to your success, has a temperament and style that will be compatible with yours, and will ultimately be your best long-term partner. Ask for references from the VCs but also hunt down founders they didn't list as references, so that you get a full picture on your prospective investors. Remember that the average length of a relationship between VC and founder is on par with the average length of a marriage in the United States.

Finding a Lead VC

Assuming that you are talking with multiple potential investors, you can generally categorize them into one of three groups: leaders, followers, and everyone else. It's important to know how to interact with each of these groups. If not, you not only will waste a lot of your time but also might be unsuccessful in your fundraising mission.

Your goal is to find a lead VC. This is the firm that is going to give you a term sheet, take a leadership role in driving to a financing, and likely be your most active new investor. It's possible to have co-leads (usually two, occasionally three) in a financing. It's also desirable to have more than one VC competing to lead your deal without them knowing who else you are talking to.

As you meet with potential VCs, you'll get one of four typical vibes. First is the VC who is clearly interested and wants to lead. Next is the VC who isn't interested and passes. These are the easy ones. Engage aggressively with the ones who want to lead and don't worry about the ones who pass. While you may think that you can change their minds with persistence and salesmanship, you will almost always be wrong.

The other two categories—the "maybe" and the "slow no"—are the hardest to deal with. The "maybe" seems interested but doesn't really step up his level of engagement. This VC seems to be hanging around, waiting to see if there's any interest in your deal. Keep this person warm by continually meeting and communicating with him but realize that this VC is not going to catalyze your investment. However, as your deal comes together with a lead, this VC is a great one to bring into the mix if you want to put a syndicate of several firms together.

The "slow no" is the hardest to figure out. These VCs never actually say no but are completely in react mode. They will occasionally respond when you reach out, but there is no perceived forward motion on their part. You always feel like you are pushing on a rope—there's a little resistance but nothing ever really moves anywhere. We recommend you think of these VCs as a "no" and don't continue spending time with them.

Keep your head up and stay optimistic throughout the process. We realize how frustrating finding a lead VC can be. We also get frustrated with VCs who aren't transparent and deal in maybes and act as slow nos. If it makes you feel any better, we face the same thing when we go out to raise money from our investors and we get just as confused and frustrated as you do. Learn from all the feedback you get and don't take any of it personally.

How VCs Decide to Invest

Let's explore how VCs decide to invest in a company and what the process normally looks like. All VCs are different, so these are generalizations but reflect the way that VCs make their decisions.

The way that you get connected to a particular VC affects the process that you go through. Some VCs will only fund entrepreneurs with whom they have a prior connection or are referred by someone they trust. Other VCs (but usually not lead VCs) prefer to be introduced to entrepreneurs by other VCs. Some VCs invest only in seasoned entrepreneurs and avoid working with first-time entrepreneurs, whereas others, like us, will fund entrepreneurs of all ages, genders, ethnicities, and experience and will try to be responsive to anyone who contacts us. Whatever the case is, you should determine quickly if you reached a particular VC through her preferred channel or are swimming upstream from the beginning.

Next, you should understand the role of the person within the VC firm who is your primary connection. If an associate reached out to you via email, consider that his job is to scour the universe looking for deals but that he probably doesn't have any real pull to get a deal done. It doesn't mean that you shouldn't meet with him, but also don't get overly excited until there is a general partner or managing director at the firm paying attention to and spending real time with you.

Your first few interactions with a VC firm will vary widely depending on whether your initial contact is the firm's style. At some point it will be apparent that the VC has more than a mild interest in exploring an investment in you and will begin a process often known as *due diligence.* This isn't a formal legal or technical diligence; rather, it's code for "I'm taking my exploration to the next level."

You can learn a lot about the attitude and culture of a VC firm by the way it conducts its diligence. For example, if you are raising your first round of financing and you have no revenue and no product, a VC who asks for a five-year detailed financial projection and then proceeds to hammer you on the numbers is probably not someone who has a lot of experience or comfort making early stage investments. If you are just starting out and the VC complains that you don't have enough traction, it's likely that you are speaking to a VC that doesn't really invest in early stage companies despite what they or their marketing materials suggest.

During this phase, a VC will ask for a lot of things, such as presentations, projections, customer pipeline or targets, development plan, competitive analysis, and team bios. This is all normal. In some cases, the VCs will be mellow and accept what you have already created in anticipation of the financing. In other cases, they will make you run around like a headless chicken and create a lot of busywork for you. At this point make sure a partner-level person (usually a managing director or general partner) is involved to ensure that you aren't the object of a fishing expedition by an associate or a data collection exercise that only has a goal of getting information about your company into the VC firm's database (or, worse, leaked to a competitor the VC has funded or is considering funding).

The Entrepreneur's Perspective

If you feel like your VC is acting like a proctologist, run for the hills.

While the VC firm goes through its diligence process on you, we suggest you return the favor and ask for things like introductions to other founders they've backed. Nothing is as illuminating as a discussion with other entrepreneurs who have worked with your potential investor. Don't be afraid to ask for entrepreneurs the VC has backed whose companies haven't worked out. Since you should expect that a good VC will ask around about you, don't be afraid to ask other entrepreneurs what they think of the VC.

The Entrepreneur's Perspective

The best VCs will give you, either proactively or reactively, a list of all the entrepreneurs they've worked with in the past and ask you to pick a few for reference checks. The best reference checks are from companies that went through hard times, maybe swapped out a founder for another CEO, or even failed, because you will learn from them how the VC handled messy and adversarial situations.

You will go through multiple meetings, emails, phone calls, and more meetings. You may meet other members of the firm. You may end up going to the VC's offices to present to the entire partnership on a Monday, a tradition known by many firms as the Monday partner meeting. In other cases, as with our firm, if things are heating up you'll meet with each of the partners relatively early in the process in one-on-one or group settings.

As things unfold, either you'll continue to work with the VC in exploring the opportunity or the VC will start slowing down the pace of communication. Be very wary of the VC who is hot on your company, then warm, then cold, but never really says no. While some VCs are quick to say no when they lose interest, many VCs don't say no because they don't see a reason to. These VCs either want to keep their options open, or are unwilling to affirmatively pass on a deal because they don't want to have to shut the door. In some cases, they are simply impolite and disrespectful to the entrepreneur. This is not dissimilar from how things work when meeting someone for the first time, so while fundraising may be new to you, use your instincts as you would in your personal life.

Ultimately, VCs will decide whether to invest. If they do, the next step in the process is for them to issue a term sheet.

The Entrepreneur's Perspective

If a VC passes on a deal with you, whether graciously or by not returning your emails and your calls, do your best to politely insist on feedback as to why. This is one of the most important lessons an entrepreneur can learn and is especially useful during the fundraising cycle. Don't worry that someone is telling you that your baby is ugly. Ask for the feedback, demand it, get it, absorb it, and learn from it.

Using Multiple VCs to Create Competition

Choice is power. Having multiple VCs interested in your company will provide insight into how different firms work and give you the negotiation leverage to improve the terms of the deal.

If you want to create a competitive process, allow at least three to six months to raise money. If you start the process earlier than this, you won't feel urgency to get a deal done, nor will your prospective investors. If you start with less time, you may not have enough time to get the financing done before you run out of money. A short window to get a financing done can lead to many VCs passing since they won't have enough time to evaluate your company. In other cases, VCs will sense desperation when you only have a few months left before running out of money, which doesn't help your negotiating position.

After you've started to engage with a particular VC, make sure you understand their process. A few will tell you, but most won't. After you've had a second meeting, ask what the process is going forward. While you might get a vague answer, you will often get some clues as to what the next steps and decision points are. If the VCs don't adhere to the process they lay out, take this as a sign that they aren't that interested in your company, they don't keep their word, or possibly that they are just extremely busy. In any case, it's a useful signal to pay attention to.

Timing is everything. While it is hard enough to get multiple parties interested, you also need to make sure that the timing of each of their processes line up. It doesn't do you any good if you get three VCs interested in you 18 months apart. If you have a sense of process, you can bias your energy toward the firms with a longer process in an effort to synchronize the delivery of term sheets.

Be careful to understand what a slow process actually means. While annoying, many VCs have a slow process because they are bad at saying no and prefer to string entrepreneurs along to give the VC firm options in the event that a deal starts to heat up. If a VC is having trouble giving you clear and timely feedback, you may be speaking to someone who doesn't have the power in their firm to get a deal done. This is another reason we suggest that you interact, as much as possible, with managing directors and general partners.

Some VCs will ask you who else you are talking to. If your goal is to create a competitive process, never answer this question. If you do, the next email a VC will send is one to someone at the firms you told them you were talking to, asking what they think of you and your deal. Sometimes this works in your favor, but only in cases where the firms compete fiercely with each other for deals or in situations where firms collaborate closely. Either way, it's better to stay quiet about other conversations early on and only make connections between firms that are known collaborators as term sheets start to fly.

Be as strategic in your fundraising as you are with your business. Talk to everyone you can about which VCs to speak to, and don't waste your time with those who don't invest in your stage or sector. Be up front and direct and get as much information as you can during the fundraising process.

Closing the Deal

The most important part of the fundraising process is to close the deal, raise the money, and get back to running your business. How do you actually close the deal?

Separate it into two activities: the first is the signing of the term sheet and the second is signing the definitive documents and receiving the cash. The next few chapters of this book are primarily about getting a term sheet signed. In our experience, most executed term sheets result in a financing that closes. Reputable VCs, especially early stage firms, can't afford to have term sheets signed and then not follow through; otherwise, they won't remain reputable for long.

This can be different for later stage firms. Often, you will agree to a term sheet, albeit a nonbinding one, but you aren't done with the deal process yet. Many later stage firms have a final formal approval step, known as their investment committee, before they actually close a deal. Over the years, we have seen multiple cases where a signed term sheet from a fund wasn't actually approved by the investment committee. In these cases, the company and VC proceeded as though the term sheet would lead to a deal and, after lots of diligence and legal drafting, the investment committee turned down the deal and the VC walked away, often putting the company in a difficult situation.

The most likely situations that derail financings are when VCs find unexpected bad facts about the company after signing a term sheet. You should assume that a signed term sheet will lead to money in the bank as long as there are no smoking guns in your company's past, the investor is a professional one, and you don't do anything stupid in the definitive document-drafting process.

The second part of closing the deal is the process of drafting the definitive agreements. Generally, the lawyers do most of the heavy lifting here. They will take the term sheet and start to negotiate the 100-plus pages of documentation that are generated from the term sheet. In the best-case scenario, you respond to due diligence requests, and one day you are told to sign some documents. The next thing you know, you have money in the bank and a new board member with whom you are excited to work.

In the worst case, however, the deal blows up. Or perhaps the deal closes, but there are hard feelings left on both sides. Throughout the process, manage it on a daily basis. Don't let the lawyers behave poorly, as this will only injure the future relationship between you and your investor. Make sure that you are responsive with requests, and never assume that because your lawyer is angry and says the other side is horrible (or stupid, or evil, or worthless) that the VC even has a clue what is going on. Many times, we have seen legal teams get completely tied up on an issue and want to kill each other when neither the entrepreneur nor the VC even cared or had any notion that there was a dustup. Before you get emotional, make a phone call or send an email to the VC and see what the real story is.

Overview of the Term Sheet

At the end of 2005, during the dark ages when venture capital was very much out of favor, we participated in an equity financing that was much more difficult than it needed to be. All of the participants were to blame, and ignorance of what really mattered in the negotiation kept things going much longer than was necessary. We talked about what to do and, at the risk of giving away super-top-secret venture capital magic tricks, decided to write a series on Brad's blog (Feld Thoughts—www.feld.com) that deconstructed a venture capital term sheet and explained each section.

That blog series was the inspiration for this book. The next few chapters cover the most frequently discussed terms in a venture capital equity term sheet. Many venture capitalists (VCs) love to negotiate hard on every term as though the health of their children depended on them getting the terms just right. Sometimes this is inexperience on the part of the VC; often, it's just a negotiating tactic.

The specific language that we refer to is from actual term sheets. In addition to describing and explaining the specific terms, we will give you examples of what to focus on and implications from the perspectives of the company, VCs, and entrepreneurs.

The Entrepreneur's Perspective

The term sheet is critical. What's in it usually determines the final deal structure. Don't think of it as a letter of intent. Think of it as a blueprint for your future relationship with your investor.

The Key Concepts: Economics and Control

In general, there are only two things that VCs really care about when making investments: economics and control. *Economics* refers to the return the investors will ultimately get in a liquidity event, usually either a sale of the company, a wind down, or an initial public offering, and the terms that have direct impact on this return. *Control* refers to the mechanisms that allow the investors either to affirmatively exercise control over the business or to veto certain decisions the company can make. If you are negotiating a deal and investors are digging their heels in on a provision that doesn't impact the economics or control, they are often blowing smoke, rather than arguing substantive issues. In general, the concept of economics and control is relevant for any type of financing you do, whether it is equity, debt, loansharking, or an initial coin offering. We'll discuss each of these structures (except for loansharking) in this book.

The Entrepreneur's Perspective

Economics and control are important things to pay attention to, in and of themselves. They rule the day. An inexperienced VC will harp on other terms needlessly. You can give in on them or not, but the mere fact that a VC focuses on unimportant terms is a sign of what that VC will be like to work with as an owner, board member, and compensation committee member.

When companies are created, the founders receive *common stock*. However, when VCs invest in companies and they purchase equity, they almost always receive *preferred stock*. The specific terms we are going to discuss are for the preferred stock, not the common stock that founders and employees normally hold. While preferred stock is special, a holder of preferred stock typically can unilaterally decide to convert to common stock and give up all of these special rights. But, once preferred stock converts to common stock, it can't go back.

If your company raises convertible debt (instead of an equity round), the intention is that this debt will convert to equity at a later date. It's important to realize that the outstanding debt is, for all intents and purposes, a temporary state until the next financing, so we will start our discussion of financings with equity, and then cover convertible debt later.

As we described earlier, separate financings are usually referred to as a series designated by a letter, such as *Series A*. The first round is often called the *Series A financing*, although recently a new round occurring before the Series A has appeared, called the Series Seed *financing*. The letter is incremented in each subsequent financing, so Series B financings follow Series A, and Series C financings follow Series B. You'll occasionally see a number added onto the letter for subsequent rounds, such as Series A-1 or Series B-2. This is generally done to try to limit how far into the alphabet you go and is often used when the same investors do subsequent rounds in a company together. While we aren't aware of the world record for number of financings in a private company, we have seen a Series K financing.

In the following chapters, we walk you through language for each term and detailed examples. Let's get started by exploring the economic terms.

CHAPTER 5

Economic Terms of the Term Sheet

When discussing the economics of a venture capital deal, one often hears the question "What is the valuation?" If you watch *Shark Tank* (or one of its many derivative programs), you know that the valuation will be some unreasonably low number that makes us cringe every time we see an episode. But while valuation is an important component of the deal, it is a mistake to focus only on this term when considering the economics of a deal.

In this chapter we will discuss all of the terms that make up the economics of the deal. These include valuation, which is often expressed in a term sheet as "price," liquidation preference, pay-to-play, vesting, the employee pool, and antidilution.

Valuation and Price

The valuation that you and your VC agree upon will determine how much of your company you are selling and, consequently, how much dilution you will take in the financing. The valuation also will determine the price per share at which you sell your stock.

There are two different ways to discuss valuation: *pre-money* and *post-money*. The pre-money valuation is what the investor is valuing the company at today, prior to the investment. The post-money valuation is simply the pre-money valuation plus the contemplated aggregate investment amount. In other words, if you raise $2 million at a $6 million pre-money valuation, your post-money valuation is

$8 million. Since the investor invested $2 million and the company is now worth $8 million post-financing, the investor just bought 25% of your company (2,000,000/8,000,000.)

Be careful not to fall into the first trap that VCs often lead entrepreneurs into. When a VC says, "I'll invest $5 million at a valuation of $20 million," the VC usually means the post-money valuation, meaning the pre-money the VC is offering you is $15 million.

In this situation, the VC's expectation is that a $5 million investment will buy 25% of a $20 million post-money company. At the same time, an entrepreneur might hear a $5 million investment at a pre-money valuation of $20 million, which would buy only 20% of the $25 million post-money company. The words are the same but the expectations are very different.

The term sheet language usually spells this out in detail. However, early in your negotiation with the VC, you will often have a verbal discussion about price. How you approach this sets the tone for a lot of the balance of the negotiation. By addressing the ambiguity up front, you demonstrate that you have knowledge about the basic terms. The best entrepreneurs we've dealt with are presumptive and say something like "I assume you mean $20 million pre-money." This forces the VC to clarify, and if in fact she did mean $20 million pre-money, it doesn't cost you anything in the negotiation.

The agreed-upon valuation will determine the price per share an investor pays. In Chapter 9 we discuss how the math is done, but for now just know that these two concepts are linked. Traditionally, the way price is represented in a term sheet follows:

> Price: $____ per share (the Original Purchase Price). The Original Purchase Price represents a fully diluted pre-money valuation of $____ million and a fully diluted post-money valuation of $____ million. For purposes of the above calculation and any other reference to fully diluted in this term sheet, fully diluted assumes the conversion of all outstanding preferred stock of the Company, the exercise of all authorized and currently existing stock options and warrants of the Company, and the increase of the Company's existing option pool by [X] shares prior to this financing.

A somewhat different way that price can be represented is by defining the amount of the financing, which backs into the price. For example:

Amount of Financing: An aggregate of $X million, representing a ___% ownership position on a fully diluted basis, including shares reserved for any employee option pool. Prior to the Closing, the Company will reserve shares of its Common Stock so that ___% of its fully diluted capital stock following the issuance of its Series A Preferred is available for future issuances to directors, officers, employees, and consultants.

Modern term sheets will address valuation very simply and say:

Pre-Money Valuation: $_____

The price per share of stock, also known as the purchase price, will often be expressed in vague terms. As long as the valuation and option pool are agreed to, then the dilution is determined and the price per share is largely irrelevant as they are a calculated number. Here is some sample language that you might see in a modern term sheet.

The per share price of the Preferred Stock (the "Purchase Price") shall be calculated by dividing the Pre-Money Valuation set forth in the Summary of Terms by the fully diluted capitalization (including the Employee Pool) as of immediately prior to the closing.

There are two additional concepts that show up in these definitions. The first is the phrase *fully diluted*, which means that when determining the price per share, all outstanding stock of the company will be used in the calculations. This includes all company stock held by any party and any rights for a party to acquire stock of the company in the future. These future rights could include warrants given to a bank or business partner and always include granted and available shares in the employee option pool of the company.

The second important concept is the employee option pool, which is inextricably linked with the concept of valuation. It deserves its own section, which follows.

Employee Option Pool

If you read earlier versions of this book, you probably are geared up for a discussion on liquidation preferences. And while liquidation preferences are important, the size of the employee option pool ultimately affects valuation more.

Both the company and the investor will want to make sure the company has sufficient equity (or *stock options*) reserved to compensate and motivate its workforce. This is also known as the *employee option pool* or *option pool*. The bigger the pool the better, right? Not so fast. Although a large option pool will make it easier to give good option packages to new hires, the size of the pool is taken into account in the valuation of the company. A large employee option pool can lower the actual pre-money valuation and is another common valuation trap.

Let's stay with our previous example of a $5 million investment at $20 million pre-money. Assume that you have an existing option pool that has options representing 10% of the outstanding stock reserved and unissued. The VCs suggest that they want to see a 20% option pool. In this case, the extra 10% will come out of the pre-money valuation, resulting in an effective pre-money valuation of $18 million.

There is no magic number for the option pool, and this is often a key point of the pricing negotiation. The typical early stage company option pool ends up in a range of 10% to 20%, with later stage companies having smaller option pools. If the investors believe that the option pool of the company should be increased, they will insist that the increase happens prior to the financing, resulting in the existing shareholders, rather than the incoming investors, being diluted by the new options.

It is important to recognize that the VC is talking about unissued options. You may have already granted options to employees. These are not included in the amount VCs are asking for the pool size, so you will also see the pool referred to as the unissued option pool.

You have several negotiating approaches: You can fight the pool size, trying to get the VCs to end up at 15% instead of 20%; you can accept a 20% pool, but negotiate on the pre-money valuation (for example, by asking for a $22 million pre-money valuation); or you can suggest that the increase in the option pool gets added to the deal post-money, which will result in the same pre-money valuation but a higher post-money valuation. Recognize that in all three of these cases, you are simply negotiating over price.

Once the financing is done, the unissued shares in the option pool are allocated periodically to new and existing employees. The primary allocator of the pool is often the CEO of the company, although option grants have to be approved by the board of directors of the company. So while the pool size could be 20%, the CEO can manage the grants to employees to 10% so that at a time of acquisition the effective dilution from the use of the pool would be only 10%. The unissued options simply vanish into thin air in this situation, giving everyone an incremental 10% ownership of the company (on a pro-rata basis, if you owned 1.0% of the company but 10% of the options vanished, you would now own 1.11% of the company).

The valuation and the size of the option pool should be part of the same discussion during the negotiation. There are three common ways that this shows up, either in the two just listed in the valuation and price section, or the following separate paragraph in the term sheet:

> Employee Pool: Prior to the Closing, the Company will reserve shares of its Common Stock so that _____% of its fully diluted capital stock following the issuance of its Series A Preferred is available for future issuances to directors, officers, employees, and consultants. The term "Employee Pool" shall include both shares reserved for issuance as stated above, as well as current options outstanding, which aggregate amount is approximately _____% of the Company's fully diluted capital stock following the issuance of its Series A Preferred.

As term sheets have continued to evolve, a modern term sheet simply says:

> Unissued Employee Pool: _____%

Let's look at one more example and see how the valuation and the option pool work together. Assume that a $2 million financing is being done at a $10 million post-money valuation. In this case, the new investors get 20% of the company for $2 million and the effective post-money valuation is $10 million. Before the financing there is a 10% unallocated option pool. However, in the term sheet, the investors put a provision that the post-financing unallocated option pool will be 20%. This results in a post-financing ownership split of 20% to the new investors, 60% to the old shareholders, and an unallocated employee pool of 20%.

In contrast, if the 10% option pool that previously existed was simply rolled over, the post-money allocation would still be 20% to new investors, but the old shareholders would get 70% and the unallocated option pool would be 10%.

While in both cases the investors end up with 20%, the old shareholders have 10% less ownership in the case of the 20% option pool. Although the additional ownership will ultimately end up in the hands of future employees, it is effectively coming from the old shareholders rather than being shared between the new investors and the old shareholders. This will result in a lower price per share for the new investors and effectively a lower pre-money valuation.

If the VC is pushing for a larger option pool to come out of the pre-money valuation but the entrepreneur feels that there is enough in the pool to meet the company's needs over the time frame of this financing, the entrepreneur should say, "Look, I strongly believe we have enough options to cover our needs. Let's go with it at my proposed level and if we should need to expand the option pool before the next financing, we will provide full antidilution protection for you to cover that."

The Entrepreneur's Perspective

VCs will want to minimize their risk of future dilution as much as possible by making the option pool as large as possible up front. When you have this negotiation, you should come armed with an *option budget*. List out all of the hires you plan on making between today and your next anticipated financing date and the approximate option grant you think it will take to land each one of them. You should be prepared to have an option pool with more options than your budget calls for, but not necessarily by a huge margin. The option budget will be critical in this conversation with your potential investor.

Warrants

Another economic term associated with financings that you will encounter, especially in later stage financings, is *warrants*. As with the employee option pool, this is another way for an investor to sneak in a lower valuation for the company. A warrant is similar to a stock option and is a right for an investor to purchase a certain number of shares at a predefined price for a certain number of years. For example, a 10-year warrant for 100,000 shares of Series A stock at $1 per share gives the warrant holder the option to buy 100,000 shares of Series A stock at $1 per share anytime in the next decade, regardless of what the stock is worth at the moment in time the investor avails himself of the warrant (which is referred to as exercising the warrant.)

Warrants as part of a venture financing, especially in an early stage investment (where they are rare), tend to create a lot of unnecessary complexity and accounting headaches down the road. If the issue is simply one of price, we recommend the entrepreneur negotiate for a lower pre-money valuation to try to eliminate the warrants. Occasionally, this may be at cross-purposes with existing investors who, for some reason, want to artificially inflate the valuation, since the warrant value is rarely calculated as part of the valuation even though it impacts the future allocation of proceeds in a liquidity event.

There is one type of financing, called a *bridge loan,* in which warrants are commonplace. A bridge loan occurs when an investor is planning to do a financing but is waiting for additional investors to participate. In the bridge loan scenario, the existing investor will make the investment as *convertible debt,* which will convert into equity at the price of the upcoming financing. Since the bridge loan investor took additional risk, he generally gets either a discount on the price of the equity (usually up to 20%) or warrants that effectively grant a discount (again, usually up to 20%, although occasionally more). In bridge round cases, it's not worth fighting these warrants as long as they are structured reasonably. We discuss convertible debt at length in Chapter 8.

The best way to negotiate a higher price is to have multiple VCs interested in investing in your company. This is Economics 101. If you have more demand (VCs interested) than supply (equity in your company to sell), then price will increase. In early rounds, your new investors will likely be looking for the lowest possible price that still leaves enough equity in the founders' and employees' hands. In later rounds, your existing investors will often argue for the highest price for new investors in order to limit the dilution of the existing investors. If there are no new investors interested in investing in your company, your existing investors will often argue for a price equal to (*flat round*) or lower than (*down round*) the price of the previous round. Finally, new investors will always argue for the lowest price they think will enable them to get a financing done, given the appetite (or lack thereof) of the existing investors for putting more money into the company. As an entrepreneur, you are faced with all of these contradictory motivations in a financing, reinforcing the truism that it is incredibly important to pick your early investors wisely, since they can materially help or hurt this process.

The Entrepreneur's Perspective

The best Plan A has a great Plan B standing behind it. The more potential investors you have interested in investing in your company, the better your negotiating position is. Spend as much time on your *best alternative to a negotiated agreement* (BATNA) as possible.

How Valuation Is Determined

By now you may be wondering how VCs value companies. It is not an exact science regardless of the number of spreadsheets involved. VCs take into account many factors when deciding how to value a potential investment. Some are quantifiable while others are completely qualitative. Following are some of the different factors, along with brief explanations of what impacts them.

- *Stage of the company.* Early stage companies tend to have a valuation range that is determined more by the experience of the entrepreneurs, the amount of money being raised, and the perception of the overall opportunity. As companies mature, the historical financial performance and future financial projections start to impact valuation. In later stage companies, supply and demand for the financing combined with financial performance dominate, as investors are beginning to look toward an imminent exit event.
- *Competition with other funding sources.* The simple time-tested rule for the entrepreneur is "more is better." When VCs feel that they are competing with other VCs for a deal, price tends to increase. However, a word of caution: don't overplay competition that doesn't exist. If you do and get caught, you'll damage your current negotiating position, potentially lose the existing investor that you have at the table, and, if nothing else, lose all of your leverage in other aspects of the negotiation. Our belief is that you should always negotiate honestly. Overrepresenting your situation rarely ends well.
- *Experience of the entrepreneurs and leadership team.* The more experienced the entrepreneurs, the less risk, and, correspondingly, the higher the valuation.

- *Size and trendiness of the market.* There will be some pricing influence depending on how large, or trendy, the market is that you are playing in.
- *The VC's natural entry point.* Some VCs are early stage investors and will invest only at low price points. For example, we know of one well-known early stage investor who publicly states the intention not to invest at a valuation above $10 million post-money. Later stage investors tend to be much less focused on a specific price level and care more about the specific status of the company. While VC firms often have stated strategies, it's also the case that they will diverge from these strategies, especially when markets heat up.
- *Numbers, numbers, numbers.* The numbers matter. Whether it is past performance; predictions of the future; revenue; earnings before interest, taxes, depreciation, and amortization (EBITDA); cash burn; or head count, they each factor into the determination of price. That being said, don't believe everything your MBA professor told you about DCF (discounted cash flow, for those of you without an MBA), especially for early stage companies. Remember, the only thing you know for sure about your financial projections at the early stages is that they are wrong.
- *Current economic climate.* Though this is out of the control of the entrepreneur, it weighs heavily on pricing. When the macro economy is in the dumps, valuations are lower. When the macro economy is growing quickly, valuations go up. Specifically, valuations often expand when there is future optimism forecasted about the macro economy. However, these events are not tightly correlated, especially in the technology sector.

Regardless of an investor's justification for the valuation they are giving you, recognize that it's a guess influenced by multiple factors. While numbers matter more in the later stages, don't be insulted if your valuation and a VC's valuation aren't the same, as each of you is coming from a different perspective. Our best advice to entrepreneurs on maximizing price is to focus on what you can control and get several different VCs interested in your financing.

The Entrepreneur's Perspective

I encourage entrepreneurs not to take valuation personally. Just because VCs say their take is that your business is worth $6 million when your take is that your business is worth $10 million, it doesn't mean that they lack appreciation for you as a CEO or for your business's future potential. It means they are negotiating a deal to their advantage, just as you would.

Liquidation Preference

The liquidation preference is another important economic term that impacts how the proceeds are shared in a liquidity event. A liquidity event is usually defined as a sale of the company or the majority of the company's assets. The liquidation preference is especially important in cases in which a company is sold for less than the amount of capital invested.

There are two components that make up what most people call the liquidation preference: the actual preference and participation. To be accurate, the term *liquidation preference* should pertain only to money returned to a particular series of the company's stock ahead of other series of stock. Consider, for instance, the following language:

> Liquidation Preference: In the event of any liquidation or winding down of the Company, the holders of the Series A Preferred shall be entitled to receive in preference to the holders of the Common Stock a per share amount equal to [X] times the Original Purchase Price plus any declared but unpaid dividends.

This is the actual preference. In this language, a certain multiple of the original investment per share is returned to the investor before the common stock receives any consideration. For many years, a 1× liquidation preference, or simply the amount of money invested, was the standard. In this situation, the investors get 100% of their money back before anyone else in the company receives any proceeds from the sale of the company. This makes sense, as an investor wouldn't want to fund a company with $5 million and have the company sold the next day for $5 million and have the proceeds split among all shareholders.

In 2001, as the Internet bubble burst, investors often increased this multiple, sometimes as high as 10× (10 times the amount of money invested). Over time, rational thought prevailed, and this number has generally returned to 1×, although you will often find higher multiples in later stage or distressed financings.

The next thing to consider is whether the investors' shares are participating. With participating stock, the investors will get their preference, which is usually their money back, but also receive additional proceeds after the preference is returned. While many people consider the term liquidation preference to refer to both the preference and the participation, it's important to separate the concepts. There are three varieties of participation: no participation, full participation, and capped participation.

Before we tackle the specifics of participation we need to discuss the concept of conversion. We mentioned earlier that preferred shareholders can convert their preferred stock into common stock at any time. The number of shares that preferred converts into common is determined by a conversion ratio. Normally, the conversion ratio is one to one, meaning that every preferred share will convert to one share of common. This conversion ratio can change, however, due to adjustments for antidilution, which we'll talk about later in the book. In the case where the conversion ratio is 1:1, a preferred holder with 20% of the company in preferred stock can convert into common stock and still hold 20% of the stock but would no longer have any of the rights that they previously had with the preferred stock, including things like liquidation preferences. But the ability to convert allows the preferred shareholder to maximize their payoff during a liquidation event, which will come into play as we explore the three different types of participation.

No participation indicates that the stock doesn't participate after receiving their liquidation preference. You'll hear this called "simple preferred" or "nonparticipating preferred." What this means is that upon a liquidation event, the investor gets its liquidation preference and receives nothing else. Wait. What? Yes, this is true. If an investor buys $5 million of 1× liquidation preference nonparticipating preferred stock and the company sells for $100 million, then the investor would receive exactly $5 million back if they elect to take their liquidation preference.

However, don't fall for the head fake. Remember that the investor can always convert their preferred stock to common stock at any time. Let's assume that the $5 million investment bought 20% of the company and the conversion ratio is 1:1. In this case the investor would convert to common and take 20% of the proceeds, or $20 million. The preference effectively provides downside protection for the investors (where their 20% ownership would be worth less than their investment) while allowing them to have the upside in an exit where they choose to convert to common stock.

On the other end of the spectrum is a fully participation-preferred stock. In this case, the stock will receive its liquidation preference (typically 1×, as we've seen above), and then share in the liquidation proceeds on an *as-converted basis*, where "as-converted" means as if the stock were converted into common stock based on its conversion ratio. The provision normally looks like this:

> Participation: After the payment of the Liquidation Preference to the holders of the Series A Preferred, the remaining assets shall be distributed ratably to the holders of the Common Stock and the Series A Preferred on a common equivalent basis.

In short, this is the "have your cake and eat it too" scenario, where the preferred holder takes their liquidation preference, then gets to share in the remaining proceeds as if they had converted to common. With our above example, the investor would take $5 million off the top and then get 20% of the remaining $95 million for a total of $24 million. Full participation stock guarantees that the preferred holder never converts to common stock unless the conversion ratio has been drastically changed by some other event.

The final form of participation is capped participation. This indicates that the stock will receive its liquidation preference and then share in the liquidation proceeds on an as-converted basis until a certain multiple of the original purchase price is reached. Once the return is greater than the cap, the participation stops. Sample language is as follows.

> Participation: After the payment of the Liquidation Preference to the holders of the Series A Preferred, the remaining assets shall be distributed ratably to the holders of the Common Stock and the Series A Preferred on a common equivalent basis,

provided that the holders of Series A Preferred will stop partici-pating once they have received a total liquidation amount per share equal to [X] times the Original Purchase Price, plus any declared but unpaid dividends. Thereafter, the remaining assets shall be distributed ratably to the holders of the Common Stock.

One interesting thing to note in this section is the actual mean-ing of the multiple of the original purchase price (the [X]). If the participation multiple is three (three times the original purchase price), it would mean that the preferred would stop participating (on a per share basis) once 300% of its original purchase price was returned, including any amounts paid out on the liquidation preference, plus any declared but unpaid dividends. This is not an additional 3× return, but rather an additional 2×, assuming the liq-uidation preference was a 1× money-back return. Perhaps this close association with the actual preference is the reason the term liqui-dation preference has come to include both the preference and participation terms. If the series is not participating, it will not have a paragraph that looks like the preceding ones.

Let's see how this plays out in real life with some examples. To keep it simple, let's assume that there has been only one round of financing (a Series A investment) of $5 million at a $10 million pre-money valuation. The post-money is $15 million in this case. The Series A investors own 33.3% of the company (which is $5,000,000/ $15,000,000), and the entrepreneurs own 66.7% of the company. We are going to look at four scenarios:

Case 1: The Series A stock has a 1× liquidation preference and no participation;

Case 2: The Series A stock has a 2× liquidation preference and no participation;

Case 3: The Series A stock has a 1× liquidation preference and is fully participating (no cap); and

Case 4: The Series A stock has a 1× liquidation preference and is participating up to a 3× cap.

For the ease of math, we'll also round the ownership numbers to 33% and 67%, respectively, instead of dealing with repeating deci-mals. In the real world, spreadsheets come in handy here.

Now, assume that the company has an offer to be acquired for $5 million. The preferred holders, as long as they have a 1× liquidation preference (regardless of any participation features), have the right to the entire consideration of the deal given that they invested $5 million and the deal size doesn't clear the investment amount. With companies that have raised a lot of money, any acquisition that doesn't clear the invested capital leaves the common shut out of the proceeds due to the preferred stockholders' liquidation preference. You'll hear this mentioned as the *liquidation preference overhang,* which is the amount of money that needs to be returned to investors to satisfy all liquidation preferences before the common holders begin to receive some of the proceeds.

Next, assume that the company has an offer to be acquired for $15 million.

> *Case 1: 1× preference, nonparticipating.* The Series A can either take its $5 million liquidation preference or convert to common and take 33% of the proceeds, which in this case is also $5 million. Note that the common gets $10 million here.
>
> *Case 2: 2× preference, nonparticipating.* The Series A can either take their 2× preference, which is $10 million, or convert to common and take 33%, which is $5 million. In this case, the Series A takes the $10 million, leaving $5 million to the common, which is half of what they would have made in Case 1.
>
> *Case 3: 1× preference, participating.* In this case, the Series A investors will get the first $5 million and then 33% of the remaining amount, or $3.3 million (33% of $10 million) for a total return of $8.3 million. The common will get 67% of the $10 million, or $6.7 million. Notice that in a fully participating security, there is never any reason for the preferred to convert. Once again, think of this situation as having your cake and eating it also.
>
> *Case 4: 1× preference, participating with a 3× cap.* In this case, the preferred will not reach the cap ($15 million), so this will be the same as Case 3.

Then, assume that the company has an offer to be acquired for $30 million.

Case 1: 1× preference, nonparticipating. In this case, the Series A converts and gets 33%, or $10 million, and the common will get 67%, or $20 million. If the Series A did not convert, they would only receive $5 million, which is why it converts.

Case 2: 2× preference, nonparticipating. In this case, the Series A investors will get 33%, or $10 million, and the common will get 67%, or $20 million. Note that both the conversion and nonconversion cases lead to the same allocation of proceeds.

Case 3: 1× preference, participating. In this case, the Series A investors will get the first $5 million and then 33% of the remaining amount, or $8.3 million (33% of $25 million) for a total return of $13.3 million. The common will get 67% of the $25 million, or $16.7 million.

Case 4: 1× preference, participating with a 3× cap. In this case, the preferred will not reach the cap ($15 million), so this will be the same as Case 3. The preferred will not convert and will take $13.3 million, with the common getting $16.7 million.

Finally, assume the purchase price is $100 million.

Case 1: 1× preference, nonparticipating. The Series A investors will get 33%, or $33 million, and the common will get 67%, or $67 million. The Series A converts, as otherwise it would only receive $5 million.

Case 2: 2× preference, nonparticipating. The Series A investors will get 33%, or $33 million, and the entrepreneurs will get 67%, or $67 million. The Series A again converts; otherwise, it would only receive $10 million.

Case 3: 1× preference, participating. Again, the Series A investors get the first $5 million and then 33% of the remaining $95 million, or $31.35 million, for a total of $36.35 million. The common get 67% of the remaining $95 million, or $63.65 million.

Case 4: 1× preference, participating with a 3× cap. In this example, the Series A makes a return better than 3× ($15 million), so the participation doesn't happen and they convert. The results are the same as in Cases 1 and 2.

As you can see from this example, the participation feature has a lot of impact at relatively low outcomes and less impact (on a percentage of the deal basis) at higher outcomes because at these higher outcomes, the preferred are better off converting into common. The participation feature will also matter a lot more as more money is raised that has the participation feature (e.g., Series B and C). To understand this, let's do one last example, this time of a company that has raised $50 million and where the investors own 60% and the entrepreneurs own 40%. Assume the company is being acquired for $100 million.

> *Case 1: 1× preference, nonparticipating.* The investors can either take $50 million or convert. They convert, since doing so results in them getting $60 million. The common gets $40 million.
>
> *Case 2: 2× preference, nonparticipating.* The investors will get $100 million, or all of the consideration, since it is 2× their invested capital. The common gets nothing. Ouch.
>
> *Case 3: 1× preference, participating.* Investors get the first $50 million and then 60% of the remaining $50 million ($30 million) for a total of $80 million. The common gets 40% of the remaining $50 million, or $20 million. Again, ouch.
>
> *Case 4: 1× preference, participating with a 3× cap.* Since the investors won't make greater than 3× ($150 million) on this deal, this is the same as Case 3.

Liquidation preferences are usually easy to understand and assess when dealing with a Series A term sheet. It gets much more complicated to understand what is going on as a company matures and sells additional series of equity, since understanding how liquidation preferences work between the various series is often mathematically, and structurally, challenging. As with many VC-related issues, the approach to liquidation preferences among multiple series of stock varies and is often overly complex for no apparent reason.

There are two primary approaches:

1. The follow-on investors will stack their preferences on top of each other (known as *stacked preferences*) where Series B gets its preference first, then Series A.

2. The series are equivalent in status (known as *pari passu* or *blended preferences*) so that Series A and B share pro-ratably until the preferences are returned.

Determining which approach to use is a black art that is influenced by the relative negotiating power of the investors involved, ability of the company to go elsewhere for additional financing, economic dynamics of the existing capital structure, and the current phase of the moon.

Let's look at an example. This time, our example company has raised two rounds of financing, a Series A ($5 million invested at a $10 million pre-money valuation) and a Series B ($20 million invested at a $30 million pre-money valuation). Now, let's deal with a low outcome, one where the liquidation preference is going to come into play, namely a sale of the company for $15 million.

If the preference is stacked, the Series B investors will get the entire $15 million. In fact, in this case it won't matter what the pre-money valuation of the Series B was; they'll get 100% of the consideration regardless.

However, if the preference is blended, the Series A will get 20% of every dollar returned (in this case $3 million) and the Series B will get 80% of every dollar returned (or $12 million), based on their relative amounts of the capital invested in the company.

In each of these cases the entrepreneurs will receive nothing regardless of whether the preference includes a participating or non-participating element since the preference is $25 million and the company is being sold for $15 million, or less than the preference.

Note that investors get either the liquidation preference and participation amounts (if any) or what they would get on a fully converted common holding, at their election; they do not get both. Realize, however, that in the fully participating case the investors get their liquidation preference amount and then receive what they would get on a fully converted common holding basis.

In early stage financings, it's actually in the best interest of both the investor and the entrepreneur to have a simple liquidation preference and no participation. In future rounds, the terms are often inherited from the early stage terms since investors love precedents from earlier rounds that favor them. So if you have a participating preferred in a seed round, you could expect to have a participating preferred in all subsequent rounds. In this case, if the seed investor doesn't participate in future rounds, his economics in many outcomes could actually be worse with the participation feature. While the early investor might think he is negotiating a great deal for himself, early investors end up looking like the common holders (in terms of returns), since their preference amounts are so small. As a result, we recommend to entrepreneurs and our VC co-investors to keep it simple and lightweight in early rounds.

Most professional investors will not want to gouge a company with excessive liquidation preferences since the greater the liquidation preference, the lower the potential value of the management or employee equity. There's a fine balance here and each case is situation specific, but a rational investor will want a combination of the best price while ensuring maximum motivation of management and employees. Obviously, what happens in the end is a negotiation and depends on the stage of the company, bargaining strength, and existing capital structure. But, in general, most companies and their investors will reach a reasonable compromise regarding these provisions. Ultimately, reputable investors will rarely leave the management team with nothing on a liquidation event that is below the liquidation preferences despite what the legal documents dictate, a situation called a *management carve-out*, which we will discuss later.

Lastly, since we've been talking about liquidation preferences, it's important to define what a *liquidation event* is. Often, entrepreneurs think of a liquidation event as a bad thing, such as a bankruptcy or a winding down of the company. In VC-speak, a liquidation is actually tied to a *liquidity event* in which the shareholders receive proceeds for their equity in a company and includes mergers, *acquisitions*, or a change of control of the company. As a result, the liquidation preference section determines the allocation of proceeds in both good times and bad. Standard language defining a liquidation event looks like this:

> Liquidation Event: A merger, acquisition, sale of voting control in which the shareholders of the Company do not own a majority of the outstanding shares of the surviving corporation or sale of all or substantially all of the assets of the Company shall be deemed to be a liquidation. Any acquisition agreement that provides for escrowed or other contingent consideration will provide that the allocation of such contingent amounts properly accounts for the liquidation preference of the Preferred Stock.

Ironically, lawyers don't necessarily agree on a standard definition of a liquidation event. Jason once had an entertaining and unpleasant debate during a guest lecture he gave at his alma mater law school (University of Michigan, for those of you wondering) with a partner from a major Chicago law firm. At the time, this partner was teaching a venture class that semester and claimed that an initial public offering (IPO) should be considered a liquidation event. His theory was that an IPO was the same as a merger, that the company was going away, and thus the investors should get their proceeds. Even if such a theory were accepted by an investment banker who would be willing to take the company public (there's not a chance, in our opinion), it makes no sense, as an IPO is simply another funding event for the company, not a liquidation of the company. In fact, in almost all IPO scenarios, the VC's preferred stock is converted to common stock as part of the IPO, eliminating the issue around a liquidity event in the first place.

The Entrepreneur's Perspective

Liquidation preference is a critical term that is part of most equity financings other than small angel financings. Participating preferred deals have become an unfortunate standard over the years, where VCs have essentially decided on a new standard floor for deals that require the repayment of principal as well as a common stock interest in the company on the sale of a company. In the mid-1990s, companies used to negotiate so-called kick-outs whereby participation rights went away as long as the company had achieved a meaningful return for the VC (2x to 3x). Entrepreneurs should band together to reinstate this as a standard!

Anything other than a straight participating preferred security, such as multiple preferences, is just greedy on the part of VCs and should be a red flag to you about the investor.

Pay-to-Play

The *pay-to-play* provision is another economic term that is usually relevant in a down round financing and can be very useful to the entrepreneur in situations where the company is struggling and needs another financing. In a pay-to-play provision, investors must keep investing pro-ratably in future financings (paying) in order to not have their preferred stock converted to common stock (playing) in the company.

A typical pay-to-play provision follows:

Pay-to-Play: In the event of a Qualified Financing (as defined below), shares of Series A Preferred held by any Investor which is offered the right to participate but does not participate fully in such financing by purchasing at least its pro rata portion as calculated under "Right of First Refusal" will be converted into Common Stock.

A Qualified Financing is the next round of financing after the Series A financing by the Company that is approved by the Board of Directors who determine in good faith that such portion must be purchased pro rata among the stockholders of the Company subject to this provision. Such determination will be made regardless of whether the price is higher or lower than any series of Preferred Stock.

At the turn of the millennium, a pay-to-play provision was rarely seen. After the dot-com bubble burst in 2001, it became ubiquitous. Interestingly, this is a term that most companies and their investors can agree on if they approach it from the right perspective.

There are various levels of intensity of the pay-to-play provision. The preceding one is pretty aggressive when compared to the following softer one:

If any holder of Series A Preferred Stock fails to participate in the next Qualified Financing (as defined below), on a pro rata basis (according to its total equity ownership immediately before such financing) of their Series A Preferred investment, then such holder will have the Series A Preferred Stock it owns converted into Common Stock of the Company. If such holder participates in the next Qualified Financing but not to the full extent of its pro rata share, then only a percentage of its Series A Preferred Stock will be converted into Common Stock (under the same terms as in the preceding sentence), with such percentage being equal to the percent of its pro rata contribution that it failed to contribute.

When determining the number of shares held by an Investor or whether this "Pay-to-Play" provision has been satisfied, all shares held by or purchased in the Qualified Financing by affiliated investment funds shall be aggregated. An Investor shall be entitled to assign its rights to participate in this financing and future financings to its affiliated funds and to investors in the Investor and/or its affiliated funds, including funds that are not current stockholders of the Company.

We believe that pay-to-play provisions are generally good for the company and its investors. It causes the investors to stand up at the time of their original investment and agree to support the company during its life cycle. If they don't, the stock they have is converted from preferred to common and they lose the rights associated with the preferred stock. When our co-investors push back on this term, we ask: "Why? Are you not going to fund the company in the future if other investors agree to?" Remember, this is not a life-time guarantee of investment; rather, if other prior investors decide to invest in future rounds in the company, there will be a strong incentive for all of the prior investors to invest or subject themselves to total or partial conversion of their holdings to common stock. A pay-to-play term ensures that all the investors agree in advance to the rules of engagement concerning future financings.

The pay-to-play provision impacts the economics of the deal by reducing liquidation preferences for the nonparticipating investors. It also impacts the control of the deal since it reshuffles the future preferred shareholder base by ensuring that only the committed investors continue to have preferred stock and the corresponding rights that go along with preferred stock.

When companies are doing well, the pay-to-play provision is often waived since a new investor wants to take a large part of the new round. This is a good problem for a company to have, as it typically means there is an up-round financing, existing investors can help drive company-friendly terms in the new round, and the investor syndicate increases in strength by virtue of new capital (and, presumably, another helpful co-investor) in the deal.

There are situations where the pay-to-play provision may not be appropriate, especially in early rounds if you have investors who generally do not participate in follow-on rounds as a matter of business practice. For instance, if a micro VC or seed fund leads your round, they often don't ever participate in future funding rounds. In these cases, a pay-to-play provision will inappropriately penalize them in the future for supporting you at the beginning when you critically needed their funding. Make sure that you understand the future funding dynamics of your VC partner and treat them accordingly.

The Entrepreneur's Perspective

This pay-to-play provision is pretty good for you as an entrepreneur, at least as it's described here. Conversion to common is no big deal in the grand scheme of things. What you want to avoid is a pay-to-play scenario where your VC has the right to force a recapitalization of the company (e.g., a financing at a $0 pre-money valuation, or something suitably low) if fellow investors don't play into a new round.

A provision like this can be particularly bad for less sophisticated angel investors (e.g., your friends and family) if they don't have the understanding or resources to back up their initial investment with future follow-on investments, and can make for uncomfortable conversations around family events.

There are many circumstances where reasonable investors who like the company can't or won't participate in a financing—their venture fund is over, or they are strategic or angel investors and don't have the funds or charter to continue investing—and you and they shouldn't be punished excessively for not participating (remember, a recapitalization hurts you, too, even if you get new options, which always carry vesting, to "top you off"). But conversion to common for lack of follow-on investment is appropriate.

Vesting

Although vesting is a simple concept, it can have profound and unexpected implications. Vesting is the concept that when an employee is granted a stock option, they don't get the entire award on their first day. Typically, stock options will vest over four years with a one-year cliff. This means that an employee will have to be around for one year to receive any vesting and on that day will receive vesting worth 25% of the award with the balance equally vested over the next three years. If the employee leaves the company before the end of the four-year period, the vesting formula applies and they get only a percentage of the stock. Founders and executives use vesting as an employee retention mechanism. VCs will also impose vesting on founder shares if there aren't any prior to a financing. Many entrepreneurs view vesting as a way for VCs to control them, their involvement, and their ownership in a company, which, while it can be true, is only a part of the story.

A typical stock-vesting clause follows:

> Stock Vesting: All stock and stock equivalents issued after the Closing to employees, directors, consultants, and other service

providers will be subject to vesting provisions below unless different vesting is approved by the majority (including at least one director designated by the Investors) consent of the Board of Directors (the "Required Approval"): 25 percent to vest at the end of the first year following such issuance, with the remaining 75 percent to vest monthly over the next three years. The repurchase option shall provide that upon termination of the employment of the shareholder, with or without cause, the Company or its assignee (to the extent permissible under applicable securities law qualification) retains the option to repurchase at the lower of cost or the current fair market value any unvested shares held by such shareholder. Any issuance of shares in excess of the Employee Pool not approved by the Required Approval will be a dilutive event requiring adjustment of the conversion price as provided above and will be subject to the Investors' first offer rights.

The outstanding Common Stock currently held by ____ and ____ (the "Founders") will be subject to similar vesting terms provided that the Founders shall be credited with [one year] of vesting as of the Closing, with their remaining unvested shares to vest monthly over three years.

Again, industry standard vesting for early stage companies is a one-year *vesting cliff* and monthly vesting thereafter for a total of four years. This means that if you leave before the first year is up, you haven't vested any of your stock. After a year, you have vested 25% (that's the cliff). Then you begin vesting monthly (or quarterly, or annually) over the remaining period. If you have a monthly vest with a one-year cliff and you leave the company after 18 months, you'll have vested 37.5% (or 18/48) of your stock.

Often, founders will get somewhat different vesting provisions than the rest of the employees. A common term is the second paragraph of the example clause, where the founders receive one year of vesting credit at the closing of the financing and then vest the balance of their stock over the remaining 36 months. This type of vesting arrangement is typical in cases where the founders started the company a year or more earlier than the VC investment and want to get some credit for existing time served. In cases where the founders started the company within a year of the first VC investment, they will occasionally be able to argue for vesting back to the inception of the company.

Unvested stock typically disappears into the ether when someone leaves the company. The equity doesn't get reallocated; rather, it gets reabsorbed and everyone, including VCs, stockholders, and option holders, benefits ratably from the increase in ownership, also known as *reverse dilution.* In the case of founders' stock, the unvested stuff just vanishes. In the case of unvested employee options, it usually goes back into the option pool to be reissued to future employees.

In some cases, founders own their stock outright through a purchase at the time that the company is established. While the description of what happens to this founders' stock is often referred to as vesting, it's actually a buy-back right of the company. Though there are technically the same outcomes, the legal language around this is somewhat different and matters for tax purposes.

The Entrepreneur's Perspective

How a founder's stock vests is important. Although simple vesting can work, you should consider alternative strategies such as the company allowing you to purchase your unvested stock at the same price as the financing if you leave, protecting your position for a termination "without cause," or treating your vesting as a *clawback* with an Internal Revenue Code Section 83(b) election so you can lock in long-term capital gains tax rates early on (which is discussed later in this book).

A key component of vesting is defining what, if anything, happens to vesting schedules upon a merger. *Single-trigger acceleration* refers to automatic accelerated vesting upon a merger. *Double-trigger acceleration* refers to two events needing to take place before accelerated vesting, specifically an acquisition of the company combined with the employee in question being fired by the acquiring company.

In VC-funded deals, a double trigger is much more common than a single trigger. Acceleration on change of control is often a contentious point of negotiation between founders and VCs, as the founders will want to get all their stock in a transaction. The founders will argue that "Hey, we earned it!" while the VCs will want to minimize the impact of the outstanding equity on their share of the purchase price. Most acquirers will want there to be some forward-looking incentive for founders, management, and employees, so they usually prefer some unvested equity to exist to help motivate folks to stick around for a period of time post acquisition. In the absence of this, the acquirer will include a separate management retention incentive as part of the deal value. Since this management retention piece is included in the value of the transaction, it effectively reduces the consideration that gets allocated to the equity owners of the company, including the VCs and any founders who are no longer actively involved in the company. This often frustrates VCs since it puts them at cross-purposes with management in an acquisition negotiation—everyone should be negotiating to maximize the value for all shareholders, not just specifically for themselves. Although the actual legal language is not very interesting, it is included here:

> In the event of a merger, consolidation, sale of assets, or other change of control of the Company and should an Employee be terminated without cause within one year after such event, such person shall be entitled to [one year] of additional vesting. Other than the foregoing, there shall be no accelerated vesting in any event.

Structuring acceleration on change-of-control terms used to be a huge deal in the 1990s when pooling of interests was an accepted form of accounting treatment, since there were significant constraints on any modifications to vesting agreements. Pooling was abolished in early 2000, and under current acquisition accounting treatment (also known as purchase accounting) there is no meaningful accounting impact of changing the vesting arrangements in a merger (including accelerating vesting). As a result, we usually recommend a balanced approach to acceleration such as a double trigger with one-year acceleration and recognize that this will often be negotiated during an acquisition. Many VCs have a distinct point of view on this; some VCs will never do a deal with single-trigger acceleration, whereas some VCs don't really care very much. As in any negotiation, make sure you are not negotiating against a point of principle, as VCs will often say, "That's how it is and we won't do anything different."

Vesting works for the founders as well as the VCs. We have been involved in a number of situations where one founder didn't stay with the company very long, either by choice or because the other founders wanted her to leave the company. In these situations, if there hadn't been vesting provisions, the person who didn't stay at the company would have walked away with all of her stock and the remaining founders would have had no differential ownership going forward. By vesting each founder, there is a clear incentive to work your hardest and participate constructively in the team, beyond the founder's moral imperative. The same rule applies to employees; since equity is another form of compensation, vesting is the mechanism to ensure the equity is earned over time.

Time to exit has a huge impact on the relevancy of vesting. In the late 1990s, when companies often reached an exit event within two years of being founded, the vesting provisions, especially acceleration clauses, mattered a huge amount to the founders. In a market where the typical gestation period of an early stage company is five to seven years, most people, especially founders and early employees who stay with a company, will be fully (or mostly) vested at the time of an exit event.

While it's easy to set up vesting as a contentious issue between founders and VCs, we recommend the founding entrepreneurs view vesting as an overall alignment tool—for themselves, their cofounders, early employees, and future employees. Anyone who has experienced an unfair vesting situation will have strong feelings about it; a balanced approach and consistency are key to making vesting provisions work for the long term in a company.

The Entrepreneur's Perspective

While single-trigger acceleration might seem appealing, double-trigger acceleration with some boundaries makes a lot of sense. Any entrepreneur who has been on the buy side of an acquisition will tell you that having one or two years' worth of guaranteed transition on the part of an acquired management team is critical to an acquisition's financial success.

Exercise Period

One provision that is not generally found in term sheets but that is closely aligned with vesting is the concept of an *exercise period*. Once stock is vested, a holder may exercise the option by paying the purchase price to the company. In other words, if you have an option for 1,000 shares of stock at $0.10 a share, you can pay $100 to the company (after all the shares have vested) and own the stock outright. Often, current employees of a company don't do this, as they want to see how successful the company will be before they use funds to purchase stock, although if the cost of exercising is low enough there's a significant tax advantage by exercising the options, as you'll now own stock that will be subject to capital gains tax treatment, instead of options, which are subject to ordinary income tax treatment.

However, once a person leaves a company, the exercise period determines how long the departed employee has to purchase their stock. Historically, this time period has been 90 days. If you leave the company for any reason (voluntarily or not), then you have up to 90 days to pay the $100 to the company for the stock; otherwise the stock would be forfeited and returned to the stock option plan to be granted to other employees.

There have been recent efforts to change this, as some feel it's not fair for recently departed employees to have to pay for their options within 90 days or forfeit the stock they earned during their employment. There are some companies that have changed their exercise periods to the maximum legal amount, which is 10 years from the date of grant.

As a current topic, it will be interesting to see how this all works out. What concerns us about the extension of the exercise period is that it allows people to change jobs frequently and acquire options in a number of companies, undermining the retention benefits of options. Furthermore, the ultimate balance of equity between early employees who leave within a year or two, but hold on to their options for a decade can get out of alignment with later employees, who stay longer, but start with fewer options.

At this point, we tend to prefer to deal with this issue on a case-by-case basis. If the employee leaving merits this type of treatment, the company can always choose to extend the exercise period as part of the termination agreement.

Antidilution

The final key economic provision is *antidilution*. While not usually contentious from a negotiation standpoint, it is important to pay attention to. This term is what will change the conversion ratio that we discussed in the liquidation preference section and is what protects investors from having their ownership diluted in certain situations. A typical antidilution clause in a term sheet follows:

> Antidilution Provisions: The conversion price of the Series A Preferred will be subject to a [full ratchet/broad-based/narrow based weighted average] adjustment to reduce dilution in the event that the Company issues additional equity securities— other than shares (i) reserved as employee shares described under the Company's option pool; (ii) shares issued for consideration other than cash pursuant to a merger, consolidation, acquisition, or similar business combination approved by the Board; (iii) shares issued pursuant to any equipment loan or leasing arrangement, real property leasing arrangement, or debt financing from a bank or similar financial institution approved by the Board; and (iv) shares with respect to which the holders of a majority of the outstanding Series A Preferred waive their antidilution rights—at a purchase price less than the applicable conversion price. In the event of an issuance of stock involving tranches or other multiple closings, the antidilution adjustment shall be calculated as if all stock was issued at the first closing. The conversion price will also be subject to proportional adjustment for stock splits, stock dividends, combinations, recapitalizations, and the like.

Yeah, we agree—that's a mouthful. It's also a clause that often trips up entrepreneurs. While the antidilution provision is usually used to protect investors in the event a company issues equity at a lower valuation than in previous financing rounds, it is also an excuse for lawyers to use a spreadsheet. There are two varieties: *weighted average antidilution* and *ratchet-based antidilution*.

Full ratchet antidilution means that if the company issues shares at a price lower than the price for the series with the full ratchet provision, then the earlier round price is effectively reduced to the price of the new issuance. One can get creative and do partial ratchets, such as half ratchets or two-thirds ratchets, which are less harsh but rarely seen.

Full ratchets came into vogue in the 2001–2003 time frame when down rounds were all the rage, but the most common antidilution provision is based on the weighted average concept, which takes into account the magnitude of the lower-priced issuance, not just the actual valuation. In a full ratchet world, if the company sold one share of its stock to someone for a price lower than the previous round, all of the previous round stock would be repriced to the new issuance price. In a weighted average world, the number of shares issued at the reduced price is considered in the repricing of the previous round.

Mathematically, it works as follows:

$$NCP - OCP * \frac{CSO - CSP}{CSO + CSAP}$$

where
      NCP = new conversion price
      OCP = old conversion price
      CSO = common stock outstanding
      CSP = common stock purchasable with consideration received by company (i.e., what the buyer should have bought if it hadn't been a down round issuance)
      CSAP = common stock actually purchased in subsequent issuance (i.e., what the buyer actually bought)

Note that despite the fact that one is buying preferred stock, the calculations are always done on an as-if-converted to common stock basis. The company is not issuing more shares; rather, it determines a new conversion price for the previous series of stock. Alternatively, the company can issue more shares, but we think this is a silly and unnecessarily complicated approach that merely increases the amount the lawyers can bill the company for the financing. Consequently, antidilution provisions usually generate a *conversion price adjustment.*

You might note the term *broad-based* in describing weighted average antidilution. What makes the provision broad-based versus narrow-based is the definition of common stock outstanding (CSO). A broad-based weighted average provision encompasses both the company's common stock outstanding (including all common stock issuable upon conversion of its preferred stock) as well as the number of shares of common stock that could be obtained by converting all other options, rights, and securities (including employee options). A narrow-based provision will not include these other convertible securities and will limit the calculation to only currently outstanding securities. The number of shares and how you count them matter; make sure you are agreeing on the same definition, since you'll often find different lawyers arguing over what to include or not include in the definitions.

In our example language, we've included a section that is generally referred to as "antidilution *carve-outs*"—the section "other than shares (i) ... (iv)." These are the standard exceptions for shares granted at lower prices for which antidilution does not apply. From a company and entrepreneur perspective, more exceptions are better, and most investors will accept these carve-outs without much argument.

One particular item to note is the last carve-out:

> (iv) shares with respect to which the holders of a majority of the outstanding Series A Preferred waive their antidilution rights.

This is a carve-out that started appearing recently, which we have found to be very helpful in deals where a majority of the Series A investors agree to further fund a company in a follow-on financing, but the price will be lower than the original Series A. In this example, several minority investors signaled they were not planning to invest in the new round, as they would have preferred to sit back and increase their ownership stake via the antidilution provision. Having the larger investors (the majority of the class) step up and vote to carve the financing out of the antidilution terms was a bonus for the company common stockholders and employees, who would have suffered the dilution of additional antidilution from investors who were not continuing to participate in financing the company. This approach encourages the minority investors to participate in the round in order to protect themselves from dilution.

Occasionally, antidilution will be absent in a Series A term sheet. Remember, investors love precedent (e.g., the new investor says, "I want what the last guy got, plus more"). In many cases, antidilution provisions hurt Series A investors more than later investors, if you assume the Series A price is the low-water mark for the company. For instance, if the Series A price is $1, the Series B price is $5, and the Series C price is $3, then the Series B benefits from the antidilution provision at the expense of the Series A. Our experience is that antidilution is usually requested despite this, as Series B investors will most likely always ask for it and, since they do, the Series A investors proactively ask for it anyway.

In addition to economic impacts, antidilution provisions can have control impacts. First, the existence of an antidilution provision will motivate the company to issue new rounds of stock at higher valuations because of the impact of antidilution protection on the common stockholders. In some cases, a company may pass on taking an additional investment at a lower valuation, although practically speaking, this happens only when a company has other alternatives to the financing. A recent phenomenon is to tie antidilution calculations to milestones the investors have set for the company, resulting in a conversion price adjustment in the case that the company does not meet certain revenue, product development, or other business milestones. In this situation, the antidilution adjustment occurs automatically if the company does not meet its objectives, unless the investor waives it after the fact. This creates a powerful incentive for the company to accomplish its investor-determined goals. We tend to avoid this approach, as blindly hitting predetermined product and sales milestones set at the time of a financing is not always best for the long-term development of a company, especially if these goals end up creating a diverging set of objectives between management and the investors as the business evolves.

Antidilution provisions are almost always part of a financing, so understanding the nuances and knowing which aspects to negotiate are an important part of the entrepreneur's tool kit. We advise you not to get hung up trying to eliminate antidilution provisions. Instead, focus on minimizing their impact and building value in your company after the financing so they don't ever come into play.

CHAPTER 6

Control Terms of the Term Sheet

The terms we discussed in the preceding chapter define the economics of a deal. The next set of terms define the control provisions of a deal. Control provisions are important to venture capitalists, since they aren't at the company on a daily basis (if they are, you have a different issue) and they want a say in actions that could materially affect their investment. Additionally, some control provisions are necessary to prevent VCs from running afoul of the fiduciary duties they owe both to their investors (their *limited partners*) and to the company. While VCs often have less than 50% ownership of a company, they usually have a variety of control terms that effectively give them control of many activities of the company.

In this chapter we discuss the following terms: *board of directors, protective provisions, drag-along,* and *conversion.*

Board of Directors

One of the key control mechanisms is the process for electing the *board of directors.* The board of directors is the most powerful element of a company's management structure and almost always has the power to fire the CEO. The board has to approve many important actions that the company takes, including budgets, option plans, mergers, IPOs, new offices, significant expenditures, financings, and hiring of C-level executives. Entrepreneurs should think carefully about the proper balance among investor, company, founder, and outside representation on the board.

The Entrepreneur's Perspective

Electing a board of directors is an important, and delicate, point. Your board is your strategic planning department, judge, jury, and executioner all at once. Some VCs are terrible board members, even if they're good investors and nice people.

A typical board of directors clause follows:

Board of Directors: The size of the Company's Board of Directors shall be set at [X]. The Board shall initially be comprised of _____, as the Investor representative[s] _____, _____, and _____. At each meeting for the election of directors, the holders of the Series A Preferred, voting as a separate class, shall be entitled to elect [X] member[s] of the Company's Board of Directors which director shall be designated by Investor, the holders of Common Stock, voting as a separate class, shall be entitled to elect [X] member[s], and the remaining directors will be [Option 1: mutually agreed upon by the Common and Preferred, voting together as a single class] [or Option 2: chosen by the mutual consent of the Board of Directors].

This paragraph is subject to negotiation. First, consider how many board members there are. In our experience, more is not merrier. Like at any meeting, there are advantages and disadvantages to having more people in a room.

As shown in the example paragraph, the election of the "remaining directors" is often hotly negotiated. There are two typical options: common and preferred voting as a single class and by mutual consent. The first of these would allow the class (common or preferred) that has the majority of the ownership of the company to elect the director, whereas the second means that everyone needs to agree.

These remaining directors are important and are independent, or *outside directors*. They are people who are not a major investor or an executive at the company. Usually these people are from a relevant industry that can help the company with networking and insights in the ecosystem they participate in. Many outside board members are former or current CEOs who can act as mentors to the executive team. And, if experienced directors, these outsiders can mediate issues that arise between the company and investor-elected board members.

VCs will often want to include a board observer as part of the agreement either instead of or in addition to an official member of the board. The value of this will depend on who the observer is. With many VC firms, the observer will be an associate in the firm. In these cases, some will be there just to learn. In the worst cases they will talk about board topics to their friends over beers in order to look cool. In the best cases they can be immensely helpful and, in some cases, even be more helpful than the VC partner on the board.

The Entrepreneur's Perspective

Be wary of observers. Sometimes they add no value, yet they do take up seats at the table. Often, it's not about who votes at a board meeting, but the discussion that occurs, so observers can sway the balance of a board. You don't want to find yourself with a prerevenue company and 15 people around the table at a board meeting.

Most investors will mandate that one of the board members chosen by common stockholders be the then-serving CEO of the company. This can be tricky if the CEO is also one of the key founders (often you'll see language giving the right to a board seat to one of the founders and a separate board seat to the then CEO, taking two of the common board seats). Then, if the CEO changes, so does that board seat.

Let's go through two examples: an early stage board for a company that has raised its first round of capital and the board of a company that is mature and contemplating an initial public offering (IPO).

In the case of the early stage board, there will typically be three to five board members:

The three-person board will typically consist of:

1. Founder/CEO
2. VC
3. An outside board member, or perhaps another founder

The five-person board will typically consist of:

1. Founder
2. CEO

3. VC
4. A second VC
5. An outside board member

These are the default cases for a balanced board that gives the VC enough influence to be comfortable without having control over the board. Correspondingly, the founder(s) and CEO will have the same number of seats as the VCs, and the outside board member will be able to help resolve any conflicts that arise as well as be a legitimately independent board member.

In the case of a mature board, you'll typically see more members (seven to nine) who are outside board members. The CEO and one of the founders are on this board along with a few of the VCs (depending on the amount of money raised). However, the majority of the additions to the board are outside board members, typically experienced entrepreneurs or executives in the domain in which the company is operating.

While it is appropriate for board members and observers to be reimbursed for their reasonable out-of-pocket costs for attending board meetings, we rarely see board members receive cash compensation for serving on the board of a private company. Outside board members are usually compensated with stock options just like key employees. In addition, they are occasionally invited to invest money in the company alongside the VCs. Usually you see these outsiders receive options to purchase 0.25% to 0.5% of the company that vest over two to four years.

We are of the opinion that VCs don't want to control boards of portfolio companies. If the board votes are really that contentious, then the company is in serious trouble. Instead of controlling the board, VCs generally use *protective provisions*, which we will discuss in the next section, to provide the control they want over the company.

We are also of the opinion that the founders are better off not controlling the board, either. Having an outside board member can be invaluable for certain corporate governance issues that one will want an impartial vote for. Also, having a true outside board member will bring diversity of thought that most insiders (including both the common and preferred holders) won't bring to the board room.

If you are interested in learning a lot more about how boards of directors work, and more importantly how to make them useful, get a copy of one of Brad's other books (edited by Jason), titled *Startup Boards: Getting the Most Out of Your Board of Directors.*

Protective Provisions

The next key control term you will encounter in the term sheet is *protective provisions.* Protective provisions are effectively veto rights that investors have on certain actions by the company. Not surprisingly, these provisions protect VCs, although unfortunately not from themselves.

Once upon a time, the protective provisions were often intensely negotiated but over time have mostly become standardized. Entrepreneurs would like to see few or no protective provisions in their documents. In contrast, VCs would like to have some veto-level control over a set of actions the company could take, especially when it impacts the VCs' economic position.

A typical protective provision clause looks as follows:

> For so long as any shares of Preferred Stock remain outstanding, consent of the Required Preferred shall be required for any action, whether directly or through any merger, recapitalization or similar event, that (i) alters or changes the rights, preferences or privileges of the Preferred Stock, (ii) increases or decreases the authorized number of shares of Common Stock or Preferred Stock, (iii) creates (by reclassification or otherwise) any new class or series of shares having rights, preferences or privileges senior to or on a parity with the Preferred Stock, (iv) results in the redemption or repurchase of any shares of Common Stock (other than pursuant to equity incentive agreements with service providers giving the Company the right to repurchase shares upon the termination of services), (v) results in any Change in Control or other liquidation of the Company, (vi) amends or waives any provision of the Company's Certificate of Incorporation or Bylaws, (vii) increases or decreases the authorized size of the Company's Board, (viii) results in the payment or declaration of any dividend on any shares of Common Stock or Preferred Stock, (ix) issues debt of the Company or any subsidiary in excess of $100,000, (x) makes any voluntary petition for bankruptcy or

assignment for the benefit of creditors, (xi) enters into any exclusive license, lease, sale, distribution or other disposition of the Company's products or intellectual property or (xii) (a) sells, issues or distributes any Company-created digital tokens, coins or cryptocurrency ("Tokens"), including through any agreement, pre-sale, initial coin offering, token distribution event or crowdfunding; or (b) develops a computer network either incorporating Tokens or permitting the generation of tokens by network participants.

Let's translate into English what the VC is trying to protect against. Simply, unless the VC agrees, the company can't:

- Change the terms of stock owned by the VC;
- Authorize the creation of more stock;
- Issue stock senior or equal to the VC's;
- Buy back any common stock;
- Sell the company;
- Change the certificate of incorporation or bylaws;
- Change the size of board of directors.
- Pay or declare a dividend;
- Borrow money;
- Declare bankruptcy without the VC's approval;
- License away the intellectual property of the company, effectively selling the company without the VC's consent;
- Consumate an initial coin offering or similar financings; or
- Create a token-based interest in the company.

Subsection (ix) of the protective provision clause is often the first thing that gets changed by raising the debt threshold to something higher, as long as the company is a real operating business rather than an early stage startup. Another easily accepted change is to add a minimum threshold of preferred shares outstanding for the protective provisions to apply, keeping the protective provisions from lingering on forever when the capital structure is changed.

Many company counsels will ask for *materiality qualifiers*—for instance, that the word "material" or "materially" be inserted in front of subsections (i), (ii), and (vi) in the example. We always decline this request, not to be stubborn, but because we don't really know what "material" means. If you ask a judge or read any case law, that will not help you, either. We believe that specificity is more important than debating reasonableness. Remember that these are protective provisions; they don't eliminate the ability to do these things, but simply require the consent of the investors. As long as the action is not bad for the company from the VC's point of view, the consent to do these things will be granted. We'd always rather be clear up front what the rules of engagement are rather than have a debate over what the word *material* means in the middle of a situation where these protective provisions might come into play. Finally, there have been several legal cases in the last decade that have all gone against VCs for not drafting language that is very specific.

The Entrepreneur's Perspective

As far as the example protective provision clause is concerned, (i) fair is fair; (ii) fair is fair; (iii) fair is fair; (iv) this should be positive for VCs, but not a big deal; (v) this is critical as long as Series A preferred holders represent, in aggregate, enough of your capitalization table to be relevant; (vi) makes sense; (vii) this is critical as long as Series A preferred holders represent, in aggregate, enough of your cap table to be relevant; (viii) you will never have to worry about this; (ix) this is fine, though you should try to get a higher limit or an exclusion for equipment financing in the normal course of business; (x) and (xi) are fine; (xii) ICOs? Who knows . . .

When future financing rounds occur (e.g., Series B, a new class of preferred stock), there is always a discussion as to how the protective provisions will work with regard to the new class. There are two cases: the Series B gets its own separate protective provisions or the Series B investors vote alongside the original investors as a single class. Entrepreneurs almost always will want a single vote for all the investors, as the separate investor class protective provision vote means the company now has two classes of potential veto constituents to deal with. Normally, new investors will ask for a separate vote, as their interests may diverge from those of the original investors due to different pricing, different risk profiles, and a false need for overall control. However, many experienced investors will align with the entrepreneur's point of view of not wanting separate class votes, since they do not want the potential headaches of another equity class vetoing an important company action. If Series B investors are the same as Series A investors, this is an irrelevant discussion and it should be easy for everyone to default to voting as a single class. If you have new investors in the Series B, be wary of inappropriate veto rights for small investors; for example, the consent percentage required is 90% instead of a majority (50.1%), enabling a new investor who owns only 10.1 percent of the financing to effectively assert control over the protective provisions through his vote.

The Entrepreneur's Perspective

Regardless of who your investors are, fight to have them vote as a single class. It's critical for your sanity. It keeps investors aligned. And as long as your capitalization table is rational, it won't matter.

Some investors feel they have enough control with their board involvement to ensure that the company does not take any action contrary to their interests, and as a result will not focus on these protective provisions. During a financing this is the typical argument used by company counsel to try to convince the VCs to back off of some or all of the protective provisions. We think this is a shortsighted approach for the investor, since, as a board member, an investor designee has legal duties (tirelessly referred to in moments of conflict as a *fiduciary duty*) to work in the best interests of the company. At the same time, VCs have a fiduciary duty to their investors as well. Sometimes the interests of the company and a particular class of shareholders diverge. Therefore, there can be times when an individual would legally have to approve something as a board member in the best interests of the company as a whole and not have a protective provision to fall back on as a shareholder. While this dynamic does not necessarily benefit the entrepreneur, it's good governance where it functionally separates the duties of a board member from those of a shareholder, shining a brighter light on an area of potential conflict.

While one could make the argument that protective provisions are at the core of the trust between a VC and an entrepreneur, we think that's a hollow and naive statement. When an entrepreneur asks, "Don't you trust me? Why do we need these things?" the simple answer is that it is not an issue of trust. Rather, we like to eliminate the discussion about who ultimately gets to make which decisions before we do a deal. Eliminating the ambiguity in roles, control, and rules of engagement is an important part of any financing, and the protective provisions cut to the heart of this. All of this legal activity is an attempt to clarify the rules of engagement and align incentives between investors and entrepreneurs.

Occasionally the protective provisions can help the entrepreneur, especially in an acquisition scenario. Since the investor can effectively block a sale of the company, this provides the entrepreneur with some addition leverage when negotiating with the buyer since the price needs to be high enough to garner the VC's consent on the deal. Of course, this assumes a reasonable position from the existing investor, but in most cases an experienced VC will support the entrepreneur's decision to sell a company.

A decade ago the protective provisions took several days to negotiate. Over time these provisions have been tested in courts of law from several important judicial decisions, so today they have become mostly boilerplate with the only extended negotiation often being around the word "materially."

The Entrepreneur's Perspective

Remember, you are negotiating this deal on behalf of the company (no matter who runs it in the future) and with the investors (no matter who owns the shares in the future). These terms are not only about your current relationship with the VC in question.

Drag-Along Agreement

Another important control provision is the *drag-along* agreement. Under certain circumstances, the company will not want a specific shareholder to vote his shares in whatever way the shareholder wants, but instead prefers to have the shares voted by a certain investor or class of investors. Unless a shareholder is on the board, he generally doesn't have a legal duty to keep the company's best interests in mind.

There are two general flavors of drag-along agreements. The first is where the preferred investors drag along the common shareholders. This agreement gives the preferred investors the ability to force, or drag along, all of the other investors and the founders to do a sale of the company, regardless of how the folks being dragged along feel about the deal.

Typical language follows:

> Drag-Along Agreement: The [holders of the Common Stock] or [Founders] and Series A Preferred shall enter into a drag-along agreement whereby if a majority of the holders of Series A Preferred agree to a sale or liquidation of the Company, the holders of the remaining Series A Preferred and Common Stock shall consent to and raise no objections to such sale.

After the Internet bubble of the early 2000s burst and companies that were at or below the liquidation preferences were sold, entrepreneurs and founders (not surprisingly) started to resist selling in these situations since they often weren't getting anything in the deal. While there are several mechanisms to address sharing consideration below the liquidation preferences, such as the notion of a *carve-out*, which we'll discuss later, the fundamental issue is that if a transaction occurs below the liquidation preferences, it's likely that some or all of the VCs are losing money on the transaction. The VC point of view on this varies widely and is often dependent on the situation; some VCs can deal with this and are happy to provide some consideration to management to get a deal done, whereas others are stubborn in their view that since they lost money, management and founders shouldn't receive anything.

In each of these situations, the VCs would much rather control their ability to compel other shareholders to support the transaction. As more of these situations appeared, the major holders of common stock (even when they were in the minority of ownership) began refusing to vote for the proposed transaction unless the holders of preferred stock waived part of their liquidation preferences in favor of the common stock. Needless to say, this particular holdout technique did not go over well in the venture community and, as a result, the drag-along agreement became more prevalent.

More recently, a second flavor of drag-along has come to exist and it is the one that we prefer. In this version, if a founder leaves the company, their stock will be dragged along by all other classes of stock. In other words, a departed founder (who may or may not harbor ill will toward the company) cannot play the hold-out on voting matters. Typical language looks like this:

> Drag-Along Agreement: When a Founder leaves the Company, such Founder shall agree to vote his Common Stock or Series A Preferred (or Common Stock acquired on conversion of Series A or Former Series A Preferred) in the same proportion as all other shares are voted in any vote.

Note that the drag-along shares are voted in proportion to all the other votes cast. If the vote is 90% yes and 10% no, the departed founder's shares will be voted in a 90/10 split. A popular approach is that the departed founder's stock is voted in the same proportion as all other common stock.

If you are faced with a drag-along situation, your ownership position will determine whether this is an important issue for you. An acquisition does not require unanimous consent of shareholders; these rules vary by jurisdiction, although the two most common situations are either majority of each class (California) or majority of all shares on an as-converted basis (Delaware). However, most acquirers will want 85% to 90% of shareholders to consent to a transaction. If you own 1% of a company and the VCs would like you to sign up to a drag-along agreement, it doesn't matter much unless there are 30 of you who each own 1%. Make sure you know what you are fighting for in the negotiation, and don't put disproportionate energy against terms that don't matter.

When a company is faced with the first flavor of a drag-along agreement in a VC financing proposal, the most common compromise position is to try to get the drag-along rights to pertain to following the majority of the common stock, not the preferred. This way, if you own common stock, you are dragged along only when a majority of the common stockholders consent to the transaction. This is a graceful position for a very small investor to take (e.g., "I'll play ball if a majority of the common plays ball") and one that we've always been willing to take when we've owned common stock in a company (e.g., "I'm not going to stand in the way of something a majority of folks who have rights equal to me want to do"). Of course, preferred investors can always convert some of their holdings to common stock to generate a majority, but this also results in a benefit to the common stockholders as it lowers the overall liquidation preference.

During the term sheet negotiation, pay attention to what your lawyer might be saying to your investor during the negotiation of a drag-along. We've seen many lawyers slam their fists on the table, rejecting any notion of a drag-along. While we clearly understand the debate why a drag-along might not be in the best interests of an individual, it's hard for us to see how this is not in the best interests of the company. In that instance we begin to wonder whether the lawyer is representing the company—who they should be representing—or the founder(s). While nuanced, the dynamic can be profoundly important, especially when there is conflict between a founder and the company.

The Entrepreneur's Perspective

This is one of those terms that matter most if things are falling apart, in which case you probably have bigger fish to fry. And it cuts both ways—if you have a lot of investors, for example, this term can force them all to agree to a deal, which might save you from a lot of agitation down the road. Of course, it is best to not be in a fire-sale situation, or at least to have enough board members whom you control (at least effectively, if not contractually) so that you can prevent a bad deal from happening in the first place.

Conversion

While many VCs posture during term sheet negotiations by saying things like "That is nonnegotiable," terms rarely are. Occasionally, though, a term will actually be nonnegotiable, and *conversion* is one such term.

The Entrepreneur's Perspective

Amen. "This is nonnegotiable" is usually a phrase thrown out by junior members of VC firms when they don't know any better. In particular, watch out for the "This is how we always do deals" or "This is a standard deal term for us" negotiating tactic as being ultra-lame and a sign that the people you're negotiating with don't really know what they are doing.

In all of the VC deals we've ever seen, the preferred shareholders have the unfettered right to convert their stake into common stock. The following is the standard language:

> Conversion: The holders of the Series A Preferred shall have the right to convert the Series A Preferred, at any time, into shares of Common Stock. The initial conversion rate shall be 1:1, subject to adjustment as provided below.

As we discussed in the liquidation preferences section, this allows the buyers of preferred to convert to common should they determine on a liquidation that they would be better off getting paid on an as-converted common basis rather than accepting the liquidation preference and the participation amount. It can also be used in certain extreme circumstances whereby the preferred wants to control a vote of the common on a certain issue. Note, however, that once converted, there is no provision for reconverting back to preferred.

A more interesting term is the automatic conversion, especially since it has several components that are negotiable.

> Automatic Conversion: All of the Series A Preferred shall be automatically converted into Common Stock, at the then applicable conversion price, upon the closing of a firmly underwritten public offering of shares of Common Stock of the Company at a per share price not less than [three] times the Original Purchase Price (as adjusted for stock splits, dividends, and the like) per share and for a total offering of not less than [$15] million (before deduction of underwriters' commissions and expenses) (a "Qualified IPO"). All, or a portion of each share, of the Series A Preferred shall be automatically converted into Common Stock, at the then applicable conversion price in the event that the holders of at least a majority of the outstanding Series A Preferred consent to such conversion.

In an IPO of a venture-backed company, the investment bankers will usually want to see everyone convert into common stock at the time of the IPO. It used to be rare for a venture-backed company to go public with multiple classes of stock, although this happens more frequently today. The thresholds for the automatic conversion are critical to negotiate. As the entrepreneur, you want them lower to ensure more flexibility, whereas your investors will want them higher to give them more control over the timing and terms of an IPO.

Regardless of the actual thresholds, it's important to never allow investors to negotiate different automatic conversion terms for different series of preferred stock. There are many horror stories of companies on the brink of going public with one class of preferred stockholders having a threshold above what the proposed offering would result in; as a result, these stockholders have an effective veto right on the offering.

For example, assume that you have an early stage investor with an automatic conversion threshold of $30 million and a later stage investor with an automatic conversion threshold of $60 million. Now, assume you are at the goal line for an IPO and it's turning out to be a $50 million offering based on the market and the demand for your company. Your early investor is ready to go, but your later stage investor suddenly says, "I'd like a little something else since I can block the deal and even though you've done all of this work to get to an IPO, I don't think I can support it unless ..." In these cases, much last-minute legal and financial wrangling ensues, given the lack of alignment between your different classes of investors. To avoid this, we strongly recommend that you equalize the automatic conversion threshold among all series of stock at each financing.

The Entrepreneur's Perspective

Understand what the norms are for new IPOs before you dig your heels in on conversion terms. There's no reason to negotiate away other, more critical terms over a $20 million threshold versus a $30 million threshold if the norm is $50 million. Besides, a board decision to pursue an IPO will put pressure on a VC to waive this provision.

CHAPTER

7

Other Terms of the Term Sheet

Up to this point we've been exploring terms that matter a lot and fall under the category of economics or control. As we get further into the term sheet, we start to encounter some terms that don't matter as much, are only impactful in a downside scenario, or don't matter at all.

This chapter covers those terms, which include *dividends, redemption rights, conditions precedent to financing, information rights, registration rights, right of first refusal, voting rights, restriction on sales, proprietary information and inventions agreement, co-sale rights, founders' activities, initial public offering shares purchase, no-shop agreement, indemnification,* and *assignment.*

Dividends

Whereas private equity guys love *dividends,* most venture capitalists, especially early stage ones, don't really care about them. In our experience, the VCs who do care about dividends either come from a private equity background or are focused on downside protection in larger deals.

Typical dividend language in a term sheet follows:

> Dividends: The holders of the Series A Preferred shall be entitled to receive [non]cumulative dividends in preference to any dividend on the Common Stock at the rate of [8%] of the Original Purchase Price per annum [when and as declared by the Board of Directors]. The holders of Series A Preferred also shall be entitled to participate pro rata in any dividends paid on the Common Stock on an as-if-converted basis.

For early stage investments, dividends generally do not provide venture returns. They are simply additional juice in a deal and will range from 5% to 15% depending on how aggressive your investor is.

Assume that a VC has negotiated hard and gotten a 10% cumulative annual dividend. In this case, the VC automatically gets the dividend every year. To keep the math simple, let's assume the dividend does not compound. As a result, each year the VC gets 10% of the investment as a dividend. Assume a home run deal, such as a 50×return on a $10 million investment in five years. Even with a 10% cumulative annual dividend, this increases the VC's return from $500 million to only $505 million (the annual dividend is $1 million, or 10% of $10 million, times five years).

While the extra money from the dividend is nice, it doesn't really move the needle in the success case. Since venture funds typically have a 10-year life, the dividend generates another 1×return only if you invest on day one of a fund and hold the investment for 10 years.

This also assumes the company can actually pay out the dividend. Usually the dividends can be paid in either stock or cash, typically at the option of the company. Obviously, the dividend could drive additional dilution if it is paid out in stock, so this is the one case in which it is important not to get head-faked by the investor. In this situation the dividend becomes another form of antidilution protection that is automatic and linked to the passage of time.

We are being optimistic about the return scenarios. In downside cases, the dividend can matter, especially as the invested capital increases. For example, take a $40 million investment with a 10% annual cumulative dividend in a company that is sold at the end of the fifth year to another company for $80 million. In this case, assume that there was a simple liquidation preference with no participation and the investor got 40% of the company for his investment (at a $100 million post-money valuation). Since the sale price was below the investment post-money valuation (i.e., a loser, but not a disaster), the investor will exercise the liquidation preference and take the $40 million plus the dividend ($4 million per year for five years, or $20 million). In this case, the difference between the return in a no-dividend scenario ($40 million) and a dividend scenario ($60 million) is material.

Mathematically, the larger the investment amount and the lower the expected exit multiple, the more the dividend matters. This is why you see dividends in private equity and buyout deals where big money is involved (typically greater than $50 million) and the expectation for return multiples on invested capital is lower.

Automatic dividends have some nasty side effects, especially if the company runs into trouble, since they typically should be included in the solvency analysis. If you aren't paying attention, an automatic cumulative dividend can put you unknowingly into the *zone of insolvency,* which is a bad place to be. Cumulative dividends can also be an accounting nightmare, especially when they are optionally paid in stock, cash, or a conversion adjustment, but that's why the accountants get paid the big bucks at the end of the year to put together the audited balance sheet.

The noncumulative dividend when declared by the board is benign, rarely declared, and an artifact of the past, so we typically leave it in term sheets just to give the lawyers something to do. We've never seen a company where the board declares an actual dividend unless it was easy for the company to pay it.

The Entrepreneur's Perspective

The thing to care about here is ensuring that dividends have to be approved by a majority—or even a supermajority—of your board of directors.

Redemption Rights

Even though *redemption rights* rarely come into play, some VCs are overly focused on them in the deal because they provide additional downside protection. In theory, redemption rights allow the investors to sell their shares back to the company for a guaranteed return. A typical redemption rights clause follows:

> Redemption at Option of Investors: At the election of the holders of at least a majority of the Series A Preferred, the Company shall redeem the outstanding Series A Preferred in three annual installments beginning on the [fifth] anniversary of the Closing. Such redemptions shall be at a purchase price equal to the Original Purchase Price plus declared and unpaid dividends.

There is some rationale for redemption rights. First, there is the fear (on the VC's part) that a company will become successful enough to be an ongoing business but not quite successful enough to go public or be acquired. In this case, redemption rights were invented to allow the investor a guaranteed exit path. However, a company that is around for a while as a going concern, while not being an attractive initial public offering (IPO) or acquisition candidate, generally won't have the cash to pay out redemption rights.

Another reason for redemption rights pertains to the life span of venture funds. The average venture fund has a 10-year life span to conduct its business. If a VC makes an investment in year five of the fund, it might be important for that fund manager to secure redemption rights in order to have a liquidity path before the fund must wind down. As with the previous case, whether the company has the ability to pay is another matter.

Often, companies will claim that redemption rights create a liability on their balance sheet and can make certain business optics more difficult. By optics, we mean how certain third parties view the health and stability of the company, such as bankers, customers, and employees. In the past few years, accountants have begun to argue more strongly that redeemable preferred stock is a liability on the balance sheet instead of an equity feature. Unless the redeemable preferred stock is mandatorily redeemable, this is not the case, and most experienced accountants will be able to recognize the difference.

There is one form of redemption that we have seen in the past few years that we view as overreaching: the *adverse change redemption*. We recommend you never agree to the following term that has recently crept into term sheets:

> Adverse Change Redemption: Should the Company experience a material adverse change to its prospects, business, or financial position, the holders of at least a majority of the Series A Preferred shall have the option to commit the Company to immediately redeem the outstanding Series A Preferred. Such redemption shall be at a purchase price equal to the Original Purchase Price plus declared and unpaid dividends.

This term effectively gives the VC a right to a redemption in the case of a "material adverse change to its ... business." The problem is that "material adverse change" is not defined, is a vague concept, is too punitive, and shifts an inappropriate amount of control to the investors based on an arbitrary judgment of the investors. If this term is being proposed and you are getting resistance on eliminating it, make sure you are speaking to a professional investor and not a loan shark.

In our experience, redemption rights are well understood by VCs and should not create a problem, except in a theoretical argument between lawyers and accountants.

The Entrepreneur's Perspective

I don't worry about redemption rights much, although the adverse change redemption clause is evil. As with dividends, just make sure you have maximum protection around your board, or all classes of preferred shareholders voting in aggregate, and not just the majority of a random class of shareholder declaring these.

Conditions Precedent to Financing

While there is a lot to negotiate, a term sheet is simply a step on the way to an actual deal. Term sheets are often nonbinding (or mostly nonbinding) and most VCs will load them up with *conditions precedent to financing*. Entrepreneurs glance over these, usually because they are in the back sections of the term sheet and seem pretty innocuous, but they occasionally have additional ways out of a deal for the investor that the entrepreneur should watch for, if only to better understand the current mind-set of the investor proposing the investment.

A typical conditions precedent to financing clause looks like this:

> Conditions Precedent to Financing: Except for the provisions contained herein entitled "Legal Fees and Expenses," "No-Shop Agreement," and "Governing Law," which are explicitly agreed by the Investors and the Company to be binding upon execution of this term sheet, this summary of terms is not intended as a legally binding commitment by the Investors, and any obligation on the part of the Investors is subject to the following conditions precedent: 1. Completion of legal documentation satisfactory to the prospective Investors; 2. Satisfactory completion of due diligence by the prospective Investors; 3. Delivery of a customary management rights letter to Investors; and 4. Submission of a detailed budget for the following twelve (12) months, acceptable to Investors.

Investors will try to make a few things binding, specifically, that legal fees get paid whether a deal happens, the company can't shop the deal once the term sheet is signed, and the governing law be set to a specific domicile. At the same time this term explicitly states that a bunch of things still have to happen before this deal is done, and the VC can back out for any reason.

The Entrepreneur's Perspective

Try to avoid conditions precedent to financing as much as possible. Again, the best Plan A has the strongest Plan B standing behind it. Your prospective VC should be willing to move quickly and snap up your deal on acceptable terms by the time the VC gets to a term sheet. At a minimum, do not agree to pay for the VC's legal fees unless the deal is completed (with a possible carve-out for you, canceling the deal).

There are three conditions to watch out for since they usually signal something nonobvious on the part of the VC. They are:

1. *Approval by investors' partnerships.* This is secret VC code for "This deal has not been approved by the investors who issued this term sheet." Therefore, even if you love the terms of the deal, you still may not have a deal. Note that we've seen cases where this isn't explicitly put in the term sheet but is still the case. When signing a term sheet, always ask your VC whether the terms have been approved by the partnership or if there is another approval step in the process. Be cautious of agreeing to go forward exclusively with a VC in situations where you still have additional approval steps in their partnership process.
2. *Rights offering to be completed by company.* This indicates that the VCs want to offer all previous investors in the company the ability to participate in the currently contemplated financing. This is not necessarily a bad thing, as in most cases it serves to protect all parties from liability, but it does add time and expense to the deal.
3. *Employment agreements signed by founders as acceptable to investors.* Be aware of what the full terms are before signing the agreement. As an entrepreneur, when faced with this, it's probably wise to understand and negotiate the form of employment agreement early in the process. You'll want to try to do this before you sign a term sheet and accept a no-shop clause, but most VCs will wave you off and say, "Don't worry

about it—we'll come up with something that works for everyone." Make sure you understand the key terms, such as compensation and what happens if you get fired.

The Entrepreneur's Perspective

Insist on spelling out key terms prior to a signed term sheet if it has a no-shop clause in it. A VC who won't spell out key employment terms at the beginning is a big red flag.

There are plenty of other wacky conditions. If you can dream it up, it has probably been done. Just make sure to look carefully at this paragraph and remember that you don't necessarily have a deal just because you've signed a term sheet.

Information Rights

We are back to another ubiquitous term that is important to the VC but shouldn't matter much to the entrepreneur. *Information rights* define the type of information the VC legally has access to and the time frame in which the company is required to deliver it to the VC.

> Information Rights: So long as an Investor continues to hold [any] shares of Series A Preferred or Common Stock issued upon conversion of the Series A Preferred, the Company shall deliver to the Investor the Company's annual budget, as well as audited annual and unaudited quarterly financial statements. Furthermore, as soon as reasonably possible, the Company shall furnish a report to each Investor comparing each annual budget to such financial statements. Each Investor shall also be entitled to standard inspection and visitation rights. These provisions shall terminate upon a Qualified IPO.

You might ask, "If these terms rarely matter, why bother?" Since you will end up having to deal with them in a VC term sheet, you might as well be exposed to them and hear that they don't matter much. Of course, from a VC perspective, "don't matter much" can also mean "Mr. Entrepreneur, please don't pay much attention to these terms. Just accept them as is." However, our view is that if an investor or the company is hotly negotiating this particular term, then time (and lawyer money) is most likely being wasted.

Information rights are generally something companies are stuck with in order to get investment capital. The only variation one sees is a threshold on the number of shares held (some finite number versus "any") for investors to continue to enjoy these rights.

The Entrepreneur's Perspective

If you care about information rights for your shareholders, you are nuts. You should run a transparent organization as much as possible in the twenty-first century. If you can't commit to sending your shareholders a budget and financial statements, you shouldn't take on outside investors. If you are of the paranoid mind-set (which I generally applaud), feel free to insist on a strict confidentiality clause to accompany your information rights.

Registration Rights

Registration rights define the rights that investors have for registering their shares in an IPO scenario as well as the obligation of the company to the VCs whenever they file additional registration statements after the IPO. This is a tedious example of something that rarely matters yet tends to take up a page or more of the term sheet. Get ready for your mind to be numbed by the following language or just skip this next section if you trust your lawyer.

> Registration Rights: Demand Rights: If Investors holding more than 50% of the outstanding shares of Series A Preferred, including Common Stock issued on conversion of Series A Preferred ("Registrable Securities"), or a lesser percentage if the anticipated aggregate offering price to the public is not less than $5 million, request that the Company file a Registration Statement, the Company will use its best efforts to cause such shares to be registered; provided, however, that the Company shall not be obligated to effect any such registration prior to the [third] anniversary of the Closing. The Company shall have the right to delay such registration under certain circumstances for one period not in excess of ninety (90) days in any twelve (12)-month period.
>
> The Company shall not be obligated to effect more than two (2) registrations under these demand right provisions, and shall

not be obligated to effect a registration (i) during the one hundred eighty (180)-day period commencing with the date of the Company's initial public offering, or (ii) if it delivers notice to the holders of the Registrable Securities within thirty (30) days of any registration request of its intent to file a registration statement for such initial public offering within ninety (90) days.

Company Registration: The Investors shall be entitled to "piggyback" registration rights on all registrations of the Company or on any demand registrations of any other investor subject to the right, however, of the Company and its underwriters to reduce the number of shares proposed to be registered pro rata in view of market conditions. If the Investors are so limited, however, no party shall sell shares in such registration other than the Company or the Investor, if any, invoking the demand registration. Unless the registration is with respect to the Company's initial public offering, in no event shall the shares to be sold by the Investors be reduced below 30% of the total amount of securities included in the registration. No shareholder of the Company shall be granted piggyback registration rights which would reduce the number of shares includable by the holders of the Registrable Securities in such registration without the consent of the holders of at least a majority of the Registrable Securities.

S-3 Rights: Investors shall be entitled to unlimited demand registrations on Form S-3 (if available to the Company) so long as such registered offerings are not less than $1 million.

Expenses: The Company shall bear registration expenses (exclusive of underwriting discounts and commissions) of all such demands, piggybacks, and S-3 registrations (including the expense of one special counsel of the selling shareholders not to exceed $25,000).

Transfer of Rights: The registration rights may be transferred to (i) any partner, member, or retired partner or member or affiliated fund of any holder which is a partnership; (ii) any member or former member of any holder which is a limited liability company; (iii) any family member or trust for the benefit of any individual holder; or (iv) any transferee who satisfies the criteria to be a Major Investor (as defined below); provided the Company is given written notice thereof.

Lockup Provision: Each Investor agrees that it will not sell its shares for a period to be specified by the managing underwriter (but not to exceed 180 days) following the effective date of the Company's initial public offering; provided that all officers, directors, and other 1% shareholders are similarly bound. Such lockup agreement shall provide that any discretionary waiver or termination of the restrictions of such agreements by the Company or representatives of underwriters shall apply to Major Investors, pro rata, based on the number of shares held.

Other Provisions: Other provisions shall be contained in the Investor Rights Agreement with respect to registration rights as are reasonable, including cross-indemnification, the period of time in which the Registration Statement shall be kept effective, and underwriting arrangements. The Company shall not require the opinion of Investor's counsel before authorizing the transfer of stock or the removal of Rule 144 legends for routine sales under Rule 144 or for distribution to partners or members of Investors.

Registration rights are something the company will almost always have to offer to investors. What is most interesting about registration rights is that lawyers seem genetically incapable of leaving this section untouched and always end up negotiating something. Perhaps because this provision is so long, they feel the need to keep their pens warm while reading. We find it humorous as long as we aren't the ones paying the legal fees. In the end, the modifications are generally innocuous, and besides, if you ever get to the point where registration rights come into play (e.g., an IPO), the investment bankers of the company are going to have a major hand in deciding how the deal is going to be structured, regardless of the contract the company entered into years before when it did an early stage financing.

The Entrepreneur's Perspective

Don't focus much energy on registration rights. This is more about upside. The world is good if you're going public.

Right of First Refusal

The *right of first refusal* defines the rights that an investor has to buy shares in a future financing. Right of first refusal is another chewy term that takes up a lot of space in the term sheet but is hard for the entrepreneur to have much impact on. The following is the typical language:

> Right of First Refusal: Prior to a Qualified IPO, Major Investors shall have the right to purchase their pro rata portions (calculated on a fully diluted basis) of any future issuances of equity securities by the Company (with overallotment rights in the event a Major Investor does not purchase its full allocation), other than (i) shares or options to purchase shares issued to employees, consultants or directors as approved by the Board; (ii) shares issued for consideration other than cash pursuant to a merger, consolidation, acquisition, or similar business combination approved by the Board; (iii) shares issued pursuant to any equipment loan or leasing arrangement, real property leasing arrangement or debt financing from a bank or similar financial institution approved by the Board; and (iv) other issuances approved by the Required Percentage of the outstanding Series A Preferred from time to time.

The right of first refusal is also known as a *pro rata right*. While almost all VCs will insist on a right of first refusal, there are two things to pay attention to in this term that can be negotiated. First, the share threshold that defines a *major investor* can be defined. It's often convenient, especially if you have a large number of small investors, not to have to give this right to them. However, since in future rounds you are typically interested in getting as much participation from your existing investors as you can, it's not worth struggling with this too much.

A more important thing to watch for is a multiple on the purchase rights (e.g., the "[X] times" listed). This is often referred to as a *super pro rata right* and is an excessive ask, especially early in the financing life cycle of a company.

The Entrepreneur's Perspective

The right of first refusal is not a big deal, and in some cases it's good for you. But make sure you define what a major investor is and give this only to them. At a minimum, you can make sure that shareholders get this right only if they play in subsequent rounds.

Voting Rights

Voting rights define how the preferred stock and the common stock relate to each other in the context of a share vote. It is another term that doesn't matter that much. The typical language follows:

> Voting Rights: The Series A Preferred will vote together with the Common Stock and not as a separate class except as specifically provided herein or as otherwise required by law. The Common Stock may be increased or decreased by the vote of holders of a majority of the Common Stock and Series A Preferred voting together on an as-if-converted basis, and without a separate class vote. Each share of Series A Preferred shall have a number of votes equal to the number of shares of Common Stock then issuable upon conversion of such share of Series A Preferred.

Most of the time the voting rights clause is simply an FYI section, as all the important rights, such as the protective provisions, are contained in other sections.

Restriction on Sales

The *restriction on sales* clause, also known as the right of first refusal on sales of common stock (or ROFR on common) defines the parameters associated with selling shares of stock when the company is a private company. The typical language follows:

> Restrictions on Sales: The Company's Bylaws shall contain a right of first refusal on all transfers of Common Stock, subject to normal exceptions. If the Company elects not to exercise its right, the Company shall assign its right to the Investors.

Historically, founders and management rarely argue against this, as it helps control the shareholder base of the company, which usually benefits all the existing shareholders, except possibly the ones who want to bail out of their private stock. However, we've found that the lawyers will often spend time arguing about how to implement this particular clause—specifically whether to include it in the bylaws or include it in each of the company's option agreements, plans, and stock sales. We find it easier to include this clause in the bylaws since then it's in one place and is hard to overlook.

In the early days of venture capital (say, until 2007) there was a strong conventional wisdom that founders and management shouldn't be able to sell their shares until the investors could sell their shares, through either an IPO or a sale of the company. As the time to liquidity for private companies stretched out and IPOs became less common, this philosophy shifted. Simultaneously, a healthy secondary market for founders and early employee shares appeared, fueled both by the rapid rise in valuation of private companies, such as Facebook, Uber, Airbnb, and Twitter, along with the emergence of private secondary markets, such as Second Market and SharesPost. Today, many more venture funds will buy secondary shares directly. The result is a lot more sales of private stock to other new and existing investors along with more scrutiny and discussion around the ROFR on common construct.

After being involved in several situations where this has come into play, we feel more strongly than ever that a ROFR on common is a good thing for the company and should be supported by the founders, management, and investors. Controlling the share ownership in a private company is important. The ROFR on common gives the company the ability to at least know what is going on and make decisions in the context of the various proposals.

Proprietary Information and Inventions Agreement

Having control of company intellectual property (IP) is crucial. For that reason, every term sheet we've ever seen has a *proprietary information and inventions agreement* clause.

> Proprietary Information and Inventions Agreement: Each current and former officer, employee, and consultant of the Company shall enter into an acceptable proprietary information and inventions agreement.

This paragraph benefits both the company and investors and is simply a mechanism that investors use to get the company to legally stand behind the representation that it owns its IP. Many pre–Series A companies have issues surrounding this, especially if the company hasn't had great legal representation prior to its first venture round. We've also run into plenty of situations (including several of ours— oops!) in which companies are loose about this between financings, and while a financing is a good time to clean this up, it's often annoying to current employees who are now told, "Hey, you need to sign this since we need it for the venture financing." It's even more important in the sale of a company, since the buyer will always insist on clear ownership of the IP. Our best advice here is that companies should build these agreements into their hiring process from the very beginning (with the advice from a good law firm) so that there are never any issues around this. VCs will always insist on this term.

The Entrepreneur's Perspective

A proprietary information and inventions agreement clause is good for the company. You should have all employees, including founders, sign something like this before you do an outside venture financing. If someone on the team needs a specific carve-out for work in progress that is unrelated to the business, you and your investors should be willing to grant it.

Co-Sale Agreement

Most investors will insist on a *co-sale* agreement, which states that if a founder sells shares, the investors will have an opportunity to sell a proportional amount of their stock as well. The typical language follows:

> Co-Sale Agreement: The shares of the Company's securities held by the Founders shall be made subject to a co-sale agreement (with certain reasonable exceptions) with the Investors such that the Founders may not sell, transfer, or exchange their stock unless each Investor has an opportunity to participate in the sale on a pro rata basis. This right of co-sale shall not apply to and shall terminate upon a Qualified IPO.

The chance of keeping this provision out of a financing is close to zero, so we don't think it's worth fighting it. Notice that this matters only while the company is private. If the company goes public, this clause no longer applies.

The Entrepreneur's Perspective

Your chances of eliminating the co-sale agreement clause may be zero, but there's no reason not to ask for a floor to it. If you or your cofounders want to sell a small amount of stock to buy a house, why should a VC hold it up? A right of first refusal on the purchase with a bona fide outside offer's valuation as the purchase price is one thing. An effective exclusion is something entirely different.

Founders' Activities

As you wind your way through a typical term sheet, you'll often see, buried near the back, a short clause concerning *founders' activities.* It usually looks something like this:

> Founders' Activities: Each of the Founders shall devote 100% of his professional time to the Company. Any other professional activities will require the approval of the Board of Directors.

It should be no surprise to a founder that your friendly neighborhood VC wants you to be spending 100% of your professional time and attention on your company. If this paragraph sneaks its way into the term sheet, the VC either has recently been burned, is suspicious, or is concerned that one or more of the founders may be working on something besides the company being funded. Or in our case, we just put it in to see if anyone pushes back on it. If someone does, it starts an interesting conversation.

Of course, this is a classic no-win situation for a founder. If you are actually working on something else at the same time and don't disclose it, you are violating the terms of the agreement in addition to breaching trust before you get started. If you do disclose other activities or push back on this clause (hence signaling that you are working on something else), you'll reinforce the concern that the VC has. So tread carefully here. Our recommendation, unless of course you are working on something else, is simply to agree to this.

In situations where we've worked with a founder who already had other obligations or commitments, we've always appreciated her being up front with us early in the process. We've usually been able to work through these situations in a way that results in everyone being happy, and in the cases where we couldn't get there, were glad that the issue came up early so that we didn't waste our time or the entrepreneur's time.

While there are situations where VCs get comfortable with entrepreneurs working on multiple companies simultaneously (usually with very experienced entrepreneurs or in situations where the VC and the entrepreneur have worked together in the past), they are a rare exception, not the norm.

The Entrepreneur's Perspective

If you can't agree to a founders' activities clause, don't look for professional VC financing. Or you can negotiate a very specific carve-out, and expect other consequences in your terms (e.g., vesting and IP rights).

Initial Public Offering Shares Purchase

One of the terms that falls into the "nice problem to have" category is the *initial public offering shares purchase.* This allows the VCs to buy shares in the IPO at the offering price. In a term sheet, it will look like this:

> Initial Public Offering Shares Purchase: In the event that the Company shall consummate a Qualified IPO, the Company shall use its best efforts to cause the managing underwriter or underwriters of such IPO to offer to [investors] the right to purchase at least [5%] of any shares issued under a "friends and family" or "directed shares" program in connection with such Qualified IPO. Notwithstanding the foregoing, all action taken pursuant to this Section shall be made in accordance with all federal and state securities laws, including, without limitation, Rule 134 of the Securities Act of 1933, as amended, and all applicable rules and regulations promulgated by the National Association of Securities Dealers, Inc. and other such self-regulating organizations.

This term blossomed in the late 1990s when anything that was VC funded was positioned as a company that would shortly go public. However, most investment bankers will push back on this term if the IPO is going to be a success, as they want to get stock into the hands of institutional investors (their clients). If the VCs get this push-back, they are usually so giddy with joy that the company is going public that they don't argue with the bankers. Ironically, if they don't get this push-back, or even worse, get a call near the end of the IPO road show in which the bankers are asking them to buy shares in the offering, they usually panic and do whatever they can to not have to buy into the offering since this means the deal is no longer a hot one.

Our recommendation on this one is don't worry about it or spend lawyer time on it.

No-Shop Agreement

As an entrepreneur, the way to get the best deal for a round of financing is to have multiple options. However, there comes a point in time when you have to choose your investor and shift from "search for an investor" mode to "close the deal" mode. Part of this involves choosing your lead investor and negotiating the final term sheet with him.

A *no-shop agreement* is almost always part of this final term sheet. Think of it as serial monogamy. Your new investor-to-be doesn't want you running around behind his back just as you are about to get hitched. A typical no-shop agreement follows:

> No-Shop Agreement: The Company agrees to work in good faith expeditiously toward a closing. The Company and the Founders agree that they will not, directly or indirectly, (i) take any action to solicit, initiate, encourage, or assist the submission of any proposal, negotiation, or offer from any person or entity other than the Investors relating to the sale or issuance of any of the capital stock of the Company or the acquisition, sale, lease, license, or other disposition of the Company or any material part of the stock or assets of the Company; or (ii) enter into any discussions or negotiations or execute any agreement related to any of the foregoing, and shall notify the Investors promptly of any inquiries by any third parties in regard to the foregoing. Should both parties agree that definitive documents shall not be executed pursuant to this term sheet, then the Company shall have no further obligations under this section.

At some level the no-shop agreement, like serial monogamy, is more of an emotional commitment than a legal one, although this term will often be part of the few terms that are binding in a term sheet. While it's hard, but not impossible, to enforce a no-shop agreement in a financing, if you get caught cheating, your financing will probably go the same way as the analogous situation when the groom or the bride-to-be gets caught in a compromising situation.

The no-shop agreement reinforces the handshake that says, "Okay, let's get a deal done. No more fooling around looking for a better or different one." In all cases, the entrepreneur should bound the no-shop agreement by a time period, which is usually 45 to 60 days, although you can occasionally get a VC to agree to a 30-day no-shop agreement. This makes the commitment bidirectional. You agree not to shop the deal and the VC agrees to get things done within a reasonable time frame.

Now, some entrepreneurs still view that as a unilateral agreement; namely, the entrepreneur is agreeing to the no-shop but the VC isn't really agreeing to anything at all. In most cases, we don't view the no-shop clause as terribly important since it can be bounded with time. Instead, we feel it's much more important for the entrepreneur to test the VC's commitment to follow through on the investment when signing up to do the deal.

Specifically, in some cases VCs put down term sheets early, well before they've got internal agreement within their partnership to do an investment. This used to be more common. Today, many early stage VCs don't want to go through the hassle of drafting the term sheet and trying to negotiate it unless they believe they will do the deal. In addition, there is a potential negative reputational impact for the VC, as word will get around that VC X puts term sheets out early, but then can't or won't close. In the age of the Internet, this type of reputation spreads like an infectious disease.

Although we've done hundreds of investments, we've seen only a few situations where the no-shop agreement had any meaningful impact on a deal in which we were involved. When we thought about the situations in which we were the VC and were negatively impacted by not having a no-shop agreement (e.g., a company we had agreed with on a term sheet went and did something else) or where we were on the receiving end of a no-shop agreement and were negatively impacted by it (e.g., an acquirer tied us up but then ultimately didn't close on the deal), we actually didn't feel particularly bad about any of the situations since there was both logic associated with the outcome and grace exhibited by the participants. Following are two examples.

We signed a term sheet to invest in Company X. We didn't include a no-shop clause in the term sheet. We were working to close the investment and we were 15 days into a 30-ish-day process. We had legal documents going back and forth between lawyers. One of the founders called us and said that they had just received an offer to be acquired and they wanted to pursue it. We told them no problem and that we'd still be there to do the deal if it didn't come together. We were very open with them about the pros and cons of doing the deal from our perspective and, given the economics, encouraged them to pursue the acquisition offer. It was a great deal for them. They ended up closing the deal and, as a token, gave us a small amount of equity in the company for our efforts, which was totally unexpected and unnecessary but appreciated.

In another situation we were already investors in a company that was in the process of closing an outside-led round at a significant step-up in valuation. The company was under a no-shop agreement with the new VC. A week prior to closing, we received an acquisition overture from one of the strategic investors in the company. We immediately told the new lead investor about it, who graciously agreed to suspend the no-shop agreement and wait to see whether we wanted to move forward with the acquisition or with the financing. We negotiated with the acquirer for several weeks, checking regularly with the new potential investor to make sure they were still interested in closing the round if we chose not to pursue the acquisition. They were incredibly supportive and patient. The company covered its legal fees up to that point (unprompted—although it was probably in the term sheet that we'd cover them; we can't recall). We ended up moving forward with the acquisition; the new investor was disappointed in the outcome but happy and supportive of what we did.

While both of these are edge cases, in almost all of our experiences the no-shop agreement ended up being irrelevant. As each of these examples shows, the quality and the character of the people involved made all the difference and were much more important than the legal term.

The Entrepreneur's Perspective

As an entrepreneur, you should also ask that the no-shop clause expire immediately if the VC terminates the process. Also, consider asking for a carve-out for acquisitions. Frequently financings and acquisitions follow each other around. Even if you're not looking to be acquired, you don't want handcuffs on conversations about an acquisition just because a VC is negotiating with you about a financing.

Indemnification

The *indemnification* clause states that the company will indemnify investors and board members to the maximum extent possible by law. It is another one that entrepreneurs just have to live with. An example follows:

> Indemnification: The bylaws and/or other charter documents of the Company shall limit board members' liability and exposure to damages to the broadest extent permitted by applicable law. The Company will indemnify board members and will indemnify each Investor for any claims brought against the Investors by any third party (including any other shareholder of the Company) as a result of this financing.

Given all of the shareholder litigation in recent years, there is almost no chance that a company will get funded without indemnifying its directors. The first sentence is simply a contractual obligation between the company and its board. The second sentence, which is occasionally negotiable, indicates the desire for the company to purchase formal liability insurance. One can usually negotiate away insurance in a Series A deal, but for any follow-on financing the major practice today is to procure directors and officers (D&O) insurance. We believe companies should be willing to indemnify their directors and will likely need to purchase D&O insurance in order to attract outside board members.

The Entrepreneur's Perspective

You should have reasonable and customary D&O insurance for yourself as much as for your VCs. While the indemnification clause is good corporate hygiene, make sure you follow it up with an appropriate insurance policy.

Assignment

We end this chapter with the *assignment* clause, another clause in a typical term sheet that isn't worth spending legal time and money negotiating.

> Assignment: Each of the Investors shall be entitled to transfer all or part of its shares of Series A Preferred purchased by it to

one or more affiliated partnerships or funds managed by it or any of their respective directors, officers, or partners, provided such transferee agrees in writing to be subject to the terms of the Stock Purchase Agreement and related agreements as if it were a purchaser thereunder.

The assignment clause simply gives VC firms flexibility over transfers that they require to be able to run their business and, as long as the VC is willing to require that any transferee agree to be subject to the various financing agreements, the company should be willing to provide for this. However, watch out for one thing: don't let the loophole "assignment without transfer of the obligation under the agreements" occur. You need to make sure that anyone who is on the receiving end of a transfer abides by the same rules and conditions that the original purchasers of the stock signed up for.

CHAPTER 8

Convertible Debt

In the past few chapters, we've gone through the exhaustive, but hopefully not exhausting, terms in a typical venture capital equity financing. As we foreshadowed previously, the popularity of convertible debt has grown over the years. Today, many angel investors and accelerators invest primarily using convertible debt. In the majority of cases, unless the company fails to raise any more money, this is a temporary state of financing, because the debt is intended to convert into equity at a later date.

So, what is convertible debt? Simple. It's debt. It's a loan. With a loan, you don't have to argue about valuation, although you may argue about potential future valuations using the concept of a *valuation cap*, which we will discuss further on. The fundamental notion is that when a company raises a future round of equity financing, the money loaned to the company via the convertible debt round converts into whatever type of stock the company sells under whatever terms it agrees to in the future. In exchange for the convertible debt, the investors get a modest interest rate and typically convert at a discount to the price to the next round.

For example, assume you raise $500,000 in convertible debt from angels with a 20% discount to the next round, and six months later a VC offers to lead a Series A round of a $1 million investment at $1 a share. Your financing will actually be for $1.5 million total, although the VCs will get 1 million Series A shares ($1 million at $1 per share) and the angels will get 625,000 Series A shares ($500,000 at $0.80 per share). The discount is appropriate, since your early investors want some reward for investing before the full Series A financing round comes together.

In this chapter, we cover the arguments for and against using convertible debt. We then go through the terms in a convertible debt deal, including the discount, valuation caps, interest rate, conversion mechanics, conversion in a sale of the company, warrants, and other terms. We briefly cover the differences between early stage and late stage dynamics and finish up with an example of when convertible debt could be dangerous to use.

Arguments for and Against Convertible Debt

Most fans of convertible debt argue that it's a much easier transaction to complete than an equity financing. Since no valuation is being set for the company, you get to avoid that part of the negotiation. Because it is debt, it has few, if any, of the rights of preferred stock offerings and you can accomplish a transaction with a lot less paperwork and legal fees. Note, however, that the legal fees argument is less persuasive these days with the many forms of standardized documents. A decade ago there could be a $50,000 pricing difference for legal fees between a seed preferred round and a convertible debt round. These days the difference is less than $10,000 since many lawyers will heavily discount the seed preferred round to get future business from the company.

The debate goes on endlessly about which structure is better or worse for entrepreneurs or investors. We aren't convinced there is a definitive answer here; in fact, we are convinced that those who think there is a definitive answer are wrong.

Since investors usually drive the decision about whether to raise an equity or a debt round, let's look at their motivations first. One of the primary reasons for an early stage investor to purchase equity is to price the stock being sold in the round. Early stage investing is a risky proposition, and investors will want to invest at low prices, although smart investors won't invest at a price at which founders are demotivated. As a result, most early stage deals get priced in a pretty tight range.

With a convertible debt structure, the stock price is not set and is determined at a later date when a larger financing occurs. By definition, if there is a later round the company must be doing something right. Having a discount is nice, but the ultimate price for the early convertible debt investors may still be higher than what they would have paid if they had bought equity in the first place. Some investors try to fix this problem by setting what is called a valuation cap on the price they will pay in the next round. In other words, as an investor, I'll take a 20% discount on the price of the next round up to a valuation of $X. If you get a valuation above $X, then my valuation is $X (hence the notion of a valuation cap).

This sounds like it fixes the problem, right? This might for the original investor, but it might not for the company and the founders. First of all, the investors coming into the next round may not like the idea that they are paying that much more than the convertible debt investors paid. Unlike equity, which is issued and can't easily be changed, the new equity investors could refuse to fund unless the debt investors remove or change the cap. Also, keep in mind that VCs will ask you during the fundraising process what your convertible note terms are. You'll say, "Oh, we have a valuation cap of X." VCs will then focus on and peg their valuation of your company on that cap. You are essentially drawing a line in the sand (albeit a small one and in some cases it doesn't actually affect the ultimate valuation) of what your company is worth in the future.

From the entrepreneur's standpoint, the choice isn't clear, either. Some argue that the convertible debt structure, by definition, leads to a higher ultimate price for the first round. We won't go as far as to say they are right, but we can see the argument that with a convertible debt feature you are allowing an inflated price based on time to positively impact the valuation for the past investors. We'd argue that this is missing half of the analysis in that a founder's first investors are sometimes the most important. These are the people who invested in you at the riskiest stage before anyone else would. You like them, you respect them, and you might even be related to them. Assume that you create a lot of value along the way and the equity investor prices the round at a number that is higher than even you expected. Your first investors will own less than anyone anticipated. At the end of the day, your biggest fans are happy about the financing, but sad that they own so little.

But does it really set a higher price? Let's go back to the example of a convertible debt round with a cap. If we were going to agree to this deal, our cap would be the price that we would have agreed to in an equity round. So, in effect, you've just sold the same amount of equity to us, but we have an option for the price to be lower than we would have offered you since there are plenty of scenarios in which the equity price is below the cap amount. Why on earth would I agree to a cap that is above the price that I'm willing to pay today? The cap amounts to a ceiling on your price. VCs will focus on that cap as well. There are plenty of situations where the VCs would have been willing to pay $X per share, but after seeing the cap number in due diligence prior to a term sheet they offer only $Y (less than $X) per share because it's within the cap. So while you may have gotten a better deal on your seed round, your Series A round (which normally sees the company raising a lot more money than a seed round) is now underpriced compared to what it could be. In the aggregate, the company actually underpriced itself in this scenario.

The Entrepreneur's Perspective

To attract seed stage investors, consider a convertible debt deal with two additional features: a reasonable time horizon on an equity financing and a forced conversion if that horizon isn't met, as well as a floor, not a ceiling, on the conversion valuation.

There's also some dissonance here since VCs spend a lot of their time valuing companies and negotiating on price. If your VC can't or won't do this, what is this telling you? Do you and the VC have radically different views of the value proposition you've created? Will this impact the relationship going forward or the way that each of you strategically thinks about your company?

The Discount

Remember that a convertible debt deal doesn't purchase equity in your company. Instead, it's simply a loan that has the ability to convert to equity based on some future financing event. Let's begin our discussion of terms for convertible debt with the most important one, the *discount*.

Until recently, we had never seen a convertible debt deal that didn't convert at a discount to the next financing round. Given some of the current excited market conditions at the seed stage, we've heard of convertible deals with no discount but view this as irregular and not sustainable over the long term.

The idea behind the discount is that investors should get, or require, more upside than just the interest rate associated with the debt for the risk that they are taking by investing early. These investors aren't banks. They are planning to own equity in the company but are simply deferring the price discussion to the next financing.

So how does the discount work? There are two approaches: the discounted price to the next round and warrants. We'll cover the discounted price approach in this section, as it's much simpler and better oriented for a seed round investment.

For the discounted price to the next round, you might see something like this in the legal documents:

> This Note shall automatically convert in whole without any further action by the Holders into such Equity Securities at a conversion price equal to eighty percent (80%) of the price per share paid by the Investors purchasing the Equity Securities on the same terms and conditions as given to the Investors.

This means that if your next round investors are paying $1 per share, then the note will convert into the same shares at a 20% discount, or $0.80 per share. For example, if you have a $100,000 convertible note, it will purchase 125,000 shares ($100,000/$0.80), whereas the new equity investor will get 100,000 shares for his investment of $100,000 ($100,000/$1).

The range of discounts we typically see is 10% to 30%, with 20% being the most common. While occasionally you'll see a discount that increases over time (e.g., 10% if the round closes in 90 days, 20% if it takes longer), we recommend entrepreneurs and investors keep this simple. It is the seed round.

Valuation Caps

We've touched on this concept, but let's go deeper. The cap is an investor-favorable term that puts a ceiling on the conversion price of the debt. The valuation cap is typically seen only in seed rounds where the investors are concerned that the next round of financing will be at a price that is at a valuation that wouldn't reward them appropriately for taking a risk by investing early in the seed round.

For example, an investor wants to invest $100,000 in a company and thinks that the pre-money valuation of the company is somewhere in the $2 million to $4 million range. The entrepreneur thinks the valuation should be higher. Either way, the investor and the entrepreneur agree to not deal with a valuation negotiation and instead decide to consummate a convertible debt deal with a 20% discount to the next round.

Nine months pass and the company is doing well. The entrepreneur is happy, and the investor is happy. The company goes to raise a round of financing in the form of preferred stock. It receives a term sheet at a $20 million pre-money valuation. In this case, the discount of 20% would result in the investor having an effective valuation of $16 million for his investment nine months ago.

On one hand, the investor is happy for the entrepreneur; but on the other hand, he is shocked by the high valuation for his investment. He realizes he made a bad decision by not pricing the deal initially, as anything below $16 million would have been better for him. Of course, this is nowhere near the $2 million to $4 million the investor was contemplating the company was worth at the time he made the convertible debt investment.

The valuation cap addresses this situation. By agreeing on a cap, the entrepreneur and the investor can still defer the price discussion but set a ceiling at which point the conversion price caps.

In our previous example, let's assume that the entrepreneur and the investor agree on a $4 million cap. Since the deal has a 20% discount, any valuation up to $5 million will result in the investor getting a discount of 20%. Once the discounted value goes above the cap, then the cap will apply. So, in the case of the $20 million pre-money valuation, the investor will get shares at an effective price of $4 million.

As we've mentioned, in some cases, caps can impact the valuation of the next round. Some VCs will look at the cap and view it as a price ceiling to the next round price, assuming that it was the high point negotiated between the seed investors and the entrepreneur. To mitigate this, entrepreneurs should try to not disclose the seed round terms until a price has been agreed to with a new VC investor. However, it's become pretty common for VCs to ask for the terms of the convertible debt round before they are willing to issue a term sheet, and it is hard for an entrepreneur to say no to a potential funding partner's request.

Clearly, entrepreneurs would prefer not to have valuation caps. However, many seed investors recognize that an uncapped note has the potential to create a big risk/return disparity, especially in frothy markets for early stage deals. We believe that over the long term caps create more alignment between entrepreneurs and seed investors as long as the price cap is thoughtfully negotiated based on the stage of the company.

Interest Rate

Since convertible debt is a loan, it usually has an *interest rate* associated with it, because that's the minimum upside an investor is going to want to have for the investment.

We believe interest rates on convertible debt should be as low as possible. This isn't bank debt, and the funders are being fairly compensated through the use of whatever type of discount has been negotiated. If you are an entrepreneur, check out what the applicable federal rates (AFRs) are to see the lowest legally allowable interest rates; bump them up just a little bit (for volatility), and suggest whatever that number is.

Realizing that the discount and the interest rate are often linked, we'll usually see an interest rate between 5% and 12% (the mean is 8%) associated with a discount between 10% and 30% (the mean is 20%).

Conversion Mechanics

Eventually the convertible debt will convert into equity. There are several nuances around how and when the note will convert. These conversion mechanics are important but can usually be configured in a way where everyone will be happy with them if they concentrate on defining them up front.

In general, debt holders have traditionally enjoyed superior control rights over companies and the ability to force nasty things like bankruptcy and involuntary liquidations. Therefore, having outstanding debt (that doesn't convert) can be a bad thing if an entrepreneur ever gets sideways with one of the debt holders. While it's not talked about that much, it happens, and we've seen situations where the debt holder has excessive power in a negotiation.

Here is typical conversion language:

> In the event that Payor issues and sells shares of its Equity Securities to investors (the "Investors") on or before [180] days from the date herewith (the "Maturity Date") in an equity financing with total proceeds to the Payor of not less than $1 million (excluding the conversion of the Notes or other debt) (a "Qualified Financing"), then the outstanding principal balance of this Note shall automatically convert in whole without any further action by the Holders into such Equity Securities at a conversion price equal to the price per share paid by the Investors purchasing the Equity Securities on the same terms and conditions as given to the Investors.

Let's take a look at what matters in this paragraph. Notice that in order for the note to convert automatically, all of the conditions must be met. If not, there is no automatic conversion.

- *Term.* Here, the company must sell equity within six months (180 days) for the debt to automatically convert. Consider whether this is enough time. If we were entrepreneurs, we'd try to get this period to be as long as possible. Many venture firms are not allowed (by their agreements with their investors) to issue debt that has a maturity date longer than a year, so don't be surprised if one year is the maximum that you can negotiate if you are dealing with a VC investor.
- *Amount.* In this case the company must raise $1 million of new money for the debt to convert because the conversion of the outstanding debt is excluded. The entrepreneur often gets to decide the amount based on the minimum the company is hoping to raise. When you determine this number, think about how long you have and how much you think you can raise in that time period.

So, what happens if the company does not achieve the milestones to automatically convert the debt? The debt stays outstanding unless the debt holders agree to convert their holdings. This is when voting control comes into play. It is important to pay attention to the amendment provision in the notes.

> Any term of this Note may be amended or waived with the written consent of Payor and the Majority Holders. Upon

the effectuation of such waiver or amendment in conformance with this Section 11, the Payor shall promptly give written notice thereof to the record Holders of the Notes who have not previously consented thereto in writing.

While one will never see anything less than a majority of holders needing to consent to an amendment (and thus a different standard for conversion), make sure the standard doesn't get too high. For instance, if you had two parties splitting $1 million in convertible debt with a 60/40 percentage split, you only need one party to consent if the majority rules, but both parties would need to consent if a supermajority must approve. Little things like this can make a big difference if the 40% holder is the one you aren't getting along with at the present moment.

Conversion in a Sale of the Company

What happens to the convertible debt if the company gets acquired before there is an equity financing and before the debt is converted to equity? There are a few different scenarios.

The lender gets its money back plus interest. If there is no specific language addressing this situation, this is what usually ends up happening. In this case, the convertible debt document doesn't allow the debt to convert into anything, but at the same time mandates that upon a sale the debt must be paid off. So the lenders don't see any of the upside on the acquisition. The potentially bad news is that if the merger is an all-stock deal, the company will need to find a way to get cash to pay back the loan or negotiate a way for the acquiring company to deal with the debt.

The lender gets its money back, plus interest plus a multiple of the original principal amount. In this case, the documents dictate that the company will pay back outstanding principal plus interest and then a multiple on the original investment. Usually we see a multiple of two to three times, but in later stage companies this multiple can be even higher. The typical language follows:

> Sale of the Company: If a Qualified Financing has not occurred and the Company elects to consummate a sale of the Company prior to the Maturity Date, then notwithstanding any provision of the Notes to the contrary (i) the Company will give the Investors

at least five days prior written notice of the anticipated closing date of such sale of the Company and (ii) the Company will pay the holder of each Note an aggregate amount equal to ___ times the aggregate amount of principal and interest then outstanding under such Note in full satisfaction of the Company's obligations under such Note.

Some sort of conversion does occur. In the case of an early stage company that hasn't issued preferred stock yet, the debt converts into stock of the acquiring company (if it's a stock deal) at a valuation subject to a cap. If it's not a stock deal, then one normally sees one of the preceding scenarios.

With later stage companies, the investors usually structure the convertible notes to have the most flexibility. They either get a multiple payout on the debt or get the equity upside based on the previous preferred round price. Note that if the acquisition price is low, the holders of the debt may usually opt out of conversion and demand cash payment on the notes.

While in many cases issuing convertible debt is easier to deal with than issuing equity, the one situation where this often becomes complex is an acquisition while the debt is outstanding. Our strong advice is to address in the documents how the debt will be handled in an acquisition.

Warrants

A few sections ago we discussed the "discounted price to the next round" approach to providing a discount on convertible debt. The other approach to a discount is to issue *warrants*. This approach is more complex and usually applies only to situations where the company has already raised a round of equity, but it occasionally pops up in early stage deals. If you are doing a seed round, we encourage you not to use this approach and instead save some legal fees. However, if you are doing a later stage convertible debt round or your investors insist on you issuing warrants, here's how it works.

Assume that once again the investor is investing $100,000 and receives warrant coverage in the amount of 20% of the amount of the convertible note. In this case the investor will get a warrant for $20,000.

This is where it can get a little tricky. What does $20,000 worth of warrants mean? A warrant is an option to purchase a certain number of shares at a predetermined price. But how do you figure out the number of warrants and the price that the warrants will be at? There are numerous different ways to calculate this, such as:

- $20,000 worth of common stock at the last value ascribed to either the common or the preferred stock;
- $20,000 worth of the last round of preferred stock at that round's price of the stock; or
- $20,000 worth of the next round of preferred stock at whatever price that happens to be.

As you can see, the actual percentage of the company associated with the warrants can vary significantly depending on the price of the security that underlies it. As a bonus, the particular ownership of certain classes may affect voting control of a particular class of stock.

If there is a standard, it's the second version, where the warrants are attached to the prior preferred stock round. If there is no prior preferred, then one normally sees the stock convert to the next preferred round unless an acquisition of the company occurs before a preferred round is consummated; in that case, it reverts to the common stock.

For example, assume that the round gets done at $1 per share as in the previous example. The investor who holds a $100,000 convertible note will get $20,000 of warrants, or 20,000 warrants at an exercise price of $1, to go along with the 100,000 shares received in the financing from the conversion of the note.

Warrants have a few extra terms that matter, such as:

- *Term length.* The length of time the warrants are exercisable, which is typically 5 to 10 years. Shorter is better for the entrepreneur and company. Longer is better for the investor.
- *Merger considerations.* What happens to the warrants in the event the company is acquired? We can't opine more strongly that all warrants should expire at a merger unless they are exercised just prior to the transaction. In other words, the warrant holder must decide to either exercise or give up the warrants if the company is acquired. Acquiring companies hate buying

companies that have warrants that survive a merger and allow the warrant holder to buy equity in the acquirer. Many mergers have been held up because warrants with this feature have upset the potential acquirer and thus as part of the closing requirements the acquirer has mandated that the company go out and repurchase or edit the terms of the warrants. This is not a good negotiating spot for the company to find itself in, as it will have to pay off warrant holders while disclosing the potential merger (so the company will have little leverage) and at the same time will have a sword hanging over its head by the acquirer until the issue is resolved.

- *Original issue discount (OID).* This is an accounting issue that is boring, yet important. If a convertible debt deal includes warrants, the warrants must be paid for separately in order to avoid the OID issue. In other words, if the debt is for $100,000 and there is 20% warrant coverage, the Internal Revenue Service (IRS) says that the warrants themselves have some value. If there is no provision for the actual purchase of the warrants, the lender will have received an original issue discount, which says that the $100,000 debt was issued at a discount since the lender also received warrants. The problem is that part of the $100,000 principal repaid will be included as interest to the lender or, even worse, it will be accrued as income over the life of the note even before any payments are made. The easy fix is to pay something for the warrants, which usually is an amount in the low thousands of dollars.

The difference between warrants and a discount is insignificant for the investor. We suppose if the investor is able to get warrants for common stock, then perhaps the ultimate value of warrants may outweigh the discount, but it's not clear. As evidenced by the number of words we have devoted to the topic, warrants add a fair amount of complexity and legal costs to the mix. However, some discounts will include valuation caps, and that can create some negative company valuation ramifications while warrants completely stay away from the valuation discussion. Warrants are not as popular as they once were, as discounts are more typically used.

Finally, in no case should an entrepreneur let an investor double dip and receive both a discount and warrants. That's not a reasonable position for investors to take—they should either get a discount or get warrants.

Other Terms

There are a few other terms that can show up in a convertible debt deal. You'll recognize these from the earlier chapters on terms in an equity financing, as they are the terms that more sophisticated angels or seed investors will insist on to preserve their rights in later financings.

The first term you'll occasionally see in a convertible debt financing is a *pro rata right*, which will allow debt holders to participate pro-ratably in a future financing. Since the dollars invested in a convertible debt deal are often small, investors may ask for super pro rata rights. For instance, if an investor invests $500,000 in a convertible debt deal and the company later raises $7 million, the investor's pro rata investment rights wouldn't allow the investor to purchase a large portion of the next round. As a result, the seed investor may ask for a pro rata right for two to four times the investor's current ownership or for a specific percentage (say 5% to 20%) of the next financing. While pro rata rights are pretty typical, if you have people asking for super pro rata rights or a specific portion of the next financing, you should be careful, as granting these will limit your long-term financing options.

Every now and then you'll see a *liquidation preference* in a convertible debt deal. It works the same way as in a preferred stock deal: the investors get their money back first, or a multiple of their money back first, before any proceeds are distributed to anyone else. This usually happens in the case when a company is struggling to raise capital and current investors offer a convertible debt (also called a bridge loan) deal to the company. Back in the good old days, usury laws prevented such terms; but in most states this is not an issue and the investors are allowed to have not only the security of holding debt, but the upside of preferred stock should a liquidation event occur.

Early Stage versus Late Stage Dynamics

Traditionally, convertible debt was issued by mid to late stage startups that needed a financing to get them to a place where they believed they could raise more money. These deals were called bridge financings. A common cliché around bridge loans is for the investor to contemplate whether it is a "bridge to the next round" or a "pier that drops into the ocean."

The terms were similar to early stage terms unless the company was performing poorly and there was doubt about the ability to raise new capital, or the bridge was to get the company to an acquisition or an orderly shutdown. In these cases, one saw terms like liquidation preferences and in some cases changes to board or voting control came into play. Some of these bridge loans also contained terms like *pay-to-play*, which we discussed in Chapter 5.

Given the traditional complexity and cost of legal fees associated with preferred stock financings, convertible debt became a common way to make seed stage investments because it tended to be simpler and less expensive from a legal perspective. Over time, equity rounds have become cheaper to consummate, and the legal fees argument doesn't carry much weight these days. In the end, the main force driving the use of convertible debt in early stage companies is the parties' desire to avoid setting a valuation.

Can Convertible Debt Be Dangerous?

One final issue with convertible debt is a technical legal one. You'll have to forgive us, but Jason is an ex-lawyer and sometimes he can't help himself.

If a company raises cash via equity, it has a positive balance sheet. It is solvent, and the board and executives have fiduciary duties to the shareholders in the efforts to maximize company value. The shareholders are all the usual suspects: the employees and VCs. Life is good and normal.

However, if a company is insolvent, the board and company may (based in large part on state law—ask your attorney) now owe fiduciary duties to the creditors of the company. By definition, if you raise a convertible debt round, your company is insolvent. You have cash, but your debt obligations are greater than your assets. Your creditors include your landlord, anyone you owe money to (including former disgruntled employees), and founders who have lawyers.

How does this change the paradigm? To be fair, we have had no personal war stories here, but it's not hard to construct some weird situations.

Let's look at the hypothetical situation.

Assume the company is not a success and fails. In the case of raising equity, the officers and directors owe a duty only to the creditors (e.g., the landlord) at such time that cash isn't large enough to pay their liabilities. If the company manages it correctly, creditors are paid off cleanly even on the downside scenario. But sometimes it doesn't happen this way and there are lawsuits. When the lawyers get involved, they'll look to establish the time in which the company went insolvent and then try to show that the actions of the board were bad during that time. If the time frame is short, it's hard to make a case against the company.

However, if you raise debt, the insolvency time lasts until your debt converts into equity. As a result, if your company ends up failing and you can't pay your creditors, the ability for a plaintiff lawyer to judge your actions has increased dramatically. And don't forget, if you have any outstanding employment litigation, all of those folks count as creditors as well.

The worst part of this is that many states impose personal liability on directors for things that occur while a company is insolvent. This means that some states will allow creditors to sue directors personally for not getting all of the money they are owed.

Now, we don't want to get too crazy here. We are talking about early stage and seed companies, and hopefully the situation is clean enough that these doomsday predictions won't happen; but our bet is that few folks participating in convertible debt rounds are actually thinking about these issues. While we don't know of any actual cases out there, we've been around this business long enough to know that there is constant innovation in the plaintiff's bar as well.

An Alternative to Convertible Debt

Over the years, in addition to efforts to standardize early stage financing documents, there have been several attempts to create a synthetic early stage financing instrument that combines the best characteristics of equity and debt. The most recent, and most popular, instrument was created several years ago by Y Combinator and is called *the safe* (Simple Agreement for Future Equity). It was followed quickly by 500 Startups' Version, called *KISS* (Keep It Simple

Security) demonstrating once again that document standardization is not a reality in the world of startups, at least as long as lawyers are involved.

The idea of the safe (yes, the phrasing "the safe" is deliberate, as it's intended to be analogous to "the note," which is how convertible notes are often referred to) is that the investor buys what effectively is an unpriced warrant in the company, as opposed to buying convertible debt. This eliminates some of the concerns around using debt, including the edge case issues around legal dynamics of debt, and eliminates some features of debt such as interest.

As with convertible debt, the safe can have a cap and/or a discount. An MFN, or *most favored nation*, clause can also be included so that if better terms are given to future investors, they are automatically inherited by the safe investors.

For investors, the safe has several disadvantages over convertible notes, such as the lack of an explicit pro rata right in the following round. As with convertible notes, this can be added, but at some level this undermines the idea of a simple, standard document.

The lack of maturity date is both an advantage and a disadvantage. While it eliminates the risk for the entrepreneur associated with a maturity date with debt, it simultaneously eliminates the requirement for the entrepreneurs to communicate with the investors at least around the timing of the maturity date. In many convertible debt situations, investors will simply extend the maturity date. However, in some situations, especially ones where companies are struggling, and the entrepreneurs are not communicating with the investors, the lack of a maturity date takes away a key leverage point—at least for a discussion—from the investors.

As with convertible debt, a safe ignores many of the key issues (the most important of these being valuation) that are addressed with an equity round enabling both founders and investors to defer, or just be lazy about, issues until the next financing round.

These structures are still fairly new and not that widespread, but we think if you understand the equity and convertible note structures, you should be able to understand these synthetic approaches. However, for the 1,183rd time in this book, make sure you involve a qualified attorney early in the process.

CHAPTER 9

The Capitalization Table

Now that we've worked through all of the specific clauses in the term sheet, let's explore how a typical capitalization table (*cap table*) works. A term sheet will almost always contain a summary cap table, which we describe in this chapter. You, your prospective investors, or occasionally your lawyers will generate a more detailed cap table.

The cap table summarizes who owns what part of the company before and after the financing. This is one area that some founders, especially those who have not been exposed in the past to cap table math, are often uncomfortable with. It's extremely important for founders to understand exactly who owns what part of a company and what the implications are in a potential funding round.

Normally when you initially set up the company, 100% will be allocated to the founders and employees, with a specific number of shares allocated to each individual. The question "What will I own if a venture capitalist invests X in my company at a Y valuation?" is rarely simple. To answer it, you need to be able to generate a cap table to truly analyze the deal presented by a particular term sheet. Following is a model to work from with a typical example.

Let's assume the following:

- 2 million shares held by founders before the VC invests
- $10 million pre-money valuation
- $5 million investment by the VC

129

In this example, the post-money valuation is $15 million ($10 million pre-money+$5 million investment). Consequently, the VCs own 33.33% of the company after the financing ($5 million investment/$15 million post-money valuation). This should be pretty straightforward so far.

Now, assume the term sheet includes a new employee option pool of 20% on a post-money basis. Remember that this means that after the financing, there will be an unallocated option pool equal to 20% of the company.

Although the post-money valuation remains the same ($15 million), the requirement for a 20% option pool will have a significant impact on the ownership of the founders. Per the following cap table, you can see how we calculate the percentage ownership for each class of owner, along with the price per share of the preferred stock. To start, we've filled in the known numbers and now have to solve for the unknowns (A, B, C, D, and E).

Class	Shares	Preferred Price	Valuation	Percentage
Founders	2,000,000			A
Employee pool	B			20%
Venture investors	C	D	$5,000,000	33.33%
Total	E	D	$15,000,000	100%

First, let's solve for A, the founders' ownership percentage: A = 100% minus the VC percentage minus the employee pool percentage, or 100% – 33.33% – 20% = 46.67%. Given that we know that the 2 million founders' shares represent 46.67% of the company, we can determine that the total shares outstanding (E = 2 million/0.4667) are 4,285,408. Now, if there are 4,285,408 shares outstanding, determining the number of shares in the employee pool becomes B = E×0.20 or 857,081.

The same math applies for C, the number of shares of preferred stock the VCs have. C = E×0.3333 or 1,428,326. Since $5 million bought 1,428,326 shares of preferred stock, then the price per share of preferred stock (D = $5 million/1,428,326) is $3.50 per share.

Finally, always check your calculation. Since we know we have a $10 million pre-money valuation, then the shares prior to the financing (2 million founders' shares plus the 20% option pool) times the price per share should equal $10 million. If you do this math, you'll see that (2 million + 857,081) × $3.50 = $9,999,783.50. Oops, we are off by $216.50, which represents 62 shares (well, 61.857 shares).

While this is close enough for an example, it's not close enough for most VCs, or for most lawyers for that matter. And it shouldn't be close enough for you. That's why most cap tables have two additional significant digits (or fractional shares)—the rounding to the nearest share doesn't happen during intermediate steps but does occur only at the very end.

As the entrepreneur, you shouldn't blindly rely on legal counsel to generate these documents. There are a lot of good lawyers out there with poor math skills, and the cap table can get messed up when left in the hands of the lawyers. Although some get it right, it's your responsibility to make sure you understand your cap table. This will be especially helpful at times when you want to expand the employee option pool and you want to be eloquent in front of your board of directors when explaining the ramifications.

Now, what happens when convertible debt is part of the equation? It can get a bit trickier. Our friends at Cooley LLP created a site called Cooley GO (www.cooleygo.com), which has a ton of resources for entrepreneurs. They recently wrote a great post about how to deal with convertible debt in a capitalization table,[1] which they've graciously allowed us to include in a mildly edited format in this book.

Price per Share with Convertible Notes

Calculating the cap table becomes more complex when you have convertible notes converting into equity. For this example, let's use the following assumptions about the financing and the terms of the convertible notes.

- **Agreed-Upon Pre-Money Valuation**: $8 million
- **Agreed-Upon Post-Money Valuation**: $10 million
- **Amount Being Invested by New Series A Investors**: $2 million

[1] "Calculating Share Price with Outstanding Convertible Notes," Derek Colla, https://www.cooleygo.com/calculating-share-price-outstanding-convertible-notes/.

- **Principal Plus Accrued Interest on Outstanding Promissory Notes**: $1 million
- **Discount Rate for Conversion of Notes**: 30%
- **Shares Outstanding on a Fully Diluted Basis, Pre-Investment**: 1 million

Since shares are issued upon conversion of the notes and the note holders will thus own some percentage of the company, once the transaction is complete either the existing stockholders will own less than 80% of the company or the investors will own less than 20%. Another way of saying this is that either the true pre-money valuation will be less than $8 million or the new investor will own less than 20% of the company after the transaction is completed. The key questions are (1) whose ownership percentage is diluted by the issuance of the shares on conversion of the notes, and (2) by how much is each party diluted.

As you can imagine, entrepreneurs and investors often have different views on how to resolve this question and a few different methods have become commonplace resolutions. Analysis of the three common methods of converting the notes—the (1) Pre-Money Method, (2) Percentage-Ownership Method, and (3) Dollars-Invested Method—follows.

Pre-Money Method

In the pre-money method, the pre-money valuation of the company is fixed and the conversion price for the notes is determined based on that. Using the assumptions above, the price per share for the new investors would be $8.00 per share ($8 million shares/1 million shares) and the conversion price for the notes would be $5.60 per share ($8.00 minus the 30% discount). The equity ownership of the company pre- and post-investment would be as follows:

Stockholder Group	Pre-Investment		Post-Investment	
	Shares	% Ownership	Shares	% Ownership
Founders	1,000,000	100%	1,000,000	70%
Noteholders	0	0.00%	178,571	12.50%
Series A Investors	0	0.00%	250,000	17.50%
Total:	1,000,000	100%	1,428,571	100%

The pre-money method causes both the founders and the Series A investors to be diluted by the shares issued upon conversion of the notes in proportion to their ownership percentage. While the pre-money valuation stays fixed at $8 million, the post-investment percentage ownership of the Series A investors is 17.5% and the post-money valuation implied by this method is $11.43 million. While this is probably the most common method, many investors dispute its use, since it results in them having less ownership of the company than that for which they believe they bargained.

Percentage-Ownership Method

In the percentage-ownership method, the percentage ownership of the company that the investor is purchasing is fixed and the other variables are computed based on that. You would come to the same result if you fixed the post-money valuation. Using the assumptions above, the price per share for the new investors would be $6.57 per share (mathematical result to arrive at 20% ownership) and the conversion price for the notes would be $4.60 per share ($6.57 minus the 30% discount). The equity ownership of the company pre- and post-investment would be as follows:

Stockholder Group	Pre-Investment		Post-Investment	
	Shares	% Ownership	Shares	% Ownership
Founders	1,000,000	100%	1,000,000	65.71%
Noteholders	0	0.00%	217,391	14.29%
Series A Investors	0	0.00%	304,348	20%
Total:	1,000,000	100%	1,521,739	100%

Dollars-Invested Method

The percentage-ownership method causes all of the dilution that results from the shares issued upon conversion of the notes to be borne by the founders. While the Series A investors' percentage ownership remains fixed at 20% and the post-money valuation remains fixed at $10 million, the pre-money valuation implied by this method is $6.57 million and the founders' ownership percentage is less than it is using the pre-money method. Unless it is expressly indicated in the term sheet, many entrepreneurs consider using this method to be a material deviation from the agreed-upon term sheet and object to its use.

The dollars-invested method is often utilized as a compromise between the pre-money method and the percentage-ownership method. In the dollars-invested method, the post-money valuation of the company is fixed to equal the agreed-upon pre-money valuation plus the dollars invested by the new investors plus the principal and accrued interest on the notes that are converting. Using the assumptions above, the post-money valuation would be fixed at $11 million and each of the other variables would be calculated from that. In this example, the price per share for the Series A investors would be $7.57 per share and the conversion price for the notes would be $5.30 per share ($7.57 minus the 30% discount). The equity ownership of the company pre- and post-investment would be as follows:

Stockholder Group	Pre-Investment		Post-Investment	
	Shares	% Ownership	Shares	% Ownership
Founders	1,000,000	100.00%	1,000,000	68.83%
Noteholders	0	0.00%	188,679	12.99%
Series A Investors	0	0.00%	264,151	18.18%
Total:	1,000,000	100.00%	1,452,830	100.00%

The dollars-invested method gives the founders credit for principal and accrued interest on the notes that are being converted into equity as if these were funds being newly invested into the company, but only the founders are diluted by the extra shares that the noteholders are receiving due to the conversion discount. The rationale is that converting debt into equity without a discount does not change the Series A investors' percentage ownership of the *enterprise value* of the company, so they are still getting the deal for which they bargained. The founders have to compromise and accept some additional dilution, but it is significantly less than what they would suffer under the percentage-ownership method.

The hardest part about calculating the price per share in a Series A financing of a company that has convertible notes converting at a discount is that it effectively reopens the discussion about the valuation of the company. Each party may have thought they had an agreement and now one (or both) needs to compromise to get the deal done.

The Entrepreneur's Perspective

If you do not have a great financially oriented founder, find someone who knows what she's doing to help you with the cap table—not just someone who knows math (a good starting point!), but someone who knows cap tables and venture capital financings.

Crowdfunding

When we wrote the first version of this book in 2011 the idea of using crowdfunding as a financing mechanism was nascent. Since then it has emerged as a powerful approach, both for product development and equity financing. In this chapter we will discuss the various crowdfunding approaches, legal implications, and how crowdfunding differs from more traditional methods.

Product Crowdfunding

Crowdfunding typically refers to two different approaches that are relevant to financing companies. The first, popularized by Kickstarter and Indiegogo, is *product crowdfunding*.

Product crowdfunding is typically used for physical products. The company puts its product idea up on Kickstarter along with content showing what the product will be and a series of different rewards for backers. In most cases, the product is in an early design stage and far from ready to ship. The rewards vary by dollar amount and often include things that, while linked to the product, are experiential or tangential to the product, such as logoed stickers and T-shirts, sponsorship recognition, or real-world events to celebrate the launch of the product.

Most campaigns have a 30-day funding target that, if not achieved, results in the campaign failing and funding not occurring. This is the hardware equivalent of building a software *minimum viable product* (MVP). If the campaign is successful, you know you have a compelling MVP. If the campaign does not reach its funding target, your potential customers are telling you that your MVP is not interesting enough to pursue.

Several high-profile products got their start on Kickstarter, including the Pebble Watch (which raised $10.2 million in 30 days), Oculus Rift (which raised $2.5 million in 30 days), and Occipital (which raised $1.3 million in 30 days). Companies have also had similar successes on Indiegogo, such as TrackR, which raised $1.7 million.

If this sounds similar to a preorder campaign, it is, and you will also hear people refer to them as "presales" or "preorders." While Kickstarter, Indiegogo, and other crowdfunding sites are growing rapidly, some companies, such as Glowforge, have decided to run their own preorder campaigns. In Glowforge's case, they raised $27.9 million in 30 days, demonstrating that if you have a compelling product and are sophisticated around marketing and promoting your product, you can run a very successful preorder campaign on your own.

The crowdfunding approach can even be rolled into your business model. When we invested in Betabrand, they were building a two-sided clothing marketplace that incorporated the notion of crowdfunding into their design process. Individual designers can create new designs that are then promoted on Betabrand's website. Customers preorder the designs and if a certain preorder threshold is met, the design is produced and becomes a permanent product in Betabrand's catalog.

In each of these cases, one of the large advantages of this approach is that the funding is nondilutive since no equity is involved. Instead of selling equity or debt, you are preselling a product and collecting the cash up front. Consequently, the crowdfunding backers are not shareholders of your company.

The downside of product crowdfunding is the situation where a campaign is successful, but the company doesn't finish building the product. In some cases, the company is able to raise additional capital, often equity, to complete the product and fulfill the preorders. In others, the company never ships the product or only fulfills some aspect of the campaign. While this situation is disappointing, the culture around product crowdfunding is such that these failures are understood to be part of the process, in the same way that investing equity in a company does not necessarily result in a successful company and a return on the investment.

Equity Crowdfunding

The second crowdfunding approach, popularized by AngelList, is equity crowdfunding. This approach pertains to the situation when an investor gives money to a company in exchange for a security (either debt or equity) through an intermediated process, often involving an online funding platform. These platforms, such as AngelList, allow companies to essentially advertise their funding or use the power of a social network to attract additional investor interest. Evolved approaches, such as AngelList Syndicates, allow individual investors to aggregate other investors to participate in their syndicate, acting like a small version of a venture capital fund.

While crowdfunding has expanded to cover many different situations, there are tight legal definitions surrounding each approach that were defined as part of the JOBS Act (the full name is the Jumpstart Our Business Startups Act) that was passed in 2012. As a result, some of the aspects of fundraising on platforms like AngelList are referred to as crowdfunding, but are really not anything new, other than the use of an online platform to connect companies with potential investors.

In the United States, if you are selling a *security*, you need to register the security with the Securities and Exchange Commission (SEC) unless you have an exemption not to. A security is any financial instrument that gives you an ownership interest in a company, including common stock, preferred stock, or convertible debt. This doesn't include revenue derived from product crowdfunding or a preorder campaign. The original rules for registering securities were defined in the Securities Act of 1933, and, while they have evolved, are still based on rules negotiated 86 years ago.

Fortunately, there are a number of exemptions that allow you to avoid an SEC registration. In general, unless you are taking a company public via initial public offering (IPO), you won't have to worry about registering your offering with the SEC. However, there are important guidelines that you must follow in order not to blow up your ability to rely on an exemption. The two most important to understand are the notion of an *accredited investor* and the process of *general solicitation*.

An accredited investor is a person who has a substantial net worth and/or income, as defined by the SEC and changed from time to time. In most cases, entities such as a VC, a corporation with meaningful assets, or a registered bank automatically qualify. An individual qualifies if she earns $200,000 per year or has a joint income with her spouse of $300,000 and this level has been earned in the previous two years and can be reasonably expected to be earned in the future. If an individual doesn't have this level of income, she can qualify if she has a net worth exceeding $1 million either alone or jointly with her spouse.

Unlike an accredited investor, the SEC does not clearly define what is considered to be general solicitation, instead leaving it open to interpretation. Historically, general solicitation referred to advertising or publicly promoting your fundraising, such as specifically making a financing ask in public at an accelerator demo day. Depending on your lawyer and how conservative you are, the line of where general solicitation is crossed is vague, but the simple test is that if you don't have a preexisting relationship with someone and encounter them through something that looks like an advertisement (which could include a mass email, rather than one-on-one introduction), then you are likely in the general solicitation bucket.

Prior to the JOBS Act, you wanted to avoid raising money from investors who were not accredited as well as avoid general solicitation. With the JOBS Act, the rules changed somewhat.

While there are an endless number of $99 courses on how to raise money for your company using crowdfunding, our friend Brad Bernthal, a law professor at CU Boulder, created the following chart as a summary of the implications of the three major crowdfunding and financing aspects of the JOBS Act. These are known as Rule 506(b), Rule 506(c)/Title II, and Title III, as shown in the table below.

	Rule 506(b)	Rule 506(c)/Title II	Title III
Aggregate cap on amount raised?	No	No	Yes ($1 million over 12 months)
General solicitation allowed?	No	Yes	No, except via a single funding portal or broker
Who can invest?	Accredited	Accredited	Accredited and nonaccredited
Broker or intermediary required?	No	No	Yes
Regulatory burden	Light	Medium	Heavy

Prior to Title II of the JOBS Act, if you generally solicited, you had broken the law and could not raise money. Prior to Title III of the JOBS Act, it was next to impossible to sell a meaningful number of securities to nonaccredited investors.

From a legal perspective, equity crowdfunding is really only Title III, where nonaccredited investors can participate. Not surprisingly, this is also the most heavily regulated approach. A company is limited to raising $1 million over a 12-month period and it can only solicit through one online funding portal or with a broker. While nonaccredited investors can participate in a Title III financing, there are limits on the size of individual investments, which, depending on the investor's net worth, can be as little as $2,000. Finally, there is a significant burden of SEC-mandated information disclosures that can easily cost a company tens of thousands of dollars to comply with.

Even though the phrase crowdfunding gets regularly applied to financings done on AngelList and other online platforms, this is often more around marketing the platform than it is around the substance of investing. Most of the financings done on AngelList happen under the 506(b) rules, which is similar to how most VC financings have historically been done. In some cases, companies use 506(c) so they can advertise more widely on a site like AngelList, but still only accept accredited investors. In these situations, there are additional regulations to ensure their investors are, indeed, accredited.

How Equity Crowdfunding Differs

A difference between equity crowdfunding and a more traditional financing is that with crowdfunding you are often setting the terms of the deal. Most sites allow you to determine the form of security you are issuing (equity versus debt) and to set all the major terms. While this is occasionally negotiated with a lead investor, in our experience most companies do not see much pushback on the terms they propose as long as they are reasonable.

While convertible debt financings are generally straightforward, they typically include a specific cap. With equity financings, a very light preferred stock with minimal protective provisions and terms are often used. Board seats, at least as part of the crowdfunding activity, are rarely offered.

The materials you put together include a traditional executive summary and a PowerPoint presentation. When raising online, you often get opportunities to spice things up with a fancy video, specific data about your recent performance, and continuous refreshes on this background information as time passes during the financing process.

In a VC-backed fundraise, you are often getting one or more self-proclaimed experts (the VC) involved in your company in an actively engaged way, either as a mentor, coach, networker, or board member. In crowdfunding situations, you are getting a crowd. While you may have a lead investor, you will now have many small investors who may, or may not, be focused on helping your company. Their investment may be a tiny dollar amount for them and they may have many separate small investments. Consequently, the responsibility for communication and engagement will be on you since it's unlikely that many of your new investors will proactively reach out to help. While this is similar to a situation where you raise money traditionally from a bunch of individual angels, it's a common dynamic in crowdfunding deals.

We've observed some companies end up being stranded after a crowdfunding round. These companies either can't, or don't, raise enough money in the crowdfunding round and find themselves without money and a noncommitted investor syndicate. Often, these companies are not mature enough to attract a VC financing and end up in a situation where they are too early for VCs, yet don't have meaningful support from their existing crowd of investors.

Finally, watch out for the jerks. We've seen situations where one or more members of a crowdfunded financing feel overly self-important, construct belief systems around the company that are delusional, or simply regret investing and try to exert pressure on the founders in inappropriate ways. While some angel investors forget that they are supposed to be "angels" instead of "devils," some crowdfunding participants don't appear to have subscribed to the angel notion to begin with. While some of this results from lack of sophistication of some investors in crowdfunding deals, there often is less concern about reputational constraints given the dynamics of crowdfunding as compared to angel or VC investing. A final challenge with crowdfunding platforms is that it's more difficult for the entrepreneur to do detailed diligence on the crowd, so beware of the squeaky wheel who can be a real pain in the neck.

Token Crowdfunding

ICOs (*initial coin offerings*) are funding mechanisms in which a company, project, or even a single person sells newly created crypto tokens in exchange for a cryptocurrency such as bitcoin or actual dollars. Wow, that was a lot of jargon. While this isn't a book about blockchain technology or cryptocurrencies, people are using these mechanisms, specifically ICOs or token offerings, to fund their companies, with the popularity (and hype) around this exploding in 2017.

Despite the excitement, ICOs are still rare when compared to other funding mechanisms. While many ICOs have raised a lot of money for little more than an idea and a whitepaper, there is a lot of skepticism around the long-term viability of many of them. In addition, the SEC is currently studying them in depth, as it appears that, based on current rules, many ICOs likely run afoul of one or more securities laws. Finally, there have already been several blatant frauds committed by companies raising ICOs. Buyer beware.

While there has been a lot of noise about ICOs replacing venture financings and there are a number of VCs, such as USV (https://www.usv.com) and Andreessen Horowitz (https://a16z.com), who have gone deep in this area, token crowdfunding is still very immature as a financing mechanism. If you are interested in crypto, take a look at this great list of things to read at: https://a16z.com/2018/02/10/crypto-readings-resources/. And, if you bought this book for help in raising your ICO, please direct all complaints to Brad.

CHAPTER

11

Venture Debt

While the phrase "raising venture capital" is often used as a synonym for equity, we have now discussed other financing mechanisms including convertible debt and crowdfunding. Another type of funding, known as *venture debt*, falls into its own category. The vast majority of venture-backed companies raise venture debt at some point in their life from specialized banks such as Silicon Valley Bank (SVB), which graciously wrote the following insider's guide to raising venture debt.

The Role of Debt versus Equity

If you are going to raise institutional venture capital to build and grow your business, it's worthwhile to consider using venture debt to complement the equity you raise. Venture debt is a type of loan offered by banks and nonbank lenders that is designed specifically for early stage, high-growth companies with venture capital backing. This chapter will provide insight on the types of loans that are available to venture capital–backed companies in the United States, how to pick the right lender for your company, the benefits typical of venture debt, what to expect on a term sheet, and tips for negotiating a successful deal. We'll also introduce you to the process and the players involved in the venture debt ecosystem, and the benefits and risks associated with this type of capital.

Identifying the right balance between equity and debt is an important part of an overall capital strategy. In Chapter 3, we emphasized the virtue of identifying how much equity you need as the starting point in the fundraising journey to increase the odds of long-term success. The same mindfulness applies to venture debt.

It's critical to understand the fundamental differences between debt and equity. For equity, repayment is usually not contractually required. While some form of liquidity event is presumed within a time frame of less than a decade, and *redemption rights* can sneak into your financing if you aren't vigilant, equity is long-term capital. The use of equity is supremely flexible—it can fund almost any legitimate business purpose. However, it is difficult to reprice or restructure equity if execution doesn't exactly match the business plan.

In comparison, debt can provide short-term or long-term capital. The structure, pricing, and duration are closely tied to the purpose of the capital. Debt can be configured to include financial covenants, defined repayment terms, and other features to mitigate credit and other risks borne by the lender. These characteristics limit the utility of debt, from the borrower's perspective, to a predefined set of business objectives, but they allow the lender to structure and price the loan to align with the borrower's current circumstances.

The first rule of venture debt is that it follows equity; it doesn't replace it. Venture lenders use venture capital support as a source of validation and the primary yardstick for underwriting a loan. Raising debt for an early stage company is more efficient when you can precisely describe the performance objectives associated with the last round of equity, the intended timing and strategy for raising the next round, and how the loan you are asking for will support or supplement those plans.

Venture debt availability and terms are always contextual. Loan types and sizes vary significantly based on the scale of your business, the quality and quantity of equity raised to date, and the objective for which the debt is being raised. The amount of venture debt available is calibrated to the amount of equity the company has raised, with loan sizes varying between 25% and 50% of the amount raised in the most recent equity round. Early stage loans to prerevenue or product validation companies are much smaller than loans available to later stage companies in expansion mode. And companies without VC investors face significant difficulties in attracting any venture debt.

The Entrepreneur's Perspective

If price were the only consideration, most entrepreneurs would fund their business exclusively with debt to avoid ownership dilution. This approach doesn't work for high-growth businesses because of the first rule of venture debt: You can bootstrap your business by shunning venture capital, but then venture debt likely won't be an option for your company. More traditional debt, such as cash-flow-based term loans or asset-based lines of credit may be an option, but they require you to generate positive cash flow.

Since venture debt is designed for companies that prioritize growth over profitability, the venture lender wants to follow in the path of investors they know and trust, rather than risk lending to a company without venture backing.

The Players

Silicon Valley Bank (SVB) was one of the first banks to create loan products for startups. It happened because SVB is based in Silicon Valley and evolved from the ground up to serve the innovation economy that surrounds it, which raises an important distinction as you explore loan options to fund your company. There are few banks that truly understand venture debt and many that don't. Many players come and go in the venture debt market, so make sure that whomever you are talking to is a long-term player. When a bank decides one day that it is no longer interested in lending venture debt, it can wreak havoc on your business.

There are a number of potential benefits when you identify the right banking partner. Banks with a focus on the innovation economy can provide startup-centric financial advice, investment and payments solutions, sector insights, and networking assistance to complement the support provided by your investors. The most experienced banks can also provide institutional resources to startups and in some cases your financial partner may become an active advocate for your business.

There are nonbank providers (referred to as *venture debt funds*), which raise capital from a variety of sources, worth considering for venture debt. Most raise private equity in a fund much like VCs do but with a lending charter. Some use public equity and are organized as a Business Development Company. Others have been organized as Small Business Investment Companies in order to leverage equity commitments from the private market with capital from the Small Business Administration. A few specialize in specific sectors, but most debt funds define their lending focus by loan size and company stage.

Understanding how a lender is capitalized and chartered is valuable because those factors exert a strong influence on the lender's cost of capital. Historically, venture debt funds have been differentiated from banks by the size of their loans and by their emphasis on yield and returns over structure. Unlike banks, which fund lending via deposits, venture debt funds typically have a higher cost of capital. As a result, debt funds usually take more risk in return for greater cash yield and warrant compensation. Conversely, banks have historically emphasized financial covenants and structure over yield, placing more limitations on maximum loan size. Venture debt is typically secured by the business pledging its assets as collateral to the lender, and lenders have a robust set of legal remedies they may apply when a borrower violates the loan agreement. Regardless of the venture debt option you pursue, a loan is rarely just a one-time transaction, but the beginning of a relationship, and ideally a long-term partnership.

Venture debt can be used as performance insurance, a lower-cost runway extension, funding for acquisitions or capital expenses and inventory, or a short-term bridge to the next round of equity. Before raising venture debt, you should discuss various options with your board, especially your VCs, since they will have a broad perspective on the use of venture debt and can provide introductions to the players.

How Lenders Think about Loan Types

To understand why you may qualify for some flavors of debt, and why the cost may be higher for you relative to other types of borrowers, it helps to know how lenders differentiate venture debt from other categories of loans.

Let's start by exploring how lenders think about sources of repayment. Regulated institutions such as banks are required, as part of the underwriting process, to identify two sources of repayment for every loan they make, noting which source is primary and which is secondary. They are also required to recognize more risk (i.e., downgrade the risk rating assigned to the loan) when the primary source of repayment exhibits weakness. If that happens, the lender has to reserve more capital to cover the potential for not receiving full repayment, which effectively reduces the profitability of the loan. Lenders categorize loans based on the primary source of repayment (PSOR) for a loan, and their return diminishes should the PSOR for such a loan begin to deteriorate.

The majority of loans to companies are term loans based on the cash flow of the company as the PSOR. The next largest category of commercial loans are revolving lines of credit that permit advances based on a percentage of the value of specific collateral (called a "borrowing base" by bankers), typically composed of accounts receivable or inventory, until the collateral converts to cash. These lines are categorized as asset-based loans because they focus on the collateral as the primary source of repayment instead of cash flow.

Those two categories describe the vast majority of commercial loans available. Neither category is a fit for preproduct startups or for companies just starting to generate revenue. In addition, cash flow loans don't work for revenue-producing companies that choose to accelerate growth at the expense of profitability. In effect, the traditional commercial loan market does not work for fast-growing startups.

Venture debt is a different type of loan that was created shortly after the birth of the venture capital industry. Venture debt relies on a company's access to venture capital as the PSOR for the loan. Instead of focusing on historical cash flow or working capital assets, venture debt emphasizes the borrower's ability to raise additional equity to fund the company's growth and repay the debt.

Most venture debt takes the form of a growth capital term loan. These loans usually have to be repaid within three to four years, but they often start out with a 6- to 12-month interest-only (I/O) period. During the I/O period, the company pays accrued interest, but not principal. When the I/O period is complete, the company begins paying down the principal balance of the loan. The duration of the I/O period and terms under which the loan can be drawn are key points in the negotiation process.

Recurring revenue loans are another category of venture debt that has gained traction in recent years. Recurring revenue underwriting is designed for companies that deliver a standardized product or service (such as software or media subscriptions) with recurring billing and consistent pricing. Those characteristics provide the ability to directly evaluate the unit economics of the business (i.e., the SaaS metrics). These metrics permit a lender to develop a model, based on assumptions founded on its market insight, to forecast the company's capital need, path to profitability, and ability to repay with greater precision. Many lenders use annual recurring revenue as a proxy for company valuation when underwriting venture term loans. Some lenders also use monthly recurring revenue and unit economics ratios to calibrate the availability of a borrowing formula under a revolving line of credit.

In a nutshell, venture debt availability, loan size, and deal terms correlate to the lender's assessment of the company's ability to raise more equity. In this context, institutional venture capital is a very transparent and predictable capital source. Lenders can understand and assess the investment behavior and track record of VC firms more readily than those of other players. Experienced lenders also have established relationships with VC firms that can help reduce the likelihood of surprises or misunderstandings. Without committed capital, institutional relationships, and an industry track record, it is difficult for a lender to determine whether a company has access to enough capital to repay a loan.

The Entrepreneur's Perspective

"Venture debt" is a catchall term referring to loans designed for companies that have raised equity from institutional sources—as opposed to capital raised from angel investors or "friends and family."

Venture debt isn't usually available to seed stage companies. Unlike most angels, most VCs (regardless of their natural entry point) typically invest in multiple equity rounds and maintain capital reserves for this purpose. Even if you can source a loan with an angel-backed profile, taking significant debt at the seed stage probably isn't optimal if substantial additional equity capital is required to fund the company. Institutional VC investors typically don't want to see a large portion of their fresh equity used to repay old debt.

And don't forget the main rule of debt. You do actually have to pay it back someday and that day may turn out to be an inconvenient day in ways you can't forecast ahead of time.

Knowing how lenders think about sources of repayment also helps you understand how they assess the performance of your company after you take the loan. Because their underwriting is based on your access to future capital, venture debt lenders focus on the same performance characteristics that VCs monitor. In fact, their number-one goal is to estimate how company performance impacts the incentives that drive investor behavior. Specifically, lenders are evaluating investor behavior based on the particular relationship that a lender has to your VC. Savvy lenders are paying attention to the subtle cues that distinguish whether your VCs will provide additional capital to the company.

Venture lenders are keenly aware that dilution is a powerful incentive, as the core value proposition of venture debt is reducing dilution for founders and management. Because access to capital is the PSOR, venture lenders evaluate your company through a similar lens as your investors, such as:

- Will additional equity be needed?
- Which metrics will influence the next-round valuation?
- What level of performance correlates to nondilutive access to capital?

Lenders closely monitor a company's burn rate and liquidity to determine the resulting number of months of capital available (often referred to as *runway*). Companies with enough momentum and liquidity to achieve milestones for the next financing are more likely to attract nondilutive next-round term sheets from outside investors. Companies with a shortfall in either category are likely to struggle to attract a new lead investor and may have to resort to an inside-led, possibly dilutive round, to continue funding the company.

Putting these pieces together will help you see your company the way a venture debt lender does: They care about who your investors are, what metrics your investors use to gauge the company's progress, how much progress is required to increase the probability of non-dilutive access to capital, and when your company will run low on liquidity in relation to those performance milestones.

Economic Terms

Debt term sheets differ in structure from equity term sheets, but once again economic and control terms should be the primary focus for most entrepreneurs. In addition, a new category, called *amortization terms,* appears so that bankers can have more tools to work with. With debt financings, there are usually several variables to analyze and aggregate in order to determine the total price of the financing.

Interest rate is the simplest of the pricing ingredients. Most venture lenders provide only floating (also known as variable) interest rates for their growth capital loans. Consequently, the interest rate will typically be quoted as a spread (i.e., 2.00%) above a specific reference index. Most venture loans are indexed to the *Prime Rate.* The floating rate structure means that the borrower absorbs the risk of interest rate fluctuation. While common in large corporate debt markets, LIBOR-indexed loans aren't used for the smaller loans typical of the venture debt market. Likewise, negotiating for a fixed-rate loan is difficult because it transfers the risk of the interest rate fluctuations to the lender.

Loan fees are the second ingredient in pricing. There is significant variation in the size and structure of loan fees, but most are triggered by the loan closing or loan utilization (the drawn balance) exceeding a defined metric. Venture loan fees generally are lower (ranging from 0.25% to 0.75% of the loan amount) than the fees on traditional cash flow loans. The venture market is oriented toward deferring cash burn as much as possible, and to that end entrepreneurs will want to negotiate fees based on when they draw the loan versus the lender's commitment when possible.

Warrants are a common piece of the lender's compensation in the venture debt market. While a no-warrant loan is preferable to both entrepreneurs and investors because it is nondilutive, in the early stage market, warrant pricing is considered a critical feature by most lenders, especially for true growth capital loans with no financial covenants. No-warrant loans may be available to strong-performing companies from some bank lenders, but those loans usually will require financial covenants as a trade-off. Debt funds rarely forgo warrants given their need to clear higher yield targets.

Warrant pricing can be complicated to figure out. Term sheets often express that the warrants are to be granted to the lender as a percentage of the loan commitment amount. For example, a term sheet for a $2 million growth capital loan might refer to "warrant coverage" of 2%. This means the value of the warrant is intended to be $40,000. Other term sheet variations will directly express the economic value the lender wants (i.e., $40,000) or will express the economic value as a percentage (or a certain number of basis points, where 100 basis points is equivalent to 1%) of fully diluted ownership. This fully diluted equivalent definition provides a consistent benchmark for expressing the warrant price regardless of the class of stock (common or preferred) used for the calculation. Using that metric, the warrant compensation in venture debt proposals from banks will typically range from 10 to 15 basis points for an early stage company to 2 to 5 basis points for a later stage company. The warrant compensation in term sheets from debt funds will be higher than those of banks because of debt funds' greater sensitivity to yield.

The next step in the pricing negotiation is to determine the class of stock into which the warrant will be converted and the corresponding strike price. Venture lenders are aware of the various protections and powers typically granted to preferred stock, but the degree to which they value those structural advantages over common stock varies. The primary value of taking warrants on preferred stock from a lender's point of view is price protection. Preferred stock warrants typically command the same antidilution provisions enjoyed by those who hold the actual preferred shares. Bank lenders have restrictions on their ability to monetize warrants. They typically wait for a liquidity event before exercising a warrant, and usually exercise the warrant under same-day sale procedures, since they don't want to hold shares in the company. Debt funds have more optionality in their behavior as warrant holders and may decide to exercise the warrant prior to a defined liquidity event, particularly if a warrant is close to expiring. They may also hold shares for longer periods after exercising the warrant. For these reasons, some of the structural advantages of preferred stock may be more valuable to the debt fund lender than a bank lender.

The strike price associated with a warrant is a key focus of negotiation. Entrepreneurs have an incentive to bargain for a strike price based on the next round of equity (subsequent to loan closing). Lenders have an incentive to use the last round as the strike price. If you assume that the entrepreneur is confident that the next-round valuation will be about two times the last round, a warrant with a $40,000 economic value, based on a last-round strike price of $0.50 per share, would provide the lender with 80,000 shares of the company. If the strike price is linked to the next-round valuation, and that turns out to be equivalent to $1.00 per share, the lender gets only 40,000 shares.

The duration of the warrant is another negotiation point. Most venture debt term sheets seek warrants expiring between 7 and 10 years from the grant date. The cost of granting the warrant is correlated to the duration under GAAP rules, so entrepreneurs have an incentive to shorten the maturity. Lenders have an incentive to push for longer maturities, particularly for early stage companies, since they have a limited ability to foresee how long it will take the company to reach a liquidity event.

Final payments are another common pricing mechanism in the venture debt market, particularly for life science, healthcare, and later stage companies. Final payments are analogous to a loan fee that is paid at the very end of the loan's life and are typically quoted as a percentage of the commitment amount (i.e., a final payment of 8% in our $2 million loan example would be $160,000). Final payments benefit the company by deferring the carrying cost of the loan, and, if your valuation is increasing over time, you naturally want to defer payment of principal and interest for as long as the lenders will agree. Final payments benefit the lender because they can provide an incentive for the company to refinance the loan with the same lender rather than taking a competing term sheet. Regardless of the amount of deferral provided by a final payment structure, the cash value of the payment should be aggregated into the loan's total price calculation.

Finally, *prepayments*, common in all types of loans including venture debt, may be a subject for negotiation. The most common prepayment fee structure is called a 3–2–1 because the prepayment fee reduces annually at the anniversary of the loan. If you pay the loan off during the first year, the fee equals 3% of the loan balance at the time of prepayment. The percentage drops to 2% of the loan's term in the second year and 1% in the third. This places an explicit value on the economic loss for the lender if the loan does not last to maturity, and prepayment fees provide lenders with a retention tool. The fee creates an additional incentive for the borrower to renegotiate the loan with the same lender instead of refinancing elsewhere.

Amortization Terms

Entrepreneurs focus their attention on loan pricing, but amortization terms are actually more critical to ensure that the debt aligns with the intended capital strategy.

The *draw period* (also called the availability period) is the time during which cash advances may be requested under the loan. This structure applies to term loans, as cash can be drawn (and paid back) at any time under revolving lines of credit. Venture lenders are willing to negotiate a delayed draw option of between 6 and 12 months after the loan closing, but prior to the need to raise additional equity, to ensure that the loan is actually used prior to closing the next equity round. A delayed draw period benefits the borrower because it guarantees the availability of the loan but minimizes the amount of interest. For the lender, the opposite is true since they have committed capital but are not earning interest on it. Accordingly, not all term loans allow for delayed draws, or the terms of the loan may provide for a fee to be paid to the lender for its unused commitment. Some lenders require the entire loan to be drawn at the time of closing.

The *interest-only (I/O) period* is also a common characteristic of venture loans and closely related to the draw period. Often the term sheet will provide the same amount of time (6 to 12 months from loan closing) during which the borrower makes only interest payments, but not principal payments, on the loan. Whereas the draw period provides optionality regarding the carrying cost of the loan, the I/O period has a much greater impact on the capital strategy of the company because it directly impacts cash burn and the runway calculation. Entrepreneurs and investors alike have incentives to defer principal amortization for as long as possible—money that is not applied to loan repayment can instead be used for growing the business. Because this benefit to the company is so substantial, I/O periods are usually linked to the cost of the loan and the warrant pricing.

In addition to a specific I/O period defined at the time of underwriting, some lenders may offer conditional I/O extensions for an additional three, six, or nine months related to the company meeting a defined performance milestone. Although these structures add complexity and increase uncertainty for the company, they can be a win/win for both parties. For the lender, aligning longer I/O periods with value-enhancing milestones that correlate to increased access to capital for the company improves the odds of full repayment. For the borrower, further extending the runway without materially increasing the cost of the loan is a big benefit. However, the downside when performance milestones are not met may be significant, since cash will now be going out the door to repay principal.

Once the I/O period has elapsed, scheduled amortization of the principal balance begins. Venture term loans tend to have maturity periods from 36 to 48 months, including the length of I/O period that is negotiated. As a result, a typical loan structure is 12 months of I/O period followed by 36 months of amortization. When principal repayment begins, most venture loans use what is called *straight-line amortization*, which means the principal balance is divided up equally among the number of payments. In the $2 million loan example, with a 12/36 split between I/O and amortization periods, this translates to accrued interest payments for the first 12 months, followed by 36 monthly payments of $55,500 plus interest.

Once again, the flexibility around amortization schedules is different between banks and debt funds. Since banks are regulated institutions, they are much more sensitive than debt funds to changing the payment schedule of a loan after origination. Instead of modifying the payment schedule of an existing loan, they prefer to refinance the facility with a new loan. When they do this, they need to be able to demonstrate to a regulator that the new loan is made on market terms and is consistent with the credit profile of the borrower, and that the borrower is able to repay the loan on both the existing and the new terms.

Bank regulators are vigilant for indications that lenders are modifying existing loans as a defensive measure to compensate for a borrower's inability to repay the loan in a commercially reasonable time frame. A body of regulatory guidance exists specifically to govern the extent and magnitude of payment modifications that banks can offer without impairing a loan, particularly with respect to deferring payments (also known as "payment holidays") for loans that have already begun to amortize principal. Regulators are also sensitive to the degree of amortization occurring under a given loan because they view cash amortization as a bright line that distinguishes senior debt from junior.

Debt funds are not as sensitive to these regulatory restrictions, although they are required by GAAP to demonstrate that each loan is a performing asset. As a result, nonbank lenders are more comfortable modifying the repayment terms of an existing loan rather than requiring a refinancing. In many instances, debt funds will prioritize optimizing the return on their loan and will be less concerned with the structure of the loan modification.

Control Terms

The defining characteristic of growth capital loans to early stage technology companies is the lack of financial covenants. Those are contractual terms that give the lender the right to cancel its commitment, accelerate the repayment schedule, or seize and liquidate collateral if the borrower's financial performance fails to stay within established parameters. The less predictable nature of early stage companies makes financial covenants impractical in many cases. Often, investors may not support putting debt on early stage portfolio companies if the loans require performance-based financial covenants.

Lenders link the need for warrants in the pricing of venture debt to the degree that enterprise value is at risk with the loan. Since loans to early stage companies have around twice the loss rate of traditional loans during positive market conditions, the lack of financial covenants amplifies the lender's reliance on the company's ability to grow enterprise value, thus increasing the need for warrant compensation to balance this risk.

While early stage companies can usually raise debt with warrants but no covenants, later stage companies can raise no-warrant debt, but the trade-off is that those deals consistently require financial covenants. The covenants allow the lender to reduce the repayment risk, either by requiring liquidity coverage relative to the debt or requiring growth targets that validate an increase in enterprise value.

Financial covenants are a subset of a broader category of contractual terms that lenders use to manage repayment risk. While term sheets may have a general reference to affirmative covenants, they are often not specifically described. Instead, most term sheets include a statement like: "Final loan documentation will include affirmative covenants customary to standard commercial practice and the specific needs of this transaction." The detailed covenant terms are included in draft loan documents and are discussed as part of the loan negotiation process.

In general, covenants are categorized as affirmative covenants or negative covenants. *Affirmative covenants* are actions that the company promises to take during the term of the financing contract. The list of potential conditions is lengthy and varies depending on the context and structure of the loan. The following are common affirmative covenants:

Regulatory compliance: Comply with applicable laws and regulations and maintain good standing with government agencies relevant to each jurisdiction and market the business operates in.

Government approvals: Obtain all approvals and licenses necessary for operation of the business.

Reporting: Provide accurate and timely financial statements and other material information to the lender.

Taxes: Pay all tax obligations timely as required and maintain good records.

Insurance: Maintain liability coverage that insures the business and the collateral of the lender.

Accounts: Maintain substantially all banking and collateral accounts with the lender or a designee (in the case of debt funds). Accounts with institutions other than the lender must be disclosed and may be subject to separate documentation to provide the lender with control over those accounts as part of the collateral.

Financial covenants: Maintain compliance with the financial criteria/ratios agreed upon in the term sheet as performance requirements.

Intellectual property (IP): Register, defend, and maintain the enforceability of any IP the company has and advise the lender of any material impairment or infringement.

Lenders also use *negative covenants* to define behaviors and actions that the company may not engage in as a condition of the loan. As a practical matter, negative covenants require the company to obtain the lender's consent for specific changes or actions. Negative covenants will include a materiality threshold (which can be ambiguous and is a good area for negotiation) that allows for ordinary activities without the lender's formal consent.

The following are common negative covenants:

Dispositions: Don't sell, transfer, or convey businesses, assets, and particularly the collateral (other than inventory in the ordinary course of business) of the lender without lender consent.

Change in control/location: Don't change the fundamental nature, location, or ownership structure of the business without lender consent.

Mergers/acquisitions: Don't buy other companies or sell all or part of your business without lender consent.

Indebtedness: Don't take on debt from other parties, beyond a list of ordinary categories defined as "permitted indebtedness" in the agreement.

Encumbrance: Don't provide a lien interest in the assets of the business to other parties, except typical exceptions set out in definition of permitted indebtedness.

Distributions/investments: Don't pay dividends or distributions or make material investments beyond a list of ordinary categories defined as "permitted investments" and "permitted distributions."

Subordinated debt: Don't make payments to a junior or subordinated creditor beyond a specific schedule of allowed payments defined in a separate "intercreditor agreement."

The most controversial control term used in the venture debt market is the Material Adverse Change (MAC) clause. The MAC clause typically appears as a condition that no MAC shall have occurred prior to funding and as an "Event of the Default" specified in the final loan documentation. The lender's intentions with regard to a MAC clause may or may not be disclosed in the term sheet. If you don't see a MAC reference in the term sheet, it should be a specific point of inquiry since the MAC is the kitchen sink of control clauses. It covers a wide range of scenarios that could become events of default under the loan agreement—even without specifically defining them in advance.

Understandably, investors are sensitive to MAC provisions in venture debt deals because they are subject to the discretion of the lender. These provisions safeguard lenders from making advances or maintaining a loan to a borrower when market or borrower-specific circumstances have changed in a manner that could not have been foreseen by the parties. They enable the lender to invoke an event of default based on the lender's interpretation of recent developments, how material they are, and how they might impact the company's ability to perform according to the terms of the loan agreement. Within the final legal agreement, most MAC provisions will include a statement like this:

> "Material Adverse Change" is (a) a material impairment in the perfection or priority of Bank's Lien in the Collateral or in the value of such Collateral; (b) a material adverse change in the business, operations, or condition (financial or otherwise) of Borrower; [or] (c) a material impairment of the prospect of repayment of any portion of the Obligations; [or] (d) Bank determines, based upon information available to it and in its reasonable judgment, that there is a reasonable likelihood that Borrower shall fail to comply with one or more of the financial covenants in Section [__] during the next succeeding financial reporting period.

The most important point that entrepreneurs should understand is that MAC provisions are not intended to undermine the flexibility of a "no-covenant" loan structure even though the scope of these provisions is so broad. Instead, they serve as a fail-safe, so lenders can underwrite to the range of anticipated circumstances without factoring for extremely remote outcomes, permitting lenders to price loans more accurately and cheaply.

Recognizing that MACs are designed to be exercised in only the most extremely adverse circumstances, many borrowers are nevertheless justifiably concerned that a lender may "sweep the cash" by taking cash out of the company's bank account to pay down the loan, based on a MAC. Next to the company's IP, cash liquidity is the most valuable asset of most startups. Whether the cause of an event of default is a MAC or a breach of another covenant, such as a financial covenant, a prudent lender will exercise its right to sweep cash when necessary to preserve value.

Including a MAC in the loan agreement only amplifies how critical it is for the entrepreneur to be familiar with the lender's track record and industry reputation. You should find out if the lender you are negotiating with has a consistent practice of using MAC provisions, or other control terms in the loan agreement, to invoke an event of default over the objections of management and investors. If a lender plays poorly with a MAC clause, it's highly unlikely the VCs involved with that company will ever work with that lender again.

It would be tempting to suggest that you should simply negotiate MAC provisions out of every debt agreement, but in many cases that may be impractical, if not impossible. Many venture debt funds, as a matter of principle, will not commit to a loan without the MAC clause. Banks will similarly demand the MAC for most venture debt loans, and certainly for higher-risk scenarios. Your ability to eliminate or modify the MAC in the loan agreement is governed primarily by three things: the context of your company, the context of the loan, and, most importantly, the relationship between your investors and the lender.

The last control feature is what is included in the security interest on the borrower's assets, specifically whether IP will be included in the lender's collateral. Investors and entrepreneurs would certainly love a world where IP was never on the table as loan collateral. But lenders will ask for a *perfected lien* on the IP for larger loans involving companies with higher-risk scenarios and in which the enterprise value is weighted heavily toward IP.

A spectrum of structures can be used to provide the lender with some control over the disposition of the IP without actually having a perfected lien on it. The most common is the "negative pledge." In this situation, the lender does not receive a lien on the IP. Instead the company pledges not to provide an IP lien to any other party. This provides the lender with an incremental measure of control because another party may not jump in front of them by placing a first-priority lien on the most valuable asset of the company. It effectively defers the conversation for another day, since it preserves a bargaining chip that the company may offer up (or the lender may demand) in loan modification negotiations.

Negotiation Tactics

A central tenet of this book, the value of reputation, is paramount. The venture capital industry is relationship-driven, which applies equally to debt and equity. Most VC-backed companies progress through a series of equity and debt financings and, as a result, are multiturn games. In negotiating each round of venture debt, as with equity, a tension exists between getting the best deal terms and getting the best relationship partner. The desire to optimize every term in every loan should be balanced against the benefit of partnering with a lender who may provide greater strategic or performance flexibility over a long period of time.

In the case of a deal-focused decision process, particularly if loan size is the priority, you are signaling that you view the lender as a vendor. Consequently, you may be more likely to select a lender with a similarly transactional posture toward adjusting loan terms once the initial loan agreement has been struck. That posture may simply translate into opportunistic pricing requests or it may directly impact your strategic options should you need to make material changes to the debt terms. Occasionally, there are cues that hint at which trait is more likely. For example, you should be particularly wary of lenders who change critical deal terms as the negotiation migrates from term sheet to final loan documents. Deal term drift is a good indication that a winner-take-all, contract-centric mind-set is that lender's standard operating procedure.

Conversely, in the example of a relationship-focused decision process, you may not get the most advantageous position on every deal term. Instead, you are counting on the lender's willingness to roll with the ups and downs that inevitably will impact your financial performance and strategy over time. This doesn't mean that deal terms don't matter, since the size and structure of the loan should be aligned with the needs and strategy of the business. However, the partnership-focused lender values being flexible and playing a long-term game, both with your company and your investors.

The process you use to seek a lender is another example of tensions between vendors versus partners. The most effective way to obtain optimal venture debt deal is to initiate a "bake off" among multiple lenders competing for your business. This entails collecting multiple rounds of term sheets from several lenders who are bidding for your business. If handled artfully, you can leverage feedback from each lender in between term sheet rounds to determine which terms you like the most.

While there are plenty of scenarios in which competition may improve the deal terms, in many cases it is not necessary, especially if your investors have a deep relationship with a specific lender.

The time invested in exploring options should be measured against the financial and strategic impact of the incremental gains. Your investors will have a view on this given the stage of your company and the magnitude of debt you are raising.

Restructuring the Deal

As we've previously said, the only thing certain about startups' financial forecasts is that 100% of them are wrong. Fortunately, experienced venture lenders know this, and their approach to tying the loan structure to your forecast should discount the specific level of performance you predict. Even so, given the overwhelming difficulty of controlling the financial performance of a startup, the probability that you will need to change the terms of the loan before the maturity date is still extremely high.

How you confront a looming need to renegotiate loan terms is crucial. Handled well, many of these scenarios add to the credibility of your management team and deepen the relationship with your lender. Handled poorly, the lender may increase costs before granting the current request, setting in motion a pattern of contractual opportunism that may impact future negotiations.

Start by taking a page out of the universal crisis management rule book: when things go sideways, do not try to hide the problem. Instead, your goal should be to communicate early and often with your lender about your performance as soon as it goes off plan. Surprise is the enemy, and transparency is your friend.

Once there is acknowledgment of the need to change the loan structure, the hard work of negotiating a solution begins. To find a win/win solution, it will help once again to be familiar with the lender's perspective. After the initial underwriting is completed, the focus of the lender (particularly so for bank lenders) will evolve from evaluating your business plan and capital requirements to monitoring how well your company is executing against those plans. In effect, the lender mind-set switches from seller (during initial loan underwriting) to buyer (during the life of the loan). In seller mode, the lender is primarily focused on aligning their proposal with your priorities because they are competing to win the mandate for the deal. In buyer mode, the lender is at least slightly more empowered to lead the conversation and put conditions on the negotiations based on their priorities. The lender will analyze your restructuring wish list based on its own practices for risk and portfolio management.

A top priority for all lenders, particularly banks, is the risk impact that restructuring or modifying the loan may have. Using the risk-rating terminology employed by bank regulators, most loans are characterized as Pass credits at the beginning. The capital reserve requirements aligned with the initial rating will not change unless conditions deteriorate, such as if the PSOR exhibits weakness. If the PSOR does wobble, the risk rating may be downgraded to Criticized or Classified, depending on the scope and depth of the circumstances driving the change. At the bottom of the risk-rating scale, when primary and secondary sources exhibit weakness or uncertainty and full repayment is no longer probable, the risk rating migrates to Impaired.

As noted earlier, capital requirements for the bank go up as the risk rating of a loan declines. At the Criticized or Classified level, this translates to a less profitable loan. However, if the loan is Impaired, it usually moves to nonaccrual status, meaning it is no longer treated as an income-earning asset under GAAP.

For venture debt, the PSOR is access to capital. As VC-backed companies progress through a series of financing cycles, the lender will typically be forced to adjust the risk rating, usually when liquidity is at a low ebb and a new round of equity hasn't yet been committed. When a loan structure is loosened relative to the standards set at origination, you may see a lower risk rating as well. Migrating through a series of risk-rating downgrades and upgrades is normal operating procedure for experienced venture debt lenders.

There is no way to avoid giving the venture lender a variety of control terms in the loan agreement. Even without a MAC, those control terms can be used to invoke an event of default. An event of default T the master control clause, the one ring that rules over all the other control terms. The issue is not whether your company will one day be in default of its loan agreement. If the evolution of your company is typical of the venture industry, you will violate some provision of your loan agreements eventually. In every venture loan portfolio, a significant number of companies are technically in default of their loan agreement at any given moment. The issue is how you and the lender handle that scenario. The chasm between what a lender could do under the terms of the loan agreement and what a good venture lender actually does is wider in restructuring scenarios than anywhere else.

Inevitably, a significant number of startups fail. There are a series of customary options (recapitalization, sale of company, sales of assets) that may be explored when the company's ability to continue operating as a going concern is in doubt. Executing on that evaluation process, known as searching for a soft landing, requires professionalism and collaboration among the company, the investors, and the lender. The first step in engineering a soft landing is self-awareness. As valuation ranges tighten and access to nondilutive capital declines, it is critical for the company and its investors to develop business strategies that include contingency plans.

The shift from Plan A (raising more equity) to Plan B (focusing on a sale) represents a major inflection point for a company. Many companies struggling with performance or valuation challenges tiptoe into Plan B by exploring options for selling the company while engaging with prospective investors.

In some cases, a sale doesn't materialize, and the company moves from Plan B (sale) to Plan C (wind-down), which is an even more difficult inflection point. It is often hard for founders, management, and investors to accept that there could be so little value in the eyes of competitors or other potential acquirers. However, for any company running out of cash, understanding the dynamics of both a sale and a wind-down is critical, especially in situations where you have any amount of debt.

This wind-down playbook is important to understand if you have a chance of formulating a less painful outcome for your investors and your lender. The venture market is a relationship-driven industry, and institutions have very long memories. You may get the chance to drive your company into a wall at high speed one time, hoping for a miracle. However, if that high-speed gambit increases the loan loss experienced by the lender, the likelihood that the same lender will want to take the same amount of risk on your next company is remote.

CHAPTER

How Venture Capital Funds Work

At this point, you should be familiar with different types of financings, the terms, and have some ideas on how to best maximize your chances to get a term sheet or three. In the next chapter we'll explore different negotiating strategies. But, before we do that, it's useful to understand the motivation of the person you'll be negotiating against, namely, the VC.

We've been asked many times to divulge the deep, dark secrets of what makes VCs tick. One night over dinner we talked through much of that with a very experienced entrepreneur who was in the middle of a negotiation for a late stage round for his company. At the end of the discussion, he implored us to put pen to paper since even though he was extremely experienced and had been involved in several VC-backed companies, our conversation helped him understand the nuances of what he was dealing with, which, until our explanation, had been confusing him.

In general, it's important to understand what drives your current and future investors since their motivations will impact your business. While the basics of how a venture fund works may be known, in this chapter we try to also cover all the nonobvious issues that play into how VCs think and behave. To do that, we'll dive into how funds are set up and managed as well as the pressures, both internally and externally, that VCs face.

Overview of a Typical Structure

Let's start by describing a typical *VC fund* structure (see the illustration on the next page). There are three basic entities that make up the fund. The first entity is the *management company* and is usually owned by the senior partners. The management company employs all of the people with whom you interact at the firm, such as the partners, associates, and support staff, and pays for all of the normal day-to-day business expenses, such as the firm's office lease, fresh fruit juicer, fancy coffee machine, endless supplies of Kind bars, and monthly Internet expense.

As a result, the management company is the franchise of the firm. While old funds are retired, and new funds are raised, the management company lives on and services each of the funds that are raised. A VC's business card typically lists the name of the management company, which is one of the reasons that the signature blocks on a term sheet often have a different name from the one you are used to associating with the firm. For example, in our case, Foundry Group is the name of our management company, not that of the actual funds that we raise and invest from.

The next entity is the *limited partnership* (LP) vehicle. When a VC talks about her "fund" or that her firm "raised a fund of $225 million," she is actually talking about a limited partnership vehicle that contains the investors in the fund (also called *limited partners,* or LPs).

The final entity is one an entrepreneur rarely hears of and is called the *general partnership* (GP) entity. This is the legal entity for serving as the actual general partner to the fund. In some partnerships, the individual managing directors play this role, but over time this has evolved into a separate legal entity that the managing directors each own on a fund-by-fund basis.

We realize this is confusing unless you are in law school, in which case you are salivating with joy over the legal complexity we are exposing you to. The key point to remember is that there is separation between the management company (the franchise) and the actual funds that it raises (the LP entities). These distinct entities will often have divergent interests and motivations, especially as managing directors join or leave the venture capital firm. One managing director may be your point of contact today, but this person may have different alignments among multiple organizations that will potentially affect you.

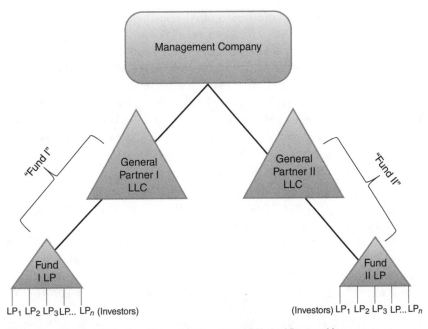

Management Company Structure: General Partnership and Limited Partnership

How Firms Raise Money

The next time you are on the fundraising trail beating your head against the wall trying to get through to a VC about how awesome your business is, remember that VCs also get to enjoy the same process when raising funds. So, while we feel your pain, we also admit that many VCs quickly forget about the whole process and inflict too much pain on the entrepreneurs raising money. In addition, many VCs within a firm don't have meaningful responsibilities for fundraising, so they feel relatively little pain. While this knowledge might help a little when you are sitting frustrated in your hotel room after another day of fundraising, we encourage you to explore the magic soothing properties of scotch.

VCs raise money from a variety of entities, including government and corporate pension funds, large corporations, banks, professional institutional investors, educational endowments, high-net-worth individuals, family offices, funds of funds, charitable organizations, and insurance companies. The arrangement between the VCs and their investors is subject to a long, complicated contract known as the *limited partnership agreement* (LPA) that makes one thing clear: VCs have bosses also—their investors, also known as their LPs.

When a VC firm makes an announcement that it has raised a $100 million fund, it is not the case that the VC has $100 million sitting in the bank waiting for a smart entrepreneur to come along. The venture capital firm normally keeps very little cash on hand and must ask its LPs every time it wants money to make an investment. This is known as a *capital call* and it typically takes two weeks from the moment the money is requested until it arrives. Note that the LPs are legally obligated under the fund agreements to send the VCs money every time they make a capital call.

If a venture capital firm requests money and its investors say no, things get tricky. The VC usually has some very draconian rights in the LPA to enforce its capital call, but we saw several moments in the past when VCs did a capital call and there was a smaller amount of money to be had than was anticipated. This is not a good thing if you are the entrepreneur relying on getting a deal done with the VC. Fortunately, this is a rare occurrence.

Why might investors refuse to fund a capital call? For one, LPs may think the VC is making bad decisions and may want to get out of the fund. More likely, something exogenous happened to the LP and they are feeling tight on cash and can't, or don't want to, comply with the capital call. This happened a number of times in the global economic crisis in the fall of 2008 (and even back in 2001) when three categories of LPs were impacted:

1. High-net-worth individuals who were feeling lower-net-worth at the time;
2. Banks that had no cash available (and quickly became parts of other banks); and
3. Endowments, foundations, and charitable organizations that had massive cash flow crises because of their ratio of illiquid investments.

In many cases, the VC will find a new LP to buy the old LP's interest. There is an active market known as a secondary market for LPs who want to sell their interest. Economically, this is almost always more attractive to the LP than not making a capital call, so except in moments of extreme stress, the VC usually ends up with the money to make an investment.

How Venture Capitalists Make Money

Now that we've explained the structure of a typical venture capital fund, let's explore how VCs get paid. The compensation dynamics of a particular fund often impact the behavior of a VC early in the life of a company, as well as later on when the company is either succeeding or struggling and needs to raise additional capital.

Management Fees

VCs' salaries come from their funds' *management fees*. The management fee is a percentage (typically between 1.5% and 2.5%) of the total amount of money committed to a fund. These fees are taken annually (paid out quarterly or semiannually) and finance the operations of the venture capital firm, including all of the salaries for the investing partners and their staff. For example, if a venture capital firm raises a $100 million fund with a 2% management fee, each year the firm will receive $2 million in management fees. While this may seem like a lot of money, it goes to pay all of the costs of the venture capital firm, including employees, partners, associates, rent, flying around the country seeing entrepreneurs, copiers, diet soda, brand-new MacBook Airs, and a new iPhone every time Apple releases a new version, even if it's only a change in color.

The percentage is usually inversely related to the size of the fund; the smaller the fund, the larger the percentage—but most funds level out around 2%. There's a slight nuance, which is the fee paid during and after the *commitment period*, or the period of time when the fund can make new investments—usually the first five years. This fee, which is usually 2% to 2.5%, begins to decrease after the end of the commitment period. The formula varies widely, but in most firms the average total fee over a 10-year period is about 15% of the committed capital. So, in our previous $100 million fund example, the typical fund will have $15 million of management fees to run its operations and pay its people.

But wait, there's more. Most venture capital firms raise multiple funds. The average firm raises a new fund every three or four years, but some firms raise funds more frequently while others have multiple different fund vehicles, such as an early stage fund, a growth stage fund, and a hot-off-the-press cryptocurrency fund. In these cases, the fees stack up across funds. If a firm raises a fund every three years, it has a new management fee that adds to its old management fee. The simple way to think of this is that the management fee is roughly 2% of total committed capital across all funds. So, if Fund 1 is a $100 million fund and Fund 2 is a $200 million fund, the management fee ends up being approximately $6 million annually ($2 million for Fund 1 and $4 million for Fund 2).

Although venture capital firms tend to grow head count (partners and staff) as they raise new funds, this isn't always the case and the head count rarely grows in direct proportion to the increased management fees. As a result, the senior partners of the venture capital firm (or the ones with a managing director title) see their base compensation rise with each additional fund. The dynamics vary widely from firm to firm, but you can assume that as the capital under management increases, so do the fees and, as a result, the salaries of some of the managing directors.

The venture capital firm gets this management fee completely independently of its investing success. Over the long term, the only consequence of investment success on the fee is the ability of the firm to raise additional funds. If the firm does not generate meaningful positive returns, over time it will have difficulty raising additional funds. However, this isn't an overnight phenomenon, as the fee arrangements for each fund are guaranteed for 10 years. We've been known to say that "it takes a decade to kill a venture capital firm," and the extended fee dynamic is a key part of this.

Carried Interest

Even though the management fees can be substantial, in a success case the real money that a VC makes, known as the *carried interest*, or *carry*, should dwarf the management fee. Carry is the profit that VCs get after returning money to their investors (the LPs). If we use our $100 million fund example, VCs receive their carry after they've returned $100 million to their LPs. Most VCs get 20% of the profits after returning capital (a 20% carry), although some long-standing or extremely successful funds take up to 30% of the profits.

Let's play out our example. Again, start with the $100 million fund. Assume that it's a successful fund and returns three times the capital, or $300 million. In this case, the first $100 million goes back to the LPs, and the remaining profit, or $200 million, is split 80% to the LPs and 20% to the GPs. The venture capital firm gets $40 million in carried interest and the LPs get the remaining $160 million. And yes, in this case everyone is very happy.

Remember that this firm received about $15 million of management fees over a decade for this fund. However, there's an interesting nuance here. If the fund is a $100 million fund and $15 million goes to management fees, doesn't that leave only $85 million to invest? In some cases it does, but VCs are allowed to recycle their management fee and subsequently reinvest it up to the total of $100 million. This assumes returns early enough in the life of the fund to recycle and in some cases careful cash flow management, but all firms should be motivated to put the entire $100 million to work. In this case, the $15 million management fee can actually be viewed as a prepayment on carry since it is essentially getting reinvested from proceeds from the fund. All LPs should favor recycling, as their goal is generally cash-on-cash return. Getting more money to work, namely the full $100 million instead of only $85 million, enhances the total return.

Note that we have been talking about the venture capital firm as a whole, not any individual managing director or other investment professional in the firm. An individual VC could quadruple the amount of money invested in his particular companies, but still receive no carry in a fund due to poor investment decisions made by the other partners. In addition, most firms do not have equal allocation of carry between partners, with the senior partners tending to get disproportionately more than the younger partners. Over time this can be a major source of friction within the firm if there is either inequitable behavior from the senior partners or other firms offer the young star performers better economic incentives and pick them off. This gets especially difficult when a fund, or a series of funds, is performing poorly yet the positive returns are coming from one or two partners.

An additional fund nuance is that the LPs expect the VCs to invest alongside the LPs in each fund, on the theory that the VCs' interests will be further aligned with the LPs' desire for a return on investment. Historically, there has been a 99%/1% split between the LPs and the GPs, where the VC partners put in their own money alongside the LPs for 1% of the fund (e.g., in our $100 million fund example, the LPs would put in $99 million and the GPs would put in $1 million). The *GP commitment* historically was 1% but has floated up over time and is occasionally as high as 5%.

While carry sounds like a wonderful thing, there is one risky situation around it called the *clawback*. Again, assume our $100 million fund. Let's also assume the VCs have called only half of the fund ($50 million). If the $50 million invested so far returns $80 million, the fund is in a profit situation where $50 million has been returned and there is $30 million in profit that the VCs have the right to take their carry on. The VCs happily pocket their $6 million, assuming the carry is 20%. But what happens if the VCs call and invest the rest of the fund and it's a bust, returning a total of only $100 million? At the end of the fund, the VCs would have invested $100 million, but returned only $100 million, and as a result should get no carry.

So, what happens to the $6 million they took in the middle of the fund life? The $6 million is clawed back from the VCs and given back to the LPs. While logical in theory, it's harder in practice. Assume the venture capital fund has four equal partners who have each received a $1.5 million carry check. These were happy days, followed by some not-so-happy days when the fund performed poorly. Along the way, two of the VCs left the firm to go to other firms, and the remaining two partners no longer talk to them. In fact, one of the remaining partners got divorced and gave half of his money to his ex-spouse. And one of the other VCs declared bankruptcy after overextending himself financially. Oh, and all four of them have paid taxes on their carry.

The LPs don't care. They want the $6 million that is owed to them, and many fund agreements state that each partner is liable for the full amount, regardless of what they actually received in profit distributions. So, it's possible that a subset of the partnership has to pay back the LPs and fight with the current and former partners for the rest. It's not pretty and we wish this were only a hypothetical situation, but it's not.

Reimbursement for Expenses

There is one other small income stream that VCs receive: reimbursements from the companies they invest in for expenses associated with board meetings. VCs will charge all reasonable expenses associated with board meetings to the company they are visiting. This usually isn't a big deal unless your VC always flies on his private plane and stays at the presidential suite at your local Four Seasons hotel. In the case where you feel your VC is spending excessively and charging everything back to the company, you should feel comfortable confronting the VC. If you aren't, enlist one of your more frugal board members to help.

How Time Impacts Fund Activity

Venture capital fund agreements have two concepts that govern the ability to invest over time. The first concept is the commitment period (also called "investment period"), which is usually five years. This is the length of time that a VC has for identifying and investing in new companies in the fund. Once the commitment period is over, the fund can no longer invest in new companies, but it can invest additional money in existing portfolio companies. This is one of the main reasons that venture capital firms typically raise a new fund every three to five years. Once they've committed to all the companies they are going to invest in from a fund, they need to raise a new fund to stay active as investors in new companies.

It's sad but true that some VCs who are past their commitment period and have not raised a new fund still meet with entrepreneurs trying to raise money. In these cases, the entrepreneur has no idea that there is no chance the VCs will invest, but the VCs get to pretend they are still actively investing and try to maintain some semblance of deal flow even though they can't invest any longer in new companies from their current fund. We first saw this in 2006 and 2007 as firms that raised their previous fund in 2000 or 2001 struggled to raise a new fund. Over time the media picked up on this dynamic and started referring to these firms as the "walking dead." These were zombie-like VCs who were still acting like VCs, earning management fees from their old funds and actively managing their old portfolios, but not making new investments.

The good zombies are open about their status; the not-so-good ones keep taking meetings with new companies even though they can't make new investments. It's usually easy to spot zombie VCs. Just ask them when they made their last new investment. If it's more than a year ago, it's likely they are a zombie. You can also ask simple questions like "How many new investments will you make out of your current fund?" or "When do you expect to be raising a new fund?" If you feel like the VCs are giving you ambiguous answers, they are probably a zombie.

The other concept is called the *investment term*, or the length of time that the fund can remain active. New investments can be made only during the commitment/investment period, but follow-on investments can be made during the investment term. A typical venture capital fund has a 10-year investment term with two one-year options to extend, although some have three one-year extensions or one two-year extension. Twelve years may sound like plenty of time, but when an early stage fund makes a new seed investment in its fifth year and the time frame for exit for an average investment can stretch out over a decade, 12 years is often a constraint. As a result, many early stage funds go on for longer than 12 years—occasionally up to as many as 20 years (or even more).

Once you get past 12 years, the LPs have to affirmatively vote every year to have the GP continue to operate the fund. In cases in which a firm has continued to raise additional funds, the LPs are generally supportive of this continued fund extension activity. There is often a negotiation over the management fee being charged to continue to manage the fund, with it ranging from a lower percentage of remaining invested capital (say, 1%) all the way to waiving the fee entirely. This isn't an issue for a firm that has raised additional funds and has the management fee from those funds to cover its operations, but it is a major issue for zombie firms that find their annual operating fees materially declining. Time is not the friend of a zombie firm, as partners begin to leave for greener pastures, spend less and less time helping the companies they've invested in, or simply start pushing the companies to sell and generate liquidity.

In some cases, entire portfolios are sold to new firms via what is called a *secondary sale* in which someone else takes over managing the portfolio through the liquidation of the companies. In these cases, the people the entrepreneurs are dealing with, including their board members, can change completely. These secondary buyers often have a very different agenda from the original investor, usually much more focused on driving the company to a speedy exit, even at a lower value than the other LPs.

The Entrepreneur's Perspective

One important thing to understand about your prospective investor's fund is how old the fund is. The closer the fund is to its end of life, the more problematic things can become for you in terms of investor pressure for liquidity (in which your interests and the investor's might not be aligned), or an investor requirement to distribute shares in your company to LPs, which could be horrible for you if the firm has a large number of LPs who then become direct shareholders.

Reserves

Reserves are the amount of investment capital that is allocated to each company that a VC invests in. This is a very important concept that most entrepreneurs don't pay proper attention to. Imagine that a VC invests $1 million in the first round of your company. When they make the investment, the VC will reserve a theoretical future amount of the fund to invest in follow-on rounds. Most VCs won't tell you this figure, but it's usually a well-defined amount within the venture capital firm.

Typically, but not always, the earlier the stage a company is at, the more reserves the VC will allocate. In the case of a late stage investment immediately prior to an initial public offering (IPO), a VC might not have any reserves allocated to a company, whereas a first-round investment might have reserves of $10 million or more associated with it.

While most VCs will ask the entrepreneur about future funding needs prior to making an investment, many VCs ignore this number and come up with their own view of the future financing dynamics and the corresponding reserves amount. In our experience, entrepreneurs are often optimistic about how much capital they need, estimating on the low side. VCs will rely on their own experience when figuring out reserves and will often be conservative and estimate high early in the life of the investment, reducing this number over time as a company ages.

Let's look at how reserve analysis can impact a company. Assume a venture capital firm has a $100 million fund and invests a total of $50 million into 10 different companies. Assume also that the venture capital firm has an aggregate of $50 million in reserves divided among the 10 companies. While it doesn't matter if the firm is accurately reserved on a company-by-company basis at the beginning, the total amount reserved and how it is deployed over time are critical. If the VC has underreserved and $70 million ends up being needed in aggregate to support the ongoing funding of the 10 companies, the venture capital firm won't have the ability to continue to fund all of the companies in which it invests. This usually results in VCs picking favorites and not supporting some of the companies. Although this can manifest itself as VCs simply walking away from their investments or being direct that they have no additional money to invest, the behavior by the VC is usually more mysterious. The less upfront VC will often actively resist additional financings, try to limit the size, and subsequently the dilution of these financings, or push you to sell the company. In cases where a pay-to-play term is in effect, you'll often see more resistance to additional financings as the venture capital firm tries to protect its position in the company, even if it's not necessarily the right thing to do for the business.

Overreserving, or reserving $50 million when you ultimately need only $30 million, is also an issue, but it doesn't impact the entrepreneurs. Overreserving results in the VC underinvesting the fund, which is economically disadvantageous to the LPs and the VCs. The LPs want all of the fund capital to be invested because it increases the chance of returning more capital. The VCs also want to get all the money to work, especially when funds become profitable, as the greater the absolute return, the greater the carry.

Most venture capital fund agreements allow a firm to raise a new fund once they are around 70% committed and reserved. While this threshold varies by firms, it is usually reasonably high. As a result, there is a slight motivation to overreserve to reach this threshold that is countered by the negative economic dynamics of not fully investing the fund. Of course, independent of the threshold, the VC still needs to have good performance and the support of the existing investors to raise a new fund.

The Entrepreneur's Perspective

You should understand how much capital the firm reserves for follow-on investments per company, or for your company in particular. If you think your company is likely to need multiple rounds of financing, you want to make sure the VC has plenty of "dry powder" in reserve for your company so you don't end up in contentious situations down the road in which your investor has no more money left to invest and is then at odds with you or with future investors.

Cash Flow

VCs have to pay as much attention to cash flow as entrepreneurs do, although many don't until they run into trouble. Remember that the capital raised by a venture firm can be used for investments in companies, management fees, and expenses of the fund, which include paying accountants for an annual audit and tax filings and paying lawyers for any litigation issues. Also remember that LPs want their VCs to invest 100% of the fund in companies.

If a VC has a $100 million fund with a typical management fee, approximately $15 million will be spent on noninvesting activity during the life of the fund. This means to fully invest the $100 million, the fund will need to generate $15 million of returns that it can recycle for future investment over the life of the fund. More importantly, timing matters since the exits that generate this additional cash are unpredictable, and as a fund gets later in its life, it can start to move into a position where it doesn't actually have the cash to recycle.

In the most extreme case, the firm will underreserve and not manage cash flow effectively. As a result, it will find itself crunched at both ends. It won't have adequate reserves to continue to support its investments and, even if it did, it won't have the cash to pay its employees through management fees. This situation can occur even in firms that have raised follow-on funds, since the cash flow dynamics of recycling are fund specific.

Cross-Fund Investing

Many venture capital firms invest out of several linked fund entities. In other words, a venture firm might raise a $100 million fund with $90 million being in the "main" fund and $10 million being kept in a "side" fund. These side funds typically have different economic arrangements than the main fund. This could be for reasons as simple as tax treatment for foreign investors, or a reduction on fees and carry to strategic investors or entrepreneurs. When you do a deal with a VC, you'll often see multiple signature blocks from these different entities, such as VC Fund III (for the main fund) and VC Entrepreneurs/Side Fund III (for the side fund).

There are also cases, however, where firms will fund out of two completely separate funds, say VC Fund III and VC Fund IV. These are called *cross-fund investments*. Typically, you'll see this when the first fund (Fund III) is underreserved and doesn't have the capital to continue to invest in a company. In this case, the firm uses the second fund (Fund IV) to fill in the gap to help the venture capital firm, as a whole, protect its position and provide support for the company.

Cross-fund investing can lead to several problems between the venture capital firm and its LPs. Cross-fund investing is rarely done from the beginning of an investment, so the later rounds are done at a different price (not always higher) than the earlier rounds. Since the underlying funds almost always have different LP composition and each fund will end up with a different return profile on the exit, the LPs won't be treated economically equally across the investment. In the upside case where the valuation is steadily increasing, this won't matter, since everyone will be happy with the positive economic outcome. However, in the downside case, or an upside case where the round that the second fund invests in is a down round, this is a no-win situation for the VC. In this situation, one fund will be disadvantaged over the other and some LPs will end up in a worse situation than they would have been in if the cross-fund investment hadn't happened. And if our friendly VC thinks too hard, the economic conflict will start to melt his brain.

Some funds do cross-fund investing through a different fund vehicle that focuses on later stage investments into well-performing portfolio companies (often called "Select" or "Opportunity" funds). In this case, the second fund's mandate is to invest in the best of the best of the VC's early stage portfolio.

Different funds will have different incentives and motivations when it comes to your company. An early stage fund may be running out of cash and time and want a quicker exit than a VC's late stage Opportunity Fund. While the same person may represent both funds, the motivations behind each fund may differ.

Departing Partners

Most venture capital firms have a *key person clause* that defines what happens in the case in which a certain number of partners or a specific partner leaves the firm. In some cases, when a firm trips the key person clause, the LPs have the right to suspend the ability of the fund to make new investments or can even shut down the fund. In cases where a partner leaves the firm but doesn't trip the key person clause, there are often contentious issues over firm economics, especially if the firm has been poorly structured, doesn't have appropriate vesting, or has a significant amount of economics in the hands of the departing partner, leaving the other partners with insignificant motivation (at least in their minds) for continuing to actively manage the firm. While the entrepreneur can't impact this, it's important to be sensitive to any potential dynamics in the structure of the firm, especially if the departing partner is the one who sits on your board or has sponsored the investment in your company.

In our experience when a VC departs a firm and leaves the board of a portfolio company, it rarely works out well for the company. In most instances, the firm forgets about the company or puts a junior person on the board to replace the departing partner. As a result, the company loses some or all of the support it once had from the venture capital firm. While there are exceptions, view the new board member in a similar way you would a new investor, and work hard to build a constructive relationship from scratch.

Corporate Venture Capital

In the past few years we have seen the emergence of numerous corporate venture capital (CVC) groups. These are VCs who have a large corporation behind them and are usually easy to identify since they go by names like Google Ventures (now GV), Intel Ventures, Qualcomm Ventures, Salesforce Ventures, and Microsoft Ventures. Today, there are several hundred CVCs. As with traditional venture capital firms, they vary in size, shape, strategy, and incentives.

CVC, however, is not a new phenomenon, and has been around for decades. There was a huge increase in the number of CVCs in the late 1990s leading up to the peak of the Internet bubble with a correspondingly rapid evaporation of these firms after the Internet bubble burst. Over the past decade (2009 to 2019) they've begun to emerge again, with a huge increase in the number of firms recently.

Unlike a traditional VC that reports to its limited partners, CVCs may answer to executive management teams, other company departments, public shareholders, or even quarterly results. While some CVCs are indistinguishable from traditional VCs, many CVCs invest off their company's balance sheet and as a result don't have a separate fund structure. When the CVC is not a separate entity, but one that reports up to the CEO or other executive of a large public company, many different pressures come into play in addition to a direct focus on financial returns. Availability of capital to invest shifts with changes in the company's stock price and balance sheet, which can have significant impact on a startup's ability to raise additional capital from the CVC.

Teams at CVCs often experience employee turnover, especially if the CVC has star performers who are incented with equity in their public company rather than economics associated with their investment returns. These CVC partners are easy pickings for many traditional venture capital firms who are looking to grow since compensation, autonomy, and authority are often significantly higher in venture capital firms than in CVCs.

Motivations around valuation, structure, and control in subsequent financings or merger and acquisition (M&A) activity is often different between VCs and CVCs. In addition to how a typical VC is motivated, CVCs often, but not always, have other interests in becoming an investor in your company, including insight into your technology, partnering around a distribution channel or go-to market approach, or locking out a competitor. As a result, CVCs are often willing to pay a higher valuation than a VC, given these additional motivations. At the same time, CVCs often look for more control, such as a *first right of refusal* on an acquisition, which is something you should never, ever give. While the higher valuation might feel good, realize that if it's too high it may negatively impact your next round of financing.

Some CVCs will take a board seat, but many do not require anything beyond an observer role on the board. Lawyers at the CVC parent company are often concerned about potential conflicts of interest that might arise along with issues around intellectual property linkage.

Compensation varies widely between CVCs and often differs significantly from the management fee/carried interest approach of VC firms. Many CVCs are simply employees of their parent company with salary, bonus, and stock option pay packages. In some cases, the CVC has a bonus plan tied to company performance, but it's rarely equivalent to the economics of a traditional venture capital firm.

Finally, be mindful of potential conflicts, especially around technology and customers. One motivation for CVCs is to have insight and/or access to innovative companies and their products, as they often are investing in companies they think can become large, long-term users of the CVC's parent company technology and products. While this can be powerful, consider what happens to the relationship when you decide to use a competitor's technology over that of your CVC or when one day you wake up and realize that the CVC's parent company has come out with a product that competes with yours.

Strategic Investors

While many CVCs also consider themselves strategic investors, there are many strategic investors that aren't formalized as venture capital investors. These are companies that aren't in the business of making venture capital investments, but for a particular reason want to invest in your company. For instance, suppose you produce a consumer device in China and your contract manufacturer tells you they want to invest in you. While flattering, there are both positive and negative aspects to this.

As with CVCs, strategic investors are incentivized differently, have different masters to answer to, and varying motivations for their investment beyond simply overall return.

Suppose you are the founder of a company called SwearJar.com, which makes a wearable device that detects foul language uttered by the wearer. Upon such detection, it automatically debits your bank account and sends 80% of the proceeds to charity and 20% to SwearJar (yup, we've seen this, and are a particularly good customer target). Your product is manufactured at ChinaFab, Inc., and they've offered to invest $1 million in your company. They have indicated that they don't care about the valuation and are happy to participate at whatever your last round was priced. You need the money, would love to be more tightly connected to your manufacturing partner, and are inclined to take it.

Before you get too excited, consider what will happen to their service to you as your manufacturer. If they have experience making strategic investments, explore whether things have gotten better or worse for the partner after they made this strategic investment. In addition to seeing some strategic investors start taking companies like SwearJar for granted after they've invested, people in the strategic partner organization begin to justify their performance as a result of having an investment in the company. Now, you want to hold them accountable by spinning up a competitive process for another contract manufacturer. At best, this is awkward and often can negatively impact your business relationship. But your strategic investor will still be an equity owner of your company, making things even more complicated.

Often the strategic investor will be helpful, and the relationship will be a constructive one. Confident strategic investors often ask for additional equity consideration for helping your company succeed. While this ignores the fact that your VC investors aren't getting additional equity compensation for helping you, strategic investors often feel entitled to something. In these cases, we encourage you to use a *performance warrant*.

As with a regular warrant, a performance warrant is an option for the strategic partner to buy stock of your company (usually common stock) at a set price (often the most recent financing round price.) Unlike a regular warrant, the performance warrant is issued only when the strategic investor accomplishes predetermined performance goals. In this situation, if they perform, you reward them with the performance warrant. If they don't perform, they still received their equity in exchange for their investment, but they didn't get the extra equity they were looking for.

Fiduciary Duties

VCs owe *fiduciary duties*, concurrently and on the same importance level, to their management company, to the GP, to the LP, and to each board that they serve on. If your investor is a CVC or strategic investor, they will owe a fiduciary duty back to their parent organization. Normally, this all works out fine if one is dealing with a credible and legitimate firm, but even in the best of cases, these duties can conflict with one another and both VCs and CVCs can find themselves in a fiduciary sandwich.

For the entrepreneur, it's important to remember that no matter how much you love your investors, they answer to other people and have a complex set of formal, legal responsibilities. Some investors understand this well, are transparent, and have a clearly defined set of internal guidelines when they find themselves in the midst of fiduciary conflicts. Others don't and subsequently act in confusing, complicated, and occasionally difficult ways.

More annoyingly to those of us who understand this dynamic, some investors pontificate about their fiduciary duties while not really knowing what to do. If you ever feel uncomfortable with the dynamic, remember that your legal counsel represents your company and can help you cut through the noise to understand what is really going on.

Implications for the Entrepreneur

VCs' motivations and financial incentives will show up in many ways that may affect their judgment or impact them emotionally, especially in times of difficult or pivotal decisions for a company. Don't be blind to the issues that affect your investment partners. More importantly, don't be afraid to discuss these issues with them; an uncomfortable yet open discussion today could save you the trauma of a surprise and company-impacting interaction later.

CHAPTER

Negotiation Tactics

Regardless of how much you know about term sheets, you still need to be able to negotiate a good deal. We've found that most people, including many lawyers, are weak negotiators. Fortunately for our current and future portfolio company executives, they can read about everything we know online and in this book, so in addition to being better negotiators, they now know all of our moves and can negotiate more effectively against us.

There are plenty of treatises on negotiation; however, this chapter walks through some negotiation tactics that have worked well for us over the years. Although this book is primarily about financings, we'll talk about a range of negotiation tactics that you can use in your life, and we illustrate some of the different types of characters you'll meet along the way.

What Really Matters?

There are only three things that matter when negotiating a financing: achieving a good and fair result, not killing your personal relationship getting there, and understanding the deal that you are striking.

It has been said that a good deal means neither party is happy. This might be true in litigation or acquisitions, but if neither party is happy following the closing of a venture financing, then you have a real problem. Remember, the financing is only the beginning of the relationship and a small part at that. Building the company together while having a productive and good relationship is what matters. A great starting point is for both sides to think they have achieved a fair result and feel lucky to be in business with one another. If you behave poorly during the financing, it's likely that tensions will be strained for some time if the deal actually gets closed. And if your lawyer behaved badly during the negotiation, it's likely that lawyer will be looking for a new client after the VC joins the board.

The Entrepreneur's Perspective

Your lawyer shouldn't be a jerk in manner or unreasonable in positions, but this doesn't mean you should advise your lawyer to behave in a milquetoast manner during negotiations, especially if she is well versed in venture financings. You need to manage this carefully as the entrepreneur, even if your eyes glaze over at legalese. This is your company and your deal, not your lawyer's.

If you are negotiating a preferred round of financing, the only two things that matter, as we've previously stated, are economics and control. We'd suggest that any significant time you are spending negotiating beyond these two core concepts is a waste of time. You can learn a lot about the person you are negotiating with by what that individual focuses on.

Start the negotiation by picking a few things that really matter. Focus on the valuation, stock option pool, liquidation preferences, board, and voting controls and just be done with it. The cliché "you never make money on terms" is especially true outside of a few key ones that we've dwelled on already. The good karma that will attach to you from the other side (assuming they aren't jerks) will be well worth it.

Preparing for the Negotiation

The single biggest mistake people make during negotiation is a lack of preparation. It's incredible to us that people will walk blindly into a negotiation when so much is on the line. And this isn't just about venture deals, as we've seen this behavior in all types of negotiations.

Many people don't prepare because they feel they don't know what they should prepare for. We'll give you some ideas but realize that you probably know how to negotiate better than you think. You already negotiate many times a day during your interactions in life, but most people just do it and don't think too hard about it. If you have a spouse, child, auto mechanic, domesticated animal, or any friends, chances are that you have dozens of negotiations every day.

When you are going to negotiate your financing (or anything, really), have a plan. Have key things that you want, understand which terms you are willing to concede, and know when you are willing to walk away. If you try to determine this during the negotiation, your emotions are likely to get the best of you and you'll make mistakes. Always have a plan.

Next, spend some time beforehand getting to know with whom you are dealing. Some people (like us) are so easy to find that you can google us and discover everything we think. If we openly state that we think people who negotiate registration rights in a term sheets are idiots (which we do), then why on earth would you or your lawyer make a big deal about it? This being said, more than 50% of the term sheet markups we get from lawyers have requested changes to the registration rights section, which makes us instantly look down on the lawyer and know that the entrepreneur isn't the one running the show. And yes, we keep a list of these law firms and don't introduce our portfolio companies to them.

If you get to know the other side ahead of time, you might also be able to play to their strengths, weaknesses, biases, curiosities, and insecurities. The saying "knowledge is power" applies here. And remember, just because you can gain the upper hand in using this type of knowledge doesn't mean that you have to, but it will serve as a security blanket and might be necessary if things go poorly. As you are getting to know the other side, try to imagine what they are doing to prepare for the negotiation. What motivates them? What are their incentives? What are their insecurities? Have multiple theories about the other side's point of view and be prepared to act on any of them in real time.

One thing to remember: everyone has an advantage over everyone else in all negotiations. There might be a David to the Goliath, but even David knew a few things that the big man didn't. Life is the same way. Figure out your superpower and your adversary's kryptonite.

If you are a first-time, 20-something entrepreneur negotiating a term sheet against a 40-something, well-weathered, and experienced

VC, what possible advantage could you have on the VC? The VC clearly understands the terms better. The VC also has a ton of market knowledge. And let's assume that this VC is the only credible funding source that you have. Sounds pretty bleak, right?

Well, yes, but don't despair. There is one immediate advantage that you probably have: time. If we generalize, it's easy to come up with a scenario of the VC having a family and lots of portfolio companies and investors to deal with. You, on the other hand, have one singular focus: your company and this negotiation. You can afford to make the process a longer one than the VC might want. In fact, most experienced VCs really hate this part of the process and will bend on terms in order to aid efficiency, although some won't and will nitpick every point (we'll deal with those folks later). Perhaps you'll want to set up your negotiation call at the end of the day, right before the VC's dinner. Or maybe you'll sweetly ask your VC to explain a host of terms that you "don't understand" and further put burdens on the VC's time. Think this doesn't happen? After we gave this advice to some of the Techstars teams in 2009, one of the teams waited until two hours before Jason left on vacation to negotiate the term sheet we gave them. Jason didn't even recognize this as their strategy and figured it was bad luck with timing. As a result, he faced time pressure that was artificially manufactured by a 20-something first-time entrepreneur. Nice job, Alex. (Alex White, former CEO of Next Big Sound, which was acquired by Pandora.)

There are advantages all over the place. Is your VC a huge Stanford fan? Strike up a conversation and find out if she has courtside seats to the game. Is your VC into a charity that you care about? Use this information to connect with her so she becomes more sympathetic to you. While simple things like this are endless, what matters is that you have a plan, know the other side, and use what natural advantages you have. In a perfect world, you won't have to use any of these tools, but if you need them and don't bring them to the actual negotiation, it's your loss.

The Entrepreneur's Perspective

Your biggest advantage is to have a solid Plan B—lots of interest and competition for your deal. VCs will fold like a house of cards on all peripheral terms if you have another comparable quality VC waiting in the wings to work with you.

A Brief Introduction to Game Theory

Everyone has a natural negotiating style. These styles have analogues that can work either well or poorly in trying to achieve a negotiated result. It's important to understand how certain styles work well together, how some conflict, and how some have inherent advantages over one another.

Before we delve into that, let's spend a little time on basic game theory. *Game theory* is a mathematical theory that deals with strategies for maximizing gains and minimizing losses within prescribed constraints, such as the rules of a card game. Game theory is widely applied in the solution of various decision-making problems, such as those of military strategy and business policy.

Game theory states that there are rules underlying situations that affect how these situations will be played out. These rules are independent of the humans involved and will predict and change how humans interact within the constructs of the situation. Knowing what these invisible rules are is of major importance when entering into any type of negotiation.

The most famous of all games is the prisoner's dilemma, which you've seen many times if you've ever watched a cop show on television. The simple form, as described in the Stanford Encyclopedia of Philosophy (http://plato.stanford.edu/entries/prisoner-dilemma/#Sym2t2PDOrdPay), is as follows:

> Tanya and Cinque have been arrested for robbing the Hibernia Savings Bank and placed in separate isolation cells. Both care much more about their personal freedom than about the welfare of their accomplice. A clever prosecutor makes the following offer to each. "You may choose to confess or remain silent. If you confess and your accomplice remains silent, I will drop all charges against you and use your testimony to ensure that your accomplice does serious time. Likewise, if your accomplice confesses while you remain silent, they will go free while you do the time. If you both confess, I get two convictions, but I'll see to it that you both get early parole. If you both remain silent, I'll have to settle for token sentences on firearms possession charges. If you wish to confess, you must leave a note with the jailer before my return tomorrow morning."

The classic prisoner's dilemma can be summarized as shown in the following table.

Classic Prisoner's Dilemma

	Prisoner B Stays Silent	Prisoner B Betrays
Prisoner A Stays Silent	Each serves 8 months	Prisoner A: 12 years Prisoner B: goes free
Prisoner A Betrays	Prisoner A: goes free Prisoner B: 12 years	Each serves 5 years

What's fascinating about this is that there is a fundamental rule in this game that demonstrates why two people might not cooperate with one another, even if it is clearly in their best interests to do so.

If the two prisoners cooperate, the outcome is best, in the aggregate, for both of them. They each get eight months of jail time and walk away. But the game forces different behavior. Regardless of what the co-conspirator chooses (silence versus betrayal), each player always receives a lighter sentence by betraying the other. In other words, no matter what the other guy does, you are always better off by ratting him out.

The other rule to this game is that it is a *single-play game*. In other words, the participants play the game once and their fate is cast. Other games are *multiplay games*. For instance, there is a lot of interesting game theory about battlegrounds. If you are in one trench fighting and we are in another, game theory would suggest that we would not fight at night, on weekends, on holidays, and during meals. Why not? It would seem logical that if we know you are sleeping, it's the absolute best time to attack.

Well, it's not, unless we can completely take you out with one strike. Otherwise, you'll most likely start attacking *us* during dinner, on holidays, or while we are watching *Westworld*. And then not only are we still fighting, but now we've both lost our free time. This tit-for-tat strategy is what keeps multiplay games at equilibrium. If you don't mess with us during our lunch break, we won't mess with you during yours. And everyone is better off. But if you do mess with us, we'll continue to mess with you until you are nice to us again.

When you are considering which game you are playing, consider not only whether there are forces at work that influence the decisions being made, like the prisoner's dilemma, but also how many times a decision will be made. Is this a one-shot deal, or will this game repeat itself, lending increased importance to precedent and reputation?

Negotiating in the Game of Financings

A venture financing is one of the easiest games there is. First, you really can have a win-win outcome where everyone is better off. Second, you don't negotiate in a vacuum like your hypothetical fellow criminal co-conspirator. Finally, this is not a single instance game. Reputation and the fear of tit-for-tat retaliation are real considerations.

Since the VC and entrepreneur will need to spend a lot of time together post investment, the continued relationship makes it important to look at the financing as just one negotiation in a very long, multiplay game. Doing anything that would give the other party an incentive to retaliate in the future is not a wise, or rational, move.

Furthermore, for the VC, this financing is but one of many that the VC will hope to complete. Therefore, the VC should be thinking about reputational factors that extend well beyond this particular interaction. With the maturation of the venture capital industry, it's easy to get near-perfect information on most VCs. Having a negative reputation can be fatal to a VC in the long run.

Not all VCs recognize that each negotiation isn't a single-round, winner-take-all game. The more experience VCs have, the better their perspective is, but this lack of a longer-term view is not limited to junior VCs. While we'll often see this behavior more from the lawyers representing the VCs or the entrepreneurs, we also see it from the business principals. When we run across people like this, at a minimum we lose a lot of respect for them and occasionally decide not to do business with them. When you encounter VCs who either have a reputation for or are acting as though every negotiation is a single-round, winner-take-all game, you should be very cautious.

The Entrepreneur's Perspective

One successful negotiating tactic is to ask VCs up front, before the term sheet shows up, what the three most important terms are in a financing for them. You should know and be prepared to articulate your top three wants as well. This conversation can set the stage for how you think about negotiating down the road, and it can be helpful to you when you are in the heat of a negotiation. If the VCs are pounding hard on a point that is not one of their stated top three, it's much easier to call them out on that fact and note that they are getting most or all of their main points.

Game theory is also useful because of the other types of negotiations you'll have. For instance, if you decide to sell your company, your acquisition discussions can be similar to the prisoner's dilemma as presented earlier. Customer negotiations usually take on the feeling of a single-round game, despite any thoughts to the contrary about partnerships. And litigation almost always takes the form of a single-round game, even when the parties will have ongoing relationships beyond the resolution of the litigation.

Remember, you can't change the game you are in, but you can judge people who play poorly within it. Using a game theory lens to view the other side is very powerful.

Negotiating Other Games

Not all other games are win-win. There are many different types of games, but three others make interesting counterpoints to the financing game. Let's start with the polar opposite of the win-win game. The "winner-takes-all" game is the classic high-stakes litigation situation. You are being sued by a patent troll or have some type of "bet-the-company" situation. In this game, reputations matter little and results are all that count. You should prepare yourself that this will be an emotionally taxing, time-draining, long, and drawn-out battle. Don't assume that the other side will have the same moral code that you do, since lying generally isn't illegal except under oath. Even then, we've all seen people lie in a courtroom deposition. These cases usually involve your lawyer becoming that attack dog that you watch in the movies. This is not fun. But, don't bring a knife to a gunfight.

The second type of case is where you have a very adversarial situation, but reputations still matter. The classic version of this is when a founder involuntarily departs a company. There will be plenty of hard feelings and lots of emotions. However, as ugly as it can get at times, this isn't a winner-take-all scenario. Both the company and the departed founder have mutual interests in that they both want their reputations to survive intact and it's highly likely that the departed founder will keep some equity in the company. Therefore, the game constrains behavior to some extent. While everyone does not have to be friends post-financing, civility will hopefully win out. In these cases, we normally see lawyers engage with respect, but firmness, on their positions. Many times, when the lawyers can't come to a solution the departed founder and company directly work out their differences.

The third of these games is the acquisition game. As we'll go into detail in Chapter 16, you will likely end up selling your company one day. In this case, you have both a winner-take-all and a win-win scenario. In one respect the pie is being divided. The negotiations of the terms of the acquisition will spell out who gets what, right down to the last penny. You also get one shot at the deal. Unlike a venture financing that is just one event in the company's life, the deal terms on the acquisition are the final outcome. This is the winner-take-all part of the game. That being said, the vast majority of management teams work for their acquirer after the deal is done. In this case, the former company executives are working next door to the people who just bought their company. In this part of the game, everyone is looking for the win-win. Acquisitions are tricky because of this and require periods of teeth gnashing as well as calm attitudes. As we'll discuss later, the various parties in an acquisition can play some or all of these roles.

Negotiating Styles and Approaches

Every person has a natural negotiating style that is often the part of your personality that you adopt when you are dealing with conflict. Age, race, gender, upbringing, mood on a particular day, the relationship you have with your significant other and kids, the relationship that you had with your parents and siblings, and many other things play into how you negotiate. Remember that you started negotiating around age two and all of these experiences have made you who you are.

There is new research showing that gender can have a large effect on negotiations. Harvard Business School reports that women don't negotiate job offers like men do for fear that negotiating will lead to reputational damage when they start their new job, damage that men experience less often. There is also data that seem to suggest that men are more comfortable with other men who negotiate agressively versus women who do and thus there can be social costs for women.[1]

We hope that by being as transparent as we can in this book about the terms, the issues, and the ways to negotiate, we can break down

---

[1] https://hbr.org/2014/06/why-women-dont-negotiate-their-job-offers.

some of these barriers. We'd encourage everyone to look inward before engaging with the other side, regardless of who you are, and make sure your biases aren't negatively impacting your approach to a negotiation.

As with anything, few people are great at several things. In the world of negotiations this means that most people don't have truly different modes for negotiation, but that doesn't mean you can't practice having a range of different behaviors that depend on the situation you are in.

Most good negotiators know where they are comfortable, but also know how to play upon and against other people's natural styles. Following are some, but not all, of the personalities you'll meet and how you might want to best work with them.

The Bully (aka UAW Negotiator)

The bully negotiates by yelling and screaming, forcing issues, and threatening the other party. Most folks who are bullies aren't that smart and don't really understand the issues; rather, they try to win by force. There are two ways to deal with bullies: punch them in the nose or mellow out so much that you sap their strength. If you can outbully the bully, go for it. But if you are wrong, then you've ignited a volcano. Unlike on the children's playground, getting hit by a bully during a negotiation generally doesn't hurt; so unless this is your natural negotiating style, our advice is to chill out as your adversary gets hotter.

The Nice Guy (aka Used-Car Salesman)

Whenever you interact with this pleasant person, you feel like they are trying to sell you something. Often, you aren't sure that you want what they are selling. When you say no, the nice guy will either be openly disappointed or will keep on smiling at you just like the audience at a Tony Robbins event. In their world, life is great as long as you acquiesce to their terms (or buy this clean 2010 Chrysler Sebring). As the negotiation unfolds, the nice guy is increasingly hard to pin down on anything. While the car salesman always needs to go talk to their manager, the nice-guy negotiator regularly responds with "Let me consider that and get back to you." While the nice guy doesn't yell at you like the bully, it's often frustrating that you can never get a real answer or seemingly make progress. Our advice is to be clear and direct and don't get worn down, as the nice guys will happily talk to you all day. If all else fails, don't be afraid to toss a little bully into the mix on your side to move things forward.

The Technocrat (aka Pocket Protector Person)

This is the technical nerd. Although they won't yell at you like the bully and you don't wonder if there is a real human being behind the facade like you do with the nice guy, you will feel like you are in endless detail hell. The technocrat has a billion issues and has a hard time deciding what's really important, since to them everything is important for some reason. Our advice is to grin and bear it and perhaps play Fortnite while you are listening to the other side drag on. Technocrats tend to cause you to lose your focus during the negotiation. Make sure you don't by remembering what you care about and conceding the other points. But make sure you cover all the points together, as the technocrat will often negotiate every point from scratch, not taking into consideration the give-and-take of each side during the negotiation. Sometimes this role is simply that: a role. Many folks have endless energy for this stuff and will use this tactic to simply tire you out during the negotiation.

The Wimp (aka George McFly)

The wimp may sound like the perfect dance partner here, but they have their own issues. Our bet is that you can take their wallet pretty easily during the negotiation, but if you get too good a deal it will come back to haunt you. And then you get to live with them on your board of directors once you close your financing. With the wimp, you end up negotiating both sides of the deal. Sometimes this is harder than having a real adversary.

The Curmudgeon (aka Archie Bunker)

With the curmudgeon, everything you negotiate sucks. No matter what you arrive at it is horrible, and every step along the way during the negotiation will feel like a dentist tugging on a tight molar at the back of your mouth. Unlike the bully, the curmudgeon won't yell; and unlike the nice guy, they will never be happy. While it'll seem like they don't care too much about the details, they are just never happy with any position you are taking. The curmudgeon is also not a wimp. They've been around the block before and will remind you of that every chance they get. In a lot of ways, the curmudgeon is like a cranky grandparent. If you are patient, upbeat, and tolerant, you'll eventually get what you want, but you'll never really please them because everyone pisses them off.

Smooth, Steady, and Smart (aka Diane Lockhart from The Good Fight)

The last of the personalities is the person who really has it all. This person can shape-shift into one or more of the personas we mentioned but has a natural calm brilliance that makes for a strong adversary. This person spends the right amount of time preparing, knows all the points at play, and has done their homework on you. They are so confident of their work product that they ooze a legitimate calm like they are walking in a park. If you've done your homework, the two of you probably will engender immediate respect and sometimes even trust. This is the best of all worlds and truly leads to a win-win outcome. On the other hand, if you haven't done your homework, they will steamroll you while making you feel good about it. Later on, that evening, you will feel differently as you commiserate with yourself over your favorite adult beverage.

The Entrepreneur's Perspective

You learn a lot about a person in a negotiation. This is one argument for doing as much of the detailed negotiation before signing a term sheet that includes a no-shop clause in it. If you find that your potential investor is a jerk to you in negotiating your deal, you may want to think twice about this person becoming a board member and part of your inner circle.

Always Be Transparent

What about the normal person? You know, the transparent, nice, smart, levelheaded human you hope to meet on the other side of the table? Though they exist, everyone has some inherent styles that will find their way into the negotiation, especially if pressed or negotiations aren't going well. Make sure you know which styles you have so you won't surprise yourself with a sudden outburst. You'll also see a lot of these behaviors come out in real time in board meetings when things aren't going quite as well as hoped.

If you are capable of having multiple negotiating personalities, which should you favor? We'd argue that in a negotiation that has reputational and relationship value, try to be the most transparent and easygoing that you can be, let the other person inside your thinking and get to know you for who you really are. If you are playing a single-round game, like an acquisition negotiation with a party you don't ever expect to do business with again, do like Al Davis said "Just win, baby." As in sports, don't ever forget that a good tactic is to change your game plan suddenly to keep the other side on their toes.

Collaborative Negotiation versus Walk-Away Threats

Of all the questions we get regarding negotiations, the most common is when to walk away from a deal. Most people's blood pressure ticks up a few points with the thought of walking away, especially after you've invested a lot of time and energy (especially emotional energy) in a negotiation. In considering whether to walk away from a negotiation, preparation is key here—know what your walk-away point is before starting the negotiation so it's a rational and deliberate decision rather than an emotional one made in the heat of the moment.

When determining your walk-away position, consider your *best alternative to negotiated agreement,* also known in business school circles as *BATNA.* Specifically, what is your backup plan if you aren't successful reaching an agreement? The answer to this varies wildly depending on the circumstances. In a financing, if you are lucky, your backup plan may be accepting your second-favorite term sheet from another VC. It could mean bootstrapping your company and forgoing a financing. Understanding BATNA is important in any negotiation, such as an acquisition (walk away as a stand-alone company), litigation (settle versus go to court), and customer contract (walk away rather than get stuck in a bad deal).

Before you begin any negotiation, make sure you know where your overall limits are, as well as your limits on each key point.

If you've thought this through in advance, you'll know when someone is trying to move you past one of these boundaries. It's also usually obvious when someone tries to pretend they are at a boundary when they really aren't. Few people are able to feign true conviction.

At some point in some negotiation, you'll find yourself up against the wall or being pushed into a zone that is beyond where you are willing to go. In this situation, tell the other party there is no deal, and walk away. As you walk away, be very clear what your walk-away point is so the other party will be able to reconsider their position. If you are sincere in walking away and the other party is interested enough in a deal, they'll be back at the table at some point and will offer you something that you can stomach. If they don't reengage, the deal wasn't meant to be.

Depending on the type of person you are negotiating with, the VC either will be sensitive to your boundaries or will force you outside these boundaries, where BATNA will come into effect. If this is happening regularly during your financing negotiation, think hard about whether this is a VC who you want to be working with, since this VC is playing a single-round game in a relationship that will have many rounds and lots of ups and downs along the way.

Finally, don't ever make a threat during a negotiation that you aren't willing to back up. If you bluff and aren't willing to back up your position, your bargaining position is forever lost in this negotiation. The 17th time we hear "and that's our final offer," we know that there's another, better offer coming if we just hold out for number 18.

Building Leverage and Getting to Yes

Besides understanding the issues and knowing how to deal with the other party, there are certain things that you can do to increase your negotiation leverage. In a venture capital financing, the best way to gain leverage is to have competing term sheets from different VCs.

If you happen to be lucky enough to have several interested parties, this will be the single biggest advantage in getting good deal terms. However, it's a tricky balance dealing with multiple parties at the same time. You have to worry about issues of transparency and timing and, if you play them incorrectly, you might find yourself in a situation where no one wants to work with you.

The Entrepreneur's Perspective

As I mentioned earlier, having a solid Plan B (and a Plan C, and a Plan D…) is one of your most effective weapons during the negotiation process. It's helpful to be transparent about that fact to all prospective investors. While it's a good practice to withhold some information, such as the names of the other potential investors with whom you're speaking since there is no reason to enable two VCs to talk about your deal behind your back, telling investors that you have legitimate interest from other firms will serve you very well in terms of speeding the process along and improving your end result.

For starters, pay attention to timing. You'll want to try to drive each VC to deliver a term sheet to you in the same time frame. This pacing can be challenging since there will be uncomfortable days when you'll end up slow-rolling one party while you seek to speed up the process of another firm. This is hard to do, but if you can get VCs to approve a financing around the same time, you're in a much stronger position than if you have one term sheet in hand that you are trying to use to generate additional term sheets.

Once you've received a term sheet from a VC, you can use this to motivate action from other VCs, but you have to walk a fine line between oversharing and being too secretive. We prefer when entrepreneurs are up front, tell us that they have other interests, and let us know where in the process they are. We never ask to see other term sheets, and we'd recommend that you don't ever show your actual term sheets to other investors. More importantly, you should never disclose to whom you are talking, since one of the first emails most interested VCs will send after hearing about other VCs who are interested in a deal is something like "Hey, I hear you are interested in investing in X—want to share notes?" As a result, you no longer have a competitive situation between the two VCs, since they will now talk about your deal and in many cases talk about teaming up. The exception, of course, is when you want them to team up and join together in a syndicate.

At the end of the day, if you have multiple term sheets, most of the deal terms will collapse into the same range (usually entrepreneur favorable), and the only real things you'll be negotiating are valuation and board control. You can signal quite effectively what your other options might be. Whatever you do, don't sign a term sheet and then pull a Brett Favre and change your mind the next day. The startup ecosystem is small, and word travels fast. Reputation is important.

Another strategy that can help you build leverage is to anchor on certain terms. Anchoring means to pick a few points, state clearly what you want, and then stick to your guns. If you anchor on positions that are reasonable while still having a little flexibility to give in the negotiation, you will get close to what you want as long as you are willing to trade away other points that aren't as important to you.

Although you should try to pace the negotiation, you should do this only after the VC has offered up the first term sheet. Never provide a term sheet to a VC, especially with a price attached, since if you do you've just capped what you can expect to get in the deal. You are always in a stronger position to react to what the VC offers, especially when you have multiple options. However, once you've gotten a term sheet, you should work hard to control the pace of the ensuing negotiation.

As with any type of negotiation, it helps to feed the ego of your partner. Figure out what the other side wants to hear and try to please them. People tend to reciprocate niceties. For example, if you are dealing with technocrats, engage them in depth on some of the deal points, even if the points don't matter to you, in order to make them happy and help them feel like you are playing their game.

When you are leading the negotiation, we highly recommend that you have a strategy about the order in which you will address the points. Your options are to address them either in the order that they are laid out in the term sheet or in some other random order of your choosing. In general, once you are a skilled negotiator, going in order is more effective, because you won't reveal which points matter most to you. Often experienced negotiators will try to get agreement on a point-by-point basis in order to prevent the other party from looking holistically at the process and determining whether a fair deal is being achieved. This strategy only really works if you have a lot of experience, and it can really backfire on you if the other party is more experienced and takes control of the discussion. Instead of being on the giving end of a divide-and-conquer strategy, you'll be on the receiving end of death by a thousand cuts.

Unless you are a very experienced negotiator, we suggest an order where you start with some important points for which you think you can get to yes quickly. This way, both parties will feel good because they are making progress toward a deal. Maybe it's liquidation preferences or the stock option plan allocation. Then dive into the minutiae. Valuation is the last subject to address, as you'll get closure on other terms but have a couple of different rounds of discussion on valuation. It is completely normal for some terms to drag out longer than others.

All of these tactics and theories assume that you are negotiating with a rational actor, one who does what is in their own best interests. An irrational actor (think toddler or hostage taker) will not offer an expected response to given inputs. While we don't see truly irrational actors much in our ecosystem, it does happen. In these cases, our strong opinion is to become an expert at empathy, much like you would negotiate with your three-year-old to go to sleep.

Things Not to Do

Since this is primarily a book about financings, we thought we would provide you with a few tips about things that you'll never want to do when negotiating a financing for your company. As we stated earlier, don't present your term sheet to a VC. In addition to signaling inexperience, you get no benefit by playing your hand first since you have no idea what the VC will offer you. The result is either you'll end up starting in a worse place than the VC would have offered, or you'll put silly terms out there that will make you look like a rookie. If your potential funding partner tells you to propose the terms, be wary, as it's an indication that you are talking to someone who isn't a professional VC, is trying to take advantage of you, or is professionally lazy.

The Entrepreneur's Perspective

You should never make an offer first. There's no reason to, unless you have another concrete one on the table. Why run the risk of aiming too low?

Next, make sure you know when to talk and when to listen. If you remember nothing else about this section, remember this: you can't lose a deal point if you don't open your mouth. Listening gives you further information about the other party, including what advantages you have over them (e.g., do they have a Little League baseball game to coach in an hour?) and which negotiation styles they are most comfortable with. Miller's Law asserts that humans can at most hold in mind seven pieces of information (plus or minus two) at any given time. Listen and calm down when you feel overwhelmed. The last thing that you want to do in this moment is speak.

The Entrepreneur's Perspective

As the old cliché goes, there's a reason you have two ears and one mouth. When you are negotiating, try to listen more than you talk, especially at the beginning of the negotiation.

If the other party is controlling the negotiation, don't address deal points in order of the legal paper. This is true of all negotiations, not just financings. If you allow a person to address each point and try to get to closure before moving on to the next point, you will lose sight of the deal as a whole. While you might feel that the resolution on each point is reasonable, when you reflect on the entire deal you may be unhappy. If a party forces you into this mode, don't concede points. Listen and let the other party know that you'll consider their position after you hear all of their comments to the document. Many lawyers are trained to do exactly this—to kill you softly point by point.

A lot of people rely on the same arguments over and over again when negotiating. People who negotiate regularly, including many VCs and lawyers, try to convince the other side to acquiesce by stating, "That's the way it is because it's market." We love hearing the market argument because then we know that our negotiating partner is a weak negotiator. Saying that "it's market" is like your parents telling you, "Because I said so," and you responding, "But everyone's doing it." These are elementary negotiating tactics that should have ended around the time you left for college.

In the world of financings, you'll hear this all the time. Rather than getting frustrated, recognize that it's not a compelling argument since the concept of market terms isn't the sole justification for a negotiation position. Instead, probe on why the market condition applies to you. In many cases, the other party won't be able to justify it and, if they can't make the argument, you'll immediately have the higher ground.

The Entrepreneur's Perspective

Understanding market terms and whether they apply to your situation is important. You can quickly get context on this by talking to other entrepreneurs in similar positions. Remember, you do only a few of these deals in your lifetime, and your VC does them for a living. Understand what market really is, and you'll be able to respond to an assertion that something is market with fact rather than with emotion.

Finally, never assume that the other side has the same ethical code as you, regardless of the game you are playing. This isn't a comment against VCs or lawyers; rather, it's a comment about life and pertains to every type of negotiation you'll find yourself involved in. Everyone has a different acceptable ethical code, and it can change depending on the context of the negotiations. For instance, if you were to lie about the current state of a key customer to a prospective VC and it was discovered before the deal closed, you'd most likely find your deal blown up. Or perhaps the deal would close, but you'd be fired afterward, and it's likely that some of your peers would hear about it. As a result, both parties (VC and entrepreneur) have solid motivation to behave in an ethical way during a financing. Note that this is directly in contrast to most behavior, at least between lawyers, in a litigation context where lies and half-truths are an acceptable part of that game. Regardless of the specific negotiation context, make sure you know the ethical code of the party you are negotiating against.

Great Lawyers versus Bad Lawyers versus No Lawyers

Regardless of how much you think you know or how much you've read, hire a great lawyer. In many cases you will be the least experienced person around the negotiating table. VCs negotiate for a living, and a great lawyer on your side will help balance things out. When choosing a lawyer, make sure he or she not only understands the deal mechanics, but also has a style that you like working with and that you are comfortable sitting alongside. This last point can't be overstated—your lawyer is a reflection of you, and if you choose a lawyer who is inexperienced, is ineffective, or behaves inconsistently, it will reflect poorly on you and decrease your negotiating credibility.

So, choose a great lawyer, but make sure you know what "great" means. Ask multiple entrepreneurs who you respect to give you referrals. Check around your local entrepreneurial community for the lawyers with the best reputations. Don't limit your exploration to billing rates, responsiveness, and intellect, but also check style and how contentious negotiations were resolved. Furthermore, it's completely acceptable to ask your VC before and after the funding what the VC's thoughts are about your lawyer.

The Entrepreneur's Perspective

Choosing a great lawyer doesn't mean hiring an expensive lawyer from a firm that your VC knows or recommends. Often for startups, going to a top-tier law firm means dealing with a second-tier or very junior lawyer, not well supervised, with high billing rates. You can hire a smaller firm with lower rates and partner attention just as well; but be sure to do your homework on them, make sure they're experienced in dealing with venture financings, and get references—even from VCs they've negotiated against in the past.

Can You Make a Bad Deal Better?

Let's say you screw up and negotiate a bad deal. You had only one term sheet, the VC was a combination bully and technocrat, and you are now stuck with deal terms that you don't love. Should you spend all of your time being depressed? Nope. There are plenty of ways to fix things after the fact that most entrepreneurs never think about.

First of all, until an exit occurs—either an acquisition or an IPO—many of the terms don't matter much. But, if you plan to raise another round led by a new investor, you have a potential ally at the time to clean up the things you negotiated poorly in the first investment. The new VC will be motivated to make sure you and your team are happy (assuming the company is performing well). If you talk to your new potential financing partner about issues that are troubling you, in many cases the new VC will concentrate on trying to bring this back into balance in the new financing. Normally the new VC will care more about the entrepreneur's happiness than that of the previous investors.

In the case where a new VC doesn't lead the next round, you still have the option of sitting down with your current VCs after you've had some run time together (again, assuming success). We've been involved in numerous cases in which these were very constructive conversations that resulted in entrepreneur-friendly modifications to a deal.

Finally, you can wait until the exit and deal with your issues then. Most acquisition negotiations include a heavy focus on retention dynamics for the management team going forward, and there are often cases of reallocating some of the proceeds from the investors to management. The style of your VCs will impact how this plays out. If they are playing a single-round game with the negotiation and they don't really care what happens after the deal closes, they will be inflexible. However, if they want to be in a position to invest with you again in the future, they'll take a top-down view of the situation and be willing to work through modifications to the deal terms to reallocate some consideration to management and employees, especially in a retention situation for the acquirer.

Recognize, however, that this dynamic cuts both ways. Many acquirers take the approach that they want to recut the economics in favor of the entrepreneur. Remember that as an entrepreneur you signed up for the deal you currently have with your investors and you have a corresponding responsibility to them. If you end up playing a single-round game with your investors where you team up with the acquirer, you run the risk of blowing up both the acquisition and your relationship with your investors. So, be thoughtful, fair, and open with your investors around the incentives and dynamics.

The Entrepreneur's Perspective

Having an open and collaborative approach with your VC in the context of an acquisition may sound a bit like a game of chicken—but it can work. Being clear with your investors about what is important to you and your team early in the negotiation can help set a tone where you and your investors are working together to reach the right deal structure, especially when the acquirer is trying to drive a wedge between you and those investors. A negotiation in a state of plenty is much easier than a negotiation in a state of scarcity.

In our experience, openness in these situations by both the entrepreneur and the VC generally results in much better outcomes. It's hard enough to engage in a negotiation, let alone one in which there are multiple parties in a negotiation at cross-purposes (e.g., acquirer, entrepreneur, and VC). We always encourage entrepreneurs and their VC backers to keep focused on doing what is right for all shareholders in the context of whatever is being offered, and as a result to continue to constructively work through any issues, especially if one party is uncomfortable with where they previously ended up.

CHAPTER

14

Raising Money the Right Way

Wwhile most people ask themselves "What should I do?" when seeking investment from a venture capitalist, there are also some things that a person should not do. Doing any of the following at best makes you look like a rookie (which is okay, we were all rookies once, but you don't want to look like one) and at worst kills any chance that you have of getting funded by the VC you just contacted. While this chapter isn't about the best way to fundraise (there are many other books covering that), we encourage you to avoid doing the following when you are raising money from VCs.

Don't Be a Machine

While you may have created the greatest technology in the world to invest in, fundraising is ultimately about the people involved. If a VC doesn't like you personally, they probably won't invest in you despite your brilliant idea.

We tell entrepreneurs that we want to fall in love with them in the style of "first date" energy. We want to feel time slip away and regret when we must go on to our next commitment. After the entrepreneur leaves, we want to keep thinking about him or her and wondering when we'll get to meet again.

Some others call this the "beer test." If we don't want to have a beer with you now, imagine how bad it will be when things inevitably get tough later on down the road. Being from Boulder, we also accept chai lattes or vitamin water. We realize that some people might not be comfortable grabbing a beer or may not want to go out for lattes. The activity is not the key point, but we do want to get to know you better than just being on the receiving end of a pitch, since we will be partners for a long time if we end up investing in your company.

So, don't be a machine. Be human. Be yourself, let us get to know you, and let us become inspired by you. Since the average relationship between a VC and an entrepreneur lasts longer than the average U.S. marriage, this is a long-term commitment. It's not just about the idea and the PowerPoint slides.

Don't Ask for a Nondisclosure Agreement

Don't ask a VC for a *nondisclosure agreement* (NDA). Although most VCs will respect how unique your idea, innovation, or company is to you, it's likely that they've seen similar things due to the sheer number of business plans that they get. If they sign an NDA regarding any company, they'd likely run afoul of it if they ended up funding a company that you consider a competitor. An NDA will also prevent a VC from talking to other VCs about your company, even ones who might be good co-investors for your financing.

However, don't be too scared about approaching a reputable VC with your idea without an NDA. The venture capital industry is small and wouldn't last long if VCs spoke out of turn, sharing people's knowledge with one another. And don't think that VCs will steal your idea and start a company, since reputational constraints as well as limits on a VC's time will eliminate this risk in most cases. Though you might occasionally run into a bad actor, do your homework and you'll be fine.

Don't Email Carpet-Bomb VCs

You might not know VCs personally, but the way to get to know them is not by buying a mailing list and sending personalized spam. And it's not good to hire an investment adviser who will do the same. VCs know when they are getting a personal pitch versus spam. We don't know any VCs who react well to spam.

Spamming looks lazy. If you didn't take the time to really think about who would be a good funding partner, what does that say about how you run the rest of the business? If you want to contact us, just email us, but make it personal to us. Be thoughtful, specific, and strategic with your first communication attempt. You don't get a second chance to make a first impression, and you are being judged for much more than your idea and your bio.

No Often Means No

While most VCs appreciate persistence, when they say they aren't interested, they usually mean it. We aren't asking you to try again. We might be saying no because your idea isn't personally interesting to us, doesn't fit our current investment themes, or is something that we think is a bad idea. Or maybe we are just too busy. Don't take a no personally. Every VC (including us) has said no plenty of times to entrepreneurs who ended up building extremely successful companies. We don't always get it right, but if we say no, please respect that.

Don't Ask for a Referral If You Get a No

VCs get a lot of inbound email pitching new investments. At our firm, we try to look at all of them and always attempt to respond within a day or two. We say no to most of them, but we are happy to be on the receiving end of them. And to be clear, dear reader, send us an email any time—just give us context that you've read this book. And yes, our email addresses are on our website.

When we say no, we try to do it quickly and clearly. We try to give an explanation, although we don't attempt to argue or debate our reason. We are sure that many of the things we say no to will get funded, and some will become incredibly successful companies. That's okay with us; even if we say no, we are still rooting for you.

However, if we say no, please don't respond and ask us to refer you to someone. You don't really want us to do this, even if you don't realize it. By referring you to someone else, at some level we are implicitly endorsing you. At the same time, we just told you that we are not interested in exploring funding your deal. These two constructs are in conflict with each other. The person we refer you to will immediately ask us if we are interested in funding your deal. We are now in the weird position of implicitly endorsing you on one side, while rejecting you on the other. This isn't necessarily comfortable for us, and it's useless to you, as the likelihood of the person we have just referred you to taking you seriously is very low. In fact, you'd probably have a better shot at it if we weren't in the mix in the first place!

The Entrepreneur's Perspective

There's one exception to it not being suitable to ask for a referral. If you have a relationship with the VC (e.g., it's not a cold request), ask why the answer is no. If the response to that question is something about the VC firm rather than your company (e.g., "You're too small for us," or "One of our portfolio companies is too competitive"), then you may ask for a referral to another firm that might be a better fit. However, be respectful here—if the VC doesn't want to make a referral, don't push it.

Somewhere in a parallel universe, someone trained a bunch of us, either at a Networking 101 event or at a Zig Ziglar seminar to always "ask for something" when you hear a "no" (e.g., keep the conversation going, get a referral, or try a different question). However, there are cases where this tactic isn't useful to you. This is one of them.

Don't Be a Solo Founder

Outside of some isolated examples, most entrepreneurs will have little chance of raising money unless they have a team. A team can be a team of two, but the solo entrepreneur raising money can be a red flag.

First, no single person can do everything. We've never met anyone who can do absolutely everything from product vision to executing on a plan, engineering development, marketing, sales, operations, and all the other random stuff starting a company entails. There are just too many mission-critical tasks in getting a successful company launched. You will be much happier if you have a partner to back you up.

Second, it's not a good sign if you can't get others excited about your plan. It's hard enough to get VCs to write checks to fund your company; if you can't find other team members with the same passion and beliefs that you have, this is a warning sign to anyone who might want to fund your company.

Finally, if you don't have a team, what is the VC investing in? Often, the team executing the idea is more important than the idea itself. Most VCs will tell you that they've made money on grade B ideas with grade A teams, but that many A ideas were left in the dustbin due to a substandard team.

The one exception would be a repeat entrepreneur. If the venture fund has had a good experience with an entrepreneur before and believes they can build a solid team post-funding, then the person has a chance to get funded as a solo entrepreneur.

Don't Overemphasize Patents

If you are a software company, don't rely on patents. We see a lot of entrepreneurs hinge their entire company's worth on their patent strategy. If you are in biotech, hardware, or medical devices, this might be entirely appropriate. When you are working on software, realize that patents are, at best, defensive weapons for others coming after you. Creating a successful software business is about having a great idea and executing well, not about having patents.

In fact, we wish that all business method and software patents didn't exist (and make a lot of noise about this on our personal blogs at www.jasonmendelson.com and www.feld.com), so if you think you are winning us over for investment in a software company by relying on your patent portfolio, you aren't. Instead, you just proved to us that you didn't do any homework on us as investors and don't really understand the value of patents versus a rock-star management team and amazing software engineers going after a big idea.

Don't Be Silent If You Witness Bad Behavior

Over the past year, we've been disgusted as we've heard reports about VCs sexually harassing female entrepreneurs. In several cases, we knew the entrepreneurs and VCs, and did our best to support the entrepreneurs in these situations. We have no tolerance for sexual harassment or, for that matter, any harassing behavior of any sort. In addition to supporting those who have been harassed, we've advocated for the removal of bad actors from our ecosystem.

That being said, we aren't naive about harassment continuing to occur. If you see something or are the subject of bad behavior, speak up. We all need to help each other root out the bad actors in this industry.

CHAPTER

Issues at Different Financing Stages

Not all financings are created equal. This is especially true when you factor in the different stages that your company will evolve through over its lifetime. While this book is primarily focused on early stage financings, and many of the issues apply to all stages, there are some key differences. This chapter touches on a few of the important ones.

Seed Deals

While seed deals have the lowest legal costs and usually involve the least contentious negotiations, they often allow for the most potential mistakes. Given how important precedent is in future financings, if you reach a bad outcome on a specific term, you might be stuck with it for the life of your company. Ironically, we've seen more cases where the entrepreneur got what at the time seemed to be too good of a deal, but ultimately ended up being bad for them.

What's wrong with getting great terms? If you can't back them up with performance when you raise your next round, you may find yourself in a difficult position with your original investor. For example, assume you are successful getting a valuation that is significantly ahead of where your business currently is. If your next round isn't at a higher valuation, you are going to be diluting your original shareholders, who are the investors who took a big risk to fund you during the seed stage. Either you'll have to make them whole or, worse, they'll vote to block the new financing. This is especially true in cases with unsophisticated seed investors who were expecting that, no matter what, the next round price would be higher.

The number and type of investors you get involved in your early rounds may also have a long-term impact on this. Assume that you are raising a $1 million seed financing and that you've been successful creating interest in your company. You have several offers—one from a venture capitalist (VC) willing to invest $750,000 alongside an AngelList syndicate that has committed the remaining $250,000. The second is from five different venture capital firms, including two very large ones, each of whom has committed to invest 20% of the round. Which is likely better for you in the long term?

In our experience, the first deal is the better one. In this situation, you have a clear lead investor who will be committed to your company and work hard for you. You also have some additional angels, ideally including some well-networked and high-profile ones who can help you. In the second scenario, which is often called a party round, you don't have a clear lead investor. Instead, each of the VCs has, in their mind, bought an option on your next financing. In the worst case, no one really pays much attention to you until you have spent most of the $1 million, at which point they evaluate whether or not you've made progress as they consider investing in the next round. Think of this as a complicated version of doubles tennis where the shot from your opponent goes right down the middle of the court while you and your partner each shout out "Yours!"

Early Stage

As with seed deals, precedent is important in early stage deals. In our experience, the terms you get in your first VC-led round will carry over to all future financings. One item that can haunt you forever is the liquidation preference. While it may not seem like a big deal to agree to a participating preferred feature, given that most early stage rounds aren't large dollar amounts, if you plan to raise larger rounds one day, these participation features can drastically reduce return characteristics for the common stockholders.

Another term to pay extra attention to at the early stage is the protective provisions. You will want to try to combine the protective provisions so that all preferred stockholders, regardless of series, vote together on them. If by your second round of financing you have two separate votes, one by each class, for the protective provisions, you are most likely stuck with a structure that will give each series of stock a separate vote and thus separate blocking rights. This can be a real pain to manage when you have multiple lead investors in multiple rounds who each have their own motivations to deal with.

This dynamic is influenced by the number of different rounds you expect to raise. If you are likely to raise only two or three rounds, the synchronization between rounds is less important. But if you expect you will raise more than three rounds, getting as many of the terms aligned across all classes of preferred shareholders will make your life a lot simpler, and better, since you won't have endless multiparty negotiations around every action that impacts your preferred stockholders. Recognize, however, that many entrepreneurs are overly optimistic about how many funding rounds they will need.

Mid and Late Stages

In your later rounds, board composition and voting control starts to come into play in a significant way. The voting control issues in the early stage deals are amplified as you wrestle with how to keep control of your board when each lead investor per round wants a board seat. Either you can increase your board size to seven, nine, or more people (which usually effectively kills a well-functioning board) or, more likely, the board will be dominated by investors. If your investors are well behaved, this might not be a problem, but you'll still be serving a lot of food at board meetings.

There isn't necessarily a good answer here. Unless you have massive negotiating power in a super-hot company, you are likely to give a board seat to each lead investor in each round. If you raise subsequent rounds, unless you've worked hard to manage this early, your board will likely expand and in many cases the founders will lose control of the board.

The Entrepreneur's Perspective

There are ways to mitigate issues of board and voting control, such as placing a cap (early on) on the number or percentage of directors who can be VCs as opposed to independent directors, preemptively offering observer rights to any director who is dethroned, or establishing an executive committee of the board that can meet whenever and wherever you'd like without everyone else around the table.

Valuation also starts to be a confounding factor in later stage rounds. While the natural instinct of any entrepreneur is to maximize valuation at each financing stage, the trade-off of a clean deal with a lower valuation against a complicated deal, with excessive control and economic characteristics (referred to as *structure*), can often make what seems like a great deal for the entrepreneur at the time become a nightmare in the future.

Much like issues that we've seen in seed deals, there have been some deals that have been too good and have forced the VCs to hold out for a huge exit price. The net effect was that by raising money at such a high valuation, the entrepreneurs forfeited the ability to sell the company at a price they would have been happy with, because of the inherent valuation-creation desires of the VCs who paid such a high price. We've seen deal terms that specifically either forbid sales below a certain value or provide for a guaranteed multiple on a VC's investment that juices up the latest round investors' return at the expense of the earlier investors, founders, and employees. The fascination with *unicorns* in the past few years has exacerbated this, as sophisticated investors demand more structure, resulting in significant outcome misalignment between early and late stage investors.

As we mentioned earlier in the book, when you get a term sheet from an early stage VC, it is almost always the case that they have full approval of their firm to move forward with the investment. This is not necessarily the case with later stage investors. They often have at least one more approval step, which often happens after the entire deal has been negotiated. We've seen multiple situations where this final approval didn't happen, and the deal died at the very end of the process.

In this case, you sign the term sheet; shut down discussions with all of the other investors you are talking with, since you have signed a term sheet with a no-shop clause; and start down the process of diligence with your prospective investor. Along the way, they inform you that they'll need approval from their investment committee and for some reason it doesn't happen. At this point you are stuck. You terminated your other investment options and now don't have a valid term sheet anymore.

Sometimes the investor will attempt to renegotiate the price or other terms knowing that they have all the leverage. We personally find this deplorable, and it was one of the motivations for us to raise our Foundry Select fund. We were tired of later stage firms playing games like this and wanted to be able to support our companies in their later stages.

There is one more factor to consider for mid and later stage deals. Remember that the fundraising paradigm shifts from the seed and early stage importance of "hope" versus the later stage importance of "results." In the early days, you can raise money with a strong team and a great idea where hope is, indeed, a strategy. In the later stages, the spreadsheets and results are what drive your potential success or failure in raising a round.

16

Letters of Intent: The Other Term Sheet

There is another type of term sheet that is important in an entrepreneur's life called the *letter of intent* (LOI). Hopefully, one day you'll receive one from a potential acquirer that will lead to fame, riches, and happiness. Or at least you'll get a new business card on heavier card stock.

Typically, the first formal step for a company that wants to acquire yours is to issue a letter of intent. This sometimes delightful and usually nonbinding document (except for things like a no-shop agreement) is also known as an indication of interest (IOI), memorandum of understanding (MOU), and even occasionally a term sheet.

As with our friend the term sheet, there are some LOI terms that matter a lot and others that don't. Once again there are plenty of mysterious words that experienced deal makers always know how and where to sprinkle so that they can later say, "But X implies Y," often resulting in much arguing between lawyers. We've had LOIs get done in a couple of hours and had others take several months to get signed. As with any negotiation, experience, knowledge, and understanding matter. The LOI negotiation is usually a first taste of the actual negotiating style you will experience from the other party.

This negotiation will be the beginning of the end of your independence as a company. Unlike a venture financing where everyone can win by expanding the pie over time, you are now negotiating for a fixed pie. Subsequently, the tone and stress around these negotiations is much tougher than that of a regular venture financing.

To keep things straightforward, we are going to focus on explaining the typical case of a two-party transaction between a buyer and a seller, which we'll refer to as an *acquisition*. As with many things in life, there are often more complex transactions, including three or more parties, but we'll save that for a different book.

By the time the buyer presents the seller with an LOI, there have been meetings, discussions, dinners, expensive bottles of wine, lots of conference calls, and an occasional argument. However, the buyer and the seller are still courting, so they tend to be on their best behavior. The LOI is typically the first real negotiation and the true icebreaker for the relationship.

In ancient times, when the first LOI was presented, someone crafted an introductory paragraph that started off with something like the following:

> Dear CEO of [Seller's Company]:
> We have greatly enjoyed our conversations to date and are honored to present you with this letter of intent to acquire [Seller's Company]. We look forward to entering into serious discussions over the next several months and reaching an agreement to acquire your company. We'd like to thank you for entertaining our proposal, which follows:

While every company has its own style, most LOIs begin with some variation of this boilerplate paragraph. Of course, you'll find later in the LOI a qualifier that states that almost everything in the LOI is nonbinding, including the appearance of civility as part of the negotiation.

Structure of a Deal

As with financings, there are only a couple of things that really matter—in this case, price and structure. Since the first question anyone involved in a deal typically asks is "What is the price?" we'll start there.

Unlike a venture financing in which price is usually pretty straightforward to understand, figuring out the price in an acquisition can be more difficult. There is usually some number floated in early discussions, but this isn't really the actual price. There are a lot of factors that can (and generally will) impact the final price of a deal by the time the negotiations are finished, and the deal is closed. It's usually a safe bet to assume that the easy-to-read number on the first page of the LOI is the best-case scenario purchase price. The following is an example of what you might see in a typical LOI:

> Purchase Price/Consideration: $100 million of cash will be paid at closing, $15 million of which will be subject to the terms of the escrow provisions described in paragraph 3 of this Letter of Intent. Working capital of at least $1 million shall be delivered at closing. Forty million dollars of cash will be subject to an earn-out and $10 million of cash will be part of a management retention pool. Buyer will not assume outstanding options to purchase Company Common Stock, and any options to purchase shares of Company Common Stock not exercised prior to the Closing will be terminated as of the Closing. Warrants to purchase shares of Company capital stock not exercised prior to the Closing will be terminated as of the Closing.

Before this paragraph was drafted, it's likely that a number around $150 million was discussed as the purchase price. The first thing that jumps out is the reference to a $15 million *escrow*. The escrow (also known as a *holdback*) is money that the buyer is going to hang on to for some period of time to satisfy any issues that come up post-financing that are not disclosed in the purchase agreement. In some LOIs, we've seen extensive details, whereas each provision of the escrow is spelled out, including the percentage of the holdback, length of time, and *carve-outs* to the indemnity agreement. In other cases, there is mention that "standard escrow and indemnity terms shall apply." We'll discuss specific escrow language later, but it's safe to say two things: first, there is no such thing as standard language; and second, whatever the escrow arrangement is, it will decrease the actual purchase price should any claim be brought under it. So, clearly, the amount and terms of the escrow and indemnity provisions are very important.

Next is the reference to $1 million of working capital. Working capital is the company's current assets minus current liabilities. While this might not seem like a big number, it's still $1 million. Many young companies end up with negative working capital at closing due to debt, deferred revenue, warranty reserves, inventory carry costs, and expenses and fees associated with the deal. As a result, these working capital adjustments directly decrease the purchase price if upon closing (or other predetermined date after the closing) the seller's working capital is less than an agreed-upon amount. Assume that unless the working capital threshold is a slam-dunk situation where the company has clearly complied with this requirement, the determination will be a battle that can have a real impact on the purchase price. In some cases, this can act in the seller's favor to increase the value of the deal if the seller has more working capital on the balance sheet than the buyer requires, but only if the clause around working capital is bidirectional (in this example it is not). Finally, it feels silly and gratuitous to us when a multibillion-dollar company asks for any working capital number above zero from a startup. We normally push back hard for working capital to be zero, with anything above that going to the shareholders of the company.

While *earn-outs* sound like a mechanism to increase price, in our experience, they are usually a tool that allows the acquirer to underpay at the time of closing and pay full value only if certain hurdles are met in the future. In our example, the acquirer suggested that it was willing to pay $150 million but is really paying only $100 million with $40 million of the deal subject to an earn-out. We'll cover earn-outs separately since there are a lot of permutations, especially if the seller is receiving stock instead of cash as its consideration.

In our example, the buyer has explicitly carved out $10 million for a management retention pool. This has become common since buyers want to make sure that management has a clear and direct future financial incentive. In this case, it's built into the purchase price (e.g., $150 million). We've found that buyers tend to be split between building it into the purchase price and putting it on top of the purchase price. In either case, it is effectively part of the deal consideration but is at risk since it'll typically be paid out over several years to the members of management who continue their role at the acquirer. If someone leaves, that portion of the management retention pool tends to vanish into the same place that socks lost in the dryer go. In addition, it's a move on the part of the buyer to allocate some percentage of the purchase price away from the formal ownership (or capitalization table) of the company as a way of driving an early negotiating wedge between management and the investors.

The Entrepreneur's Perspective

By the time someone is offering you a lot of money to buy your company, you should have good counsel or advisers or independent board members to help you navigate the terms. The structure of the deal is very important. You should be willing to stand behind your *representations and warranties* with a reasonable 12- to 18-month escrow at a minimum. If you can't, you'll look like you're hiding something. Management retention pool, working capital, and earn-outs are just negotiation points around the certainty and price of a deal.

Finally, there are a bunch of words in our example about the buyer not assuming stock options and warrants. We'll explain this in more detail later, but, like the working capital clause, it can impact the overall value of the deal based on what people are expecting to receive.

Asset Deal versus Stock Deal

While price is usually the first issue on every seller's mind, structure should be second. Lawyers talk about two types of deals, asset deals and stock deals, but there are numerous structural issues surrounding each type of deal. Let's begin by discussing the basics of an asset deal and a stock deal.

In general, all sellers want to do stock deals and all buyers want to do asset deals. Just to increase the confusion level, a stock deal can be done for cash and an asset deal can be done for stock. Don't confuse the type of deal with the actual consideration received.

Sarcastic VCs on the seller side will refer to an asset deal as a situation "when buying a company is not really buying a company." Buyers will request this structure, with the idea that they will buy only the particular assets that they want out of a company, leave certain liabilities (read: "warts") behind, and live happily ever after. If you engage lawyers and accountants in this discussion, they'll ramble on about something regarding taxes, accounting, and liabilities, but our experience is that most of the time the acquirer is just looking to buy the crown jewels, explicitly limit its liabilities, and craft a simpler deal for itself at the expense of the seller. We notice that asset deals are more popular in shaky economic times since acquirers are trying to avoid creditor issues and successor liability. One saw relatively few asset deals in the late 1990s, but in early 2000 asset deals became much more popular; yet by 2018 asset deals were once again rarely seen and only in distressed situations.

While asset deals can work for a seller, the fundamental problem for the seller is that the company hasn't actually been sold! The assets have left the company (and are now owned by the buyer), but there is still a shell corporation with contracts, liabilities, potential employees, and tax forms to file. Even if the company is relatively clean from a corporate hygiene perspective, it may take several years (depending on tax, capital structure, and jurisdictional concerns) to wind down the company. During this time, the officers and directors of the company are still on the hook, and the company presumably has few assets to use to operate the business since they were sold to the buyer.

In the case of a stock deal, the acquirer is buying the entire company. Once the acquisition is closed, the seller's company disappears into the corporate structure of the buyer and there is nothing left, except possibly some T-shirts that found their way into the hands of spouses and the company sign that used to be on the door just before the deal closed. There is nothing to wind down, and the company is history.

So is an asset deal bad or is it just a hassle? It depends. It can be really bad if the seller has multiple subsidiaries, numerous contracts, employees with severance commitments, disgruntled shareholders, or it is close to insolvency. In the case of insolvency, the officers and directors may be taking on fraudulent conveyance liability by consummating an asset deal. In other words, if the company is nearly dead and there are creditors who are owed money, the company can't sell its assets unless it is in the best interests of the creditors. If they do, the officers and directors can have personal liability.

If the company is in relatively good shape, has few shareholders, or is very small, it's merely a hassle. Of course, if any of these things are true, then the obvious rhetorical question is "Why doesn't the acquirer just buy the whole company via a stock deal?"

In our experience, we see stock deals the vast majority of the time. Often, the first draft of the LOI is an asset deal, but it's also frequently the first point raised by sophisticated sellers, who may succeed in getting a stock deal except in extreme circumstances, such as when the company is in dire straits. Many buyers go down a path to discuss all the protection they get from an asset deal. This is generally nonsense, since a stock deal can be configured to provide functionally equivalent protection for the buyer with a lot less hassle for the seller. In addition, asset deals are no longer the protection they used to be with regard to successor liability in a transaction. Courts are much more eager to find a company that purchases substantial assets of another company to be a so-called successor in interest with respect to liabilities of the seller.

The structure of the deal is also tied closely to the tax issues surrounding a deal. Once you start trying to optimize for structure and taxes, you end up defining the type of consideration (stock or cash) the seller can receive. It can get complicated very quickly, and pretty soon you can feel like you are climbing up a staircase in an Escher drawing. We'll dig into tax and consideration in a bit. Just realize that they are all linked together and usually ultimately impact price, which is, after all, what the seller usually cares most about.

The Entrepreneur's Perspective

If your company is in bad shape, you will probably have no choice but to do an asset sale and deal with the liabilities and associated winding down of the entity yourself. You should be prepared for this situation and constantly be calculating the expense and hassle of an asset deal to understand what kind of alternatives you're willing to consider.

Form of Consideration

Imagine the following conversation between an entrepreneur and a VC:

Entrepreneur: "I just received an offer for the company for $15 million from Company X."

VC: "Awesome. Who's Company X? I've never heard of them."

Entrepreneur: "It's a private company funded by Venture Firm Y."

VC: "Cool—$15 million. Is it a cash deal?"

Entrepreneur: "No, it's all stock."

VC: "Hmmm—are you getting preferred or common stock?"

Entrepreneur: "Common stock. Why?"

VC: "How much money has the company raised?"

Entrepreneur: "$110 million."

VC: "What's the liquidation preference? Is it a participating preferred? What's the valuation of the company?"

Entrepreneur: "Oh, I'm not worried about that stuff. The valuation is $300 million, and they say they are going public soon."

If you paid attention to the first part of this book, you know where this is going. The entrepreneur just received an offer for his company for 5% of the acquirer (actually 4.76% on a post-transaction basis) in an illiquid stock in a private company that is sitting under $110 million of liquidation preferences that are probably participating. If our friend calls his friendly neighborhood financial appraiser to do a valuation analysis, he'll find out the $15 million he thinks he is getting is actually valued at a lot less (probably good for tax purposes, not so good for buying beer, sports cars, and second houses).

The form of consideration matters a lot. Cash is king. Everything else is something less. And it can be a lot less. Did you hear the one where the acquirer offered "free software products" up to a certain amount in exchange for the company's assets? Gee, er, thanks.

Obviously, cash is easy to understand and to value. Stock can be more complicated. If it's stock in a private company, understanding the existing capital structure is a critical first step to understanding what you are getting. If it's stock in a public company, you'll want to ask a variety of questions, including whether the stock is freely tradable, registered, or subject to a lockup agreement. If it's freely tradable, will you be considered an insider after the transaction and have any selling restrictions? If it's not freely tradable, what kind of registration rights will you have? It can get messy quickly, especially if you try to optimize for tax (there's that tax thing again).

It's important to realize that the value of your company and the price you are getting paid may not be the same. Don't let yourself be locked into a price early in the negotiation until you understand the form of consideration you are receiving.

Assumption of Stock Options

After considering price and structure, it is time to discuss other major deal points generally found in an LOI. One item to note here: absence of these terms in your particular LOI may not be a good thing, as in our experience detailed LOIs are better than vague ones (but be careful not to overlawyer the LOI). During the LOI discussions most of the negotiating is between the business principals of the deal, not their lawyers, who will become the main deal drivers after the signing of the term sheet. Our experience is that leaving material business points to the lawyers will slow down the process, increase deal costs, and cause much unneeded pain and angst. Our suggestion would be to always have most of the key terms clearly spelled out in the LOI and agreed to by the business principals before the lawyers bring out their clubs, quivers, and broadswords.

The way stock options are handled (regardless of how you address the 409A issues, which we'll discuss later) can vary greatly in the LOI. Over the past five years, the practice of what happens to stock options in a merger has changed greatly. Let's start by discussing some history.

Prior to 2010 nearly all well-drafted option plans provided for automatic assumption of the plan. If a company was acquired, the plan would automatically be assigned to and assumed by the acquirer; otherwise, all the unvested options would immediately vest and the employees would cash out immediately. This approach provided an incentive to all parties to have the options assumed. Since nothing is free in this world, the costs to assume the plan (not the legal costs, but the total consideration owed to employees under the plan) was netted against the purchase price. Simply stated, if the assumed plan converted to options of the acquirer worth $10 million, then $10 million would come off the purchase price.

The theory behind this approach was to protect the employees of the company who are not at the bargaining table during an acquisition. In the last decade, acquirers began to substitute forms of consideration they viewed as comparable rather than simply assuming the option plan. Instead of options, they might create a cash-backed incentive plan for employees. Or, they'd choose restricted stock units (RSUs) instead of options because of arcane tax laws that force companies to expense options. Regardless, acquirers wanted flexibility to incentivize their new employees rather than being forced into a specific approach.

In some cases, acquirers did not assume the plan, sometimes due to tax laws, and all of the employees' options vested. While that sounds employee-friendly (it is), it can cause significant friction among employees. For instance, consider an employee who had been at the company for three years and was mostly vested. This employee saw relatively little vesting (one year) in contrast to the employee who joined the company a month earlier and now receives three years and 11 months of vesting.

As time passed, option plans evolved. Today, the general approach is that option plans allow for the assumption or substitution of similar plans, but explicitly state that the acquirer has no obligation to do much at all. The board of the acquired company can vote to accelerate the options if it chooses but there are no longer guaranteed protections for employees with stock options. Usually, this doesn't matter, as the parties (both the buyer and the seller, along with their respective boards of directors) do the right thing by employees. But this is not always the case.

We've seen situations where the buyer refused to assume the option plan or provide any meaningful substitute consideration. In this case, the employees with options get cheated and those who are vested get all the consideration. In these cases the acquirer only cares about technology, the management team, and long-serving employees.

We've seen other cases where the acquirer offered to either assume or substitute (again with RSUs) the option plan, but then asked key members of the team to "revest" their options. Revesting means that even if an employee has vested a certain amount of their options, they have to stick around for a predetermined period of time to vest them again. For example, presume that the acquirer wants everyone to revest all of their options over two years. It doesn't matter how many options you've already vested. You now start the vesting clock over. Typically, the acquirer will do something more complicated, like give everyone vesting credit for up to two years but then revest any remaining options over four years. This costs the acquirer nothing but has a meaningful impact on potential consideration for employees that is dependent on how long they stay.

Another issue impacting stock options is whether the acquisition is in cash, public company stock, or private company stock. We're going to ignore tax considerations for the moment (although you shouldn't ignore them in a real-world acquisition). If I'm an employee of a seller, I'm going to value cash differently from public stock (restricted or unrestricted), and public stock options differently from private stock (or options). If the buyer is public or is paying cash, the calculation is straightforward and can be easily explained to the employee. If the buyer is private, this becomes much more challenging and is something that management and the representatives of the seller who are structuring the transaction should think through carefully.

The *basis of stock options* (also known as the *strike price* or *barter element*)—and who pays for it—should also be considered, since it reduces the value of the stock options. Specifically, if the value of a share of stock in a transaction is $1 and the basis of the stock option is $0.40, the actual value of the stock option at the time of the transaction is $0.60. Many sellers forget to try to recapture the value of the barter element in the purchase price and allow the total purchase price to be the gross value of the stock options (vested and unvested) rather than getting incremental credit on the purchase price for the barter element.

Let's assume you have a $100 million cash transaction with $10 million going to option holders, 50% of whom are vested and 50% of whom are unvested. For the sake of simplicity, we'll say that the buyer is assuming unvested options but including them in the total purchase price (the $100 million), and that the total barter element of the vested stock is $1 million and the barter element of the unvested stock is $3 million. The vested stock has a value of $4 million ($5 million value minus $1 million barter element), and the unvested stock has a value of $2 million ($5 million value minus $3 million barter element). So the option holders are going to net only $6 million total. Often, the seller will catch the vested stock amount (e.g., vested options will account for $4 million of the $100 million), but the full $5 million will be allocated to the unvested options (instead of the actual value/cost to the buyer of $2 million). This is a material difference (e.g., the difference between $91 million going to the non–option holders versus $94 million).

Of course, all of this assumes that the stock options are in the money. If the purchase price of the transaction puts the options out of the money (e.g., the purchase price is below the liquidation preference), all of this is irrelevant since the options are worthless.

While this is dense stuff, it's important to address it during the LOI phase to make sure you are doing the right thing in the context of the deal for both your employees and your investors. It's easy to punt this until later in the process, only to find that you are now stuck in the middle of a multiparty negotiation between the buyer, your investors, and your employees with no obvious way to satisfy everyone. Also, by this time you've stopped negotiations with other suitors and have no real negotiation leverage.

The Entrepreneur's Perspective

In most cases, your employees got your company to where it is. Do not sell them short in an exit, whether or not there is an earn-out that compels you to keep them happy. Your reputation as an entrepreneur is at stake here, plus you want to do the right thing.

Representations, Warranties, and Indemnification

Every LOI will have some mention of *representations and warranties,* also called "reps and warranties" or just "reps" by those in the know. The reps and warranties are the facts and assurances about the business that one party gives the other. In other words, the buyer and seller make promises about themselves to the other. The reps that the sellers make are far longer, more intense, and more important. In most LOIs, the language in this paragraph is light in substance, but this section can have a profound effect on the deal and consume a ridiculous amount of legal time during the negotiation of the definitive agreement.

The first thing to note is who is making the representations. Does the LOI say the selling company will be making the reps, or does it say the selling company and its shareholders are on the hook? Or, more typically, is it silent as to who exactly is stepping up to the plate? Given that many shareholders (including VCs and individuals who hold stock in the selling company) are unwilling or unable to represent and warrant to the seller's situation, it's important to resolve in the LOI who is actually making the reps. Optimally you can get this solved before the lawyers start fighting over this, since most buyers will eventually accept that the company, instead of the underlying shareholders in the company, is making the reps.

All LOIs will have something regarding *indemnification* in the event that one of the reps or warranties is breached. Considering how important this provision is to the seller in an acquisition, it's often the case that the buyer will try to sneak past the following language in the LOI.

> The Company shall make standard representations and warranties and provide standard indemnification to Acquirer.

This is code for:

> We are really going to negotiate hard on the indemnification terms, but don't want to tell you at this stage so that you'll sign the LOI and become committed to doing the deal. Really. Trust us. Our deal guys and lawyers are nice and cuddly.

Depending on the situation of the seller (perhaps the seller is in a position where it wants to get the buyer committed more than vice versa and is willing to take its chances with the lawyers arguing), we'd suggest that you at least sketch out what the indemnification will look like. Again, once the lawyers get involved, arguments like "It's market and it's nonnegotiable" or "I get this on all of my deals" get bantered about endlessly.

The buyer usually makes some reps as well, but since it is paying for the seller, these are typically pretty lightweight unless the buyer is paying in private company stock. If you are a seller and you are getting private stock from the buyer, a completely logical starting point is to make all the reps and warranties reciprocal.

While many of these reps and warranties may look similar to the ones in your venture financing documents, VCs almost never sue companies they invest in. However, in acquisitions the reps and warranties often come into play after the merger is completed, so you should understand them and take them seriously. Given the existence of an escrow, there is a way for the buyer to recoup money from breaches of reps without the need for a lawsuit.

The Entrepreneur's Perspective

As long as most of your reps and warranties are qualified by a phrase like "to the extent currently known ...," you should have no problem signing them. Arguing against them is a big red flag to investors or buyers.

Escrow

The escrow is another hotly negotiated term that often is left ambiguous in the LOI. The escrow (also known as a holdback) is money that the buyer is going to hang on to for some period of time to satisfy any issue that comes up post-acquisition that is not disclosed in the purchase agreement.

In some LOIs we've seen extensive details with each provision of the escrow agreement spelled out, including the percentage of the holdbacks, length of time, and carve-outs to the indemnity agreement. In other cases, there is simply a declaration that "standard escrow and indemnity terms shall apply." Since there really isn't any such thing as a standard term, this is another buyer-centric trap for deferring what can become a brutal negotiation in the post-LOI stage. Whatever the escrow arrangement is, it will decrease the actual purchase price should any claim be brought under it. The terms of the agreement can be very important since they directly impact the value that the seller receives.

In our experience over hundreds of acquisitions, an escrow is typically set up as the sole remedy for breaches of the reps and warranties, with a few exceptions, known as carve-outs or *fundamental reps*. Normally between 10% and 20% of the aggregate purchase price is set aside for between 12 and 24 months to cure any breaches of the reps. While this is usually where the escrow terms end up (and are usually described as the *escrow caps*), it can take a herculean effort to get there. Buyers often try to overreach, especially if the parameters are not defined in the LOI, by asking for things such as uncapped indemnity if anything goes wrong, personal liability of company executives and major shareholders, and even the ability to capture more value than the deal is worth.

The Entrepreneur's Perspective

Buyers overreaching on the escrow terms are silly, especially if you have a well-run business with audited financials and outside directors. Remember, when a public company gets acquired, its reps and warranties usually expire at the closing!

The carve-outs (or fundamental reps) to the escrow caps typically include fraud, capitalization, and taxes. Often, especially due to the risk of attack by patent trolls, a buyer will press for intellectual property ownership to be carved out. We've also started to see liabilities resulting from lack of 409A compliance be carved out in escrow agreements under the argument that 409A is equivalent to taxes. In all cases, the maximum of the carve-out should be the aggregate deal value, as the seller shouldn't have to come up with more than it was paid in the deal to satisfy an escrow claim.

A lot of buyers will say something like "Well, I can't figure the specifics out until I do more due diligence." We say baloney to that, as we've yet to meet a buyer who was unable to put an initial escrow proposal, with some detail and caps defined, in the LOI. This language is still subject to due diligence but is harder to retrade after it has been agreed to, since something of substance has to emerge for there to be a legitimate discussion about it.

Finally, the form of consideration of the escrow is important. In a cash deal, it's easy. It's cash. However, in a stock deal or a deal that has a combination of cash and stock, the value of the escrow will float with the stock price, and the value can vary even more dramatically over time if it's private company stock. There are lots of permutations on how to best manage this on the seller side. You should be especially thoughtful about this if you have concerns that the buyer's stock is particularly volatile. Imagine the situation where the stock price declines but the buyer's escrow claims are of greater value than the stock in escrow represents. Reasonable people should be able to agree that the seller doesn't have to come up with extra money to satisfy the claims.

Confidentiality/Nondisclosure Agreement

While VCs will almost never sign nondisclosure agreements (NDAs) in the context of an investment, NDAs are almost always mandatory in an acquisition. If the deal falls apart and ultimately doesn't happen, both parties (the seller and the buyer) are left in a position where they have sensitive information regarding the other. Furthermore, it's typically one of the few legally binding provisions in an LOI other than the location of jurisdiction for any legal issues and breakup fees. If the deal closes, this provision largely becomes irrelevant since the buyer now owns the seller.

Both the buyer and the seller should be aligned in their desire to have a comprehensive and strong confidentiality agreement, since both parties benefit. If you are presented with a weak (or one-sided) confidentiality agreement, it could mean that the acquirer is attempting to learn about your company through the due diligence process and may or may not be intent on closing the deal.

Generally, a one-sided confidentiality agreement makes no sense. This should be a term that both sides are willing to sign up to with the same standard. Public companies are often very particular about the form of the confidentiality agreement. While we don't recommend sellers sign just anything, if it's bidirectional you are probably in a pretty safe position.

Employee Matters

Although the board of a company has a fiduciary responsibility to the shareholders of a company, it's unfortunately not always the case that management and the board are looking out for the employees and all the shareholders in an acquisition. In public company acquisitions you often hear about egregious cases of senior management looking out for themselves (and their board members helping them line their pockets) at the expense of shareholders. This can also happen in acquisitions of private companies, where the buyer knows it needs the senior executives to stick around and is willing to pay something extra for it. Of course, the opposite can happen as well, where the consideration in an acquisition is slim and the investors try to grab all the nickels for themselves, leaving management with little or nothing.

It's important for management and the board to have the proper perspective on their individual circumstances in the context of the specific deal that is occurring. Whenever we are on the board of a company that is a seller, we prefer to defer the detailed discussion about individual compensation until after the LOI is signed and the managements of the buyer and the seller have time to do due diligence on each other, build a working relationship, and understand the logical roles of everyone going forward. Spending too much time up front negotiating management packages often results in a lot of very early deal fatigue, typically makes buyers uncomfortable with the motivation of the management team for the sale, and can often create a huge wedge between management and the other shareholders on the seller's side. We aren't suggesting that management and employees shouldn't be taken care of appropriately in a transaction; rather, we believe there won't be an opportunity to take care of everyone appropriately if you don't actually get to the transaction. Overnegotiating this too early often causes a lot of unnecessary stress, especially between management and their investors.

While we don't recommend negotiating the employment agreements too early in the process, we also don't recommend leaving them to the very end of the process. Many buyers do this so they can exert as much pressure as possible on the key employees of the seller. Everyone is ready to get the deal done and the only thing holding it up is the employment agreements. Ironically, many sellers view the situation exactly the opposite way (i.e., now that the deal is basically done, we can ask for a bunch of extra stuff from the buyer). Neither of these positions is very effective, and both usually result in unnecessary tension at the end of the deal process and occasionally create a real rift between buyer and seller post-transaction.

This is a particular situation where balance is important. When it comes to employee matters, there's nothing wrong with a solid negotiation. Just make sure that it happens in the context of a deal or you may never actually get the deal done.

Conditions to Close

Buyers normally include certain conditions to closing in the LOI. These can be generic phrases such as "Subject to Board approval by Acquirer," "Subject to the Company not having a material adverse change," or "Subject to due diligence and agreement on definitive documents." There can also be phrases that are specific to the situation of the seller such as "Subject to the Company settling outstanding copyright litigation," or "Subject to Company liquidating its foreign subsidiaries." We generally don't get too concerned about this provision, because any of these are very easy to trigger should the buyer decide that it doesn't want to do the deal.

Instead of worrying about whether the provision is part of the LOI, we tend to focus on the details of the conditions to close since this is another data point about the attitude of the buyer. If the list of conditions is long and complex, you likely have a suitor with very particular tastes. In this case it's worth pushing back early on a few of these conditions to close, especially the more constraining ones, to learn about what your negotiation process is going to be like.

The Entrepreneur's Perspective

Remember, once buyers are in a significant legal and due diligence process with you, they are as emotionally and financially committed to a deal as you are (and in many cases, their reputation is on the line, too).

As the seller, you should expect that once you've agreed to specific conditions to close, you will be held to them. It's worth addressing these early in the due diligence process so you don't get hung up by something unexpected when you have to liquidate a foreign subsidiary or some other bizarre condition to close, especially if you've never done this before.

The No-Shop Clause

Signing a letter of intent starts a serious and expensive process for both the buyer and the seller. As a result, you should expect that a buyer will insist on a no-shop provision similar to the one that we discussed around term sheets. In the case of an acquisition, no-shop provisions are almost always unilateral, especially if you are dealing with an acquisitive buyer.

As the seller you should be able to negotiate the length of time into a reasonable zone such as 45 to 60 days. If the buyer is asking for more than 60 days, you should push back hard since it's never in a seller's interest to be locked up for an extended period of time. In addition, most deals should be able to be closed within 60 days from signing of the LOI, so having a reasonable deadline forces everyone to be focused on the actual goal of closing the deal.

Since most no-shop agreements will be unilateral, the buyer will typically have the right but not the obligation to cancel the no-shop if the buyer decides not to go forward with the deal. As a result, the time window is particularly important since the seller is likely to be tied up for the length of the no-shop even if the deal doesn't proceed. In some cases, an honorable buyer who has decided not to move forward with a deal will quickly agree to terminate the no-shop. However, it's more likely that the buyer will simply drag its feet until the no-shop expires.

In cases in which the deal is actively in process and the no-shop period ends, the seller should expect a call from the buyer a few days before the expiration of the no-shop with a request to extend it. There is often some additional leverage that accrues to the seller at this moment in time, including relief from a working capital threshold, potential short-term financing from the buyer, or even very specific concessions around reps and warranties that have been held up in the negotiation. The seller should be careful not to overreach at this moment since the tone for the final phase of the negotiation can be set by the behavior around the extension of the no-shop. If the seller asks for too much at this point in time, it can expect the buyer to tighten down on everything else through the close of the deal.

Rather than fight the no-shop, we've found it more effective to limit the duration of the no-shop period and carve out specific events, most notably financings (at the minimum financings done by the existing syndicate), to keep some pressure on the buyer.

The Entrepreneur's Perspective

As with no-shops with VCs, no-shops with potential buyers should also have an automatic out if the buyer terminates the process.

Fees, Fees, and More Fees

The LOI will usually be explicit about who pays for which costs and what limits exist for the seller to run up transaction costs in the acquisition. Transaction costs associated with an agent or a banker, the legal bill, and any other seller-side costs are typically included in the transaction fee section. Though it's conceivable that the buyer will punt on worrying about who covers transaction fees, most savvy buyers are very focused on making sure the seller ends up eating these, especially if they are meaningful amounts.

Occasionally, the concept of a breakup fee comes up for situations where the deal doesn't close or the seller ends up doing a deal with another buyer. Breakup fees are rare in private company venture capital–backed deals but prevalent in deals where one public company acquires another public company. We generally resist any request of a buyer to institute a breakup fee and tell the potential buyer to rely on the no-shop clause instead. Most buyers of venture capital–backed companies are much larger and more resource rich than the seller it seeks to acquire, so it strikes us as odd that the buyer would receive a cash windfall if the deal does not close, especially since both parties will have costs incurred in the process. When we are the seller, we rarely ask for a breakup fee.

The Entrepreneur's Perspective

There are some rare circumstances in which a seller can reasonably ask for a breakup fee. If the buyer is competitive and the seller is concerned that the buyer may be entering the process as a fishing expedition as opposed to a good-faith effort to buy the company, or if the seller incurs a massive amount of customer or employee risk by entering into the deal, a breakup fee may be appropriate.

Registration Rights

When a public company is buying a private company for stock, it's important for the seller to understand the registration characteristics and rights associated with the stock it will be receiving. Some buyers will try to ignore this. A good seller should work hard up front to get agreement on what it will be receiving. Just because a company is public doesn't mean all of their stock is tradable on a stock market. If you are receiving stock in an acquisition, you'll often receive unregistered stock that will need to be registered before you can sell it.

If the buyer offers unregistered stock, it should come with a promise to register the shares. It's important that the seller recognize that this is almost always a nonbinding promise since the buyer can't guarantee when it can register the shares because it is dependent on the Securities and Exchange Commission (SEC) for this and it doesn't control the SEC. The history of the buyer with the SEC is crucial, including knowing the current status of SEC filings, any outstanding registration statements, and any promises that the buyer has made to shareholders of other companies it has acquired.

We've experienced several cases in which buyers promised a quick registration only to drag their feet on the filing after the deal or have the filing get hung up at the SEC. In today's regulatory environment, we've been amazed by the poor behavior of several of the large accounting firms when they state they don't have time to work on acquisition accounting questioned by the SEC, especially in situations in which the accounting firm is not going to be working with the acquirer after the acquisition.

Pursuant to securities laws, if you receive unregistered stock and hold it for a year, then you can sell it on the stock market on which the company is listed. A year, however, can be a long time and involve a lot of volatility, especially in a thinly traded stock. Make sure you are getting what you think you are getting.

Shareholder Representatives

Acquisitions are not actually finished when the deal closes and the money trades hands. There are issues such as managing the escrow, dealing with earn-outs, working capital adjustments, and even litigation concerning reps and warranties that will last long into the future. In every acquisition, there is someone who is referred to as the shareholder representative. This person is appointed to be the representative of all the former shareholders of the seller to deal with these issues.

This lucky person, who is generally not paid anything for his services, gets to deal with all the issues that arise between the buyer and the seller after the transaction. These issues can be based around buyer's remorse or be legitimate issues, but are often time consuming and expensive to deal with, and impact the ultimate financial outcome of the deal.

Traditionally, either an executive from the seller or one of the venture capital board members takes on this role. If nothing ever comes up, it's a complete nonevent for this person. However, when something goes awry, for example, the buyer makes a claim on the escrow or threatens to sue the former shareholders of the company, this job often becomes a giant time-wasting nightmare. The shareholder rep typically has a full-time job, limited money to hire professionals to help her, and usually isn't a subject matter expert in anything that is at issue. Despite this, this person gets to lock horns with the buyer over any issues that come up and is legally responsible for dealing with the issues. If the shareholder rep is a former executive of the seller, she might still be working for the buyer, which can make things uncomfortable. In any case, this person is now making decisions that impact all of the shareholders and subsequently ends up spending time and energy communicating with them. Finally, some buyers, in an effort to exert even more pressure on the system, sue the shareholder rep directly.

We've each been shareholder reps many times, involved in numerous escrow battles, and even several lawsuits over escrows and earn-outs. Several years ago, we decided never to be shareholder reps again, as we see no upside in taking on this responsibility.

If you somehow end up being the shareholder rep, make sure you negotiate a pool of money into the merger agreement that you can dip into to hire professionals to support you should something arise that you have to deal with. We often see a separate escrow that is used exclusively to pay for the expenses of the shareholder representative. If nothing else, this works to be a good shield to a bad-acting buyer since it will see that you have money to hire lawyers to yell at its lawyers.

Never ask someone who will be working for the buyer post-transaction to be the shareholder rep. If you do this, you are asking this person to get into a winner-takes-all fight against his current employer, and that is not a happy position for anyone to be in. The only time this ever works is if the shareholder rep has a role that is critical to the buyer, and so the threat of the rep quitting will help influence the outcome in a way positive to the seller. Regardless, this is a stressful and uncomfortable position to be in.

You should also be wary of letting a VC take on this role. Escrow and litigation dynamics are time sensitive, and we've had experiences where other VCs involved as the shareholder rep paid little or no attention to their responsibilities since they didn't fully understand or appreciate the legal dynamics surrounding their role. We've had some bizarre experiences, including a shareholder rep who was a VC (a co-investor in a deal with us) who blew an escrow situation by ignoring the notice he received from the buyer that a claim had been breached. The notice period was 30 days, and 31 days after receiving the notice, the VC received another letter saying the escrow had been deducted by the amount of the claim. Fortunately, we had a good relationship with the lawyer on the side of the buyer and were able to get an exception made, but the buyer had no obligation to do this other than as a result of goodwill that existed between the parties.

As a result of our experience with this over the years, Jason co-founded a company called SRS Acquiom (www.srsacquiom.com/), which is an organization that acts as a shareholder rep. The cost, relative to the overall value of the deal, of using a firm like SRS is modest and you get professionals who spend 100% of their time playing the role of shareholder rep. When there is litigation, they get sued and deal with all of the details. Given the wide range of deals they've worked on as shareholder reps, they tend to have diverse and extensive experience with both buyers and their lawyers.

How to Engage an Investment Banker

We've talked about investment bankers throughout this book. In general, we are against using them in early stage financings, neutral in later stage financings, and strongly supportive in an acquisition context. While investment bankers aren't cheap, they can add tremendous value in many acquisition scenarios. Because of this, we solicited the help of Rex Golding, Managing Director of Golding Partners LLC, to provide thoughts on how to best find, engage, and compensate investment bankers. We've known and worked with Rex for over 20 years and value his wisdom and experience on this topic.

Why Hire an Investment Banker?

Your company has reached a classic decision point: raise another round of financing to scale the business or find the right acquirer that can immediately scale the business and provide liquidity to your shareholders. Maybe you can't raise more money and you are looking for a better solution than just giving up. Should you hire an investment banker to give you the right answer? No. Determining an exit strategy is the job of your board of directors, the CEO, and the founders of the company. However, once your board has made the decision to seek an acquirer, an investment banker can play an important role in managing the mergers and acquisitions (M&A) process to a successful conclusion.

Should you always bring in a banker? No. There are situations where a banker will not necessarily be additive or can even be detrimental. For example, you may receive a very attractive preemptive acquisition bid from the perfect acquirer of your company. At this point there may be more risk than reward in bringing in an outside adviser to optimize that deal. Another example would be a very low-value or liquidation-style exit. Bankers are generally too expensive and poorly equipped to manage such transactions, which are better suited to specialists in winding down companies. If you are an M&A-savvy CEO who has extensive prior experience in managing a sale process and are well connected with the logical acquirers of your company, it will be difficult for a banker to add sufficient value to justify the fees involved. But beyond these edge cases there a number of reasons you should consider hiring a banker for a typical sale of a company (also known as a "sell-side process") where you want to contact a broad universe of potential acquirers and negotiate the optimal exit for your shareholders.

The best reason for hiring a banker is to maximize your company's exit value by exposing it to the largest number of logical acquirers. Just as shares of public companies benefit from stock exchanges comprised of broad, liquid markets, your company's equity value will benefit from an analogous private market discovery process managed by your banker, which usually involves contacting 50 or more potential acquirers. Such a broad outreach usually eliminates second-guessing from shareholders who may have been expecting a higher exit value. Since the banker is an independent third party serving the company as a whole, this lessens conflict of interest concerns, such as a fear that an insider or founder may have biased the process to the advantage of a favored acquirer.

Additionally, your banker will shoulder a good portion of the heavy workload that is part of any sell-side process. Selling your company can be likened to taking on a second full-time job in addition to that job you currently have—running the company. If you hire a banker, you should expect to offload much of the logistical and processing-related tasks, such as making initial calls, scheduling meetings, updating presentation materials, and managing an online data room.

Finally, your banker can act as an important buffer and occasional bad guy in the sale process, which enables you and the senior executive team to build and preserve your relationship with the acquiring team without sacrificing negotiations on behalf of your shareholders. In most acquisition scenarios today, acquirers are looking to retain the core senior executives of the target company. Having a banker deal with some of the negotiation, especially the contentious parts, can help smooth over rough spots that could later interfere with the long-term working relationships between parties.

How to Choose an M&A Adviser

At first glance there seem to be lots of options for choosing an M&A adviser, from Wall Street behemoths like Morgan Stanley, to brand-name and specialized boutique firms, to small one- and two-person advisory firms. However, it's often difficult to find the right fit for your needs and budget. The biggest firms will likely be too expensive for most companies, as their minimum fees are in the millions of dollars. Unless you can reasonably expect a large exit exceeding $500 million, you should look elsewhere. Similarly, the best-known advisory boutiques are generally looking to execute transactions in excess of $100 million and size their fees accordingly, generally charging minimum fees of $1 million or more. What remains for most companies, who are contemplating exits of $100 million or less, is a vast and diverse set of lesser-known advisory firms with widely divergent qualifications and credentials.

Choosing the right banker for your company is subjective, based on perceived fit and chemistry but also guided by some important criteria, as follows:

Referrals and references. Your best source of banker candidates will be the people you already trust: your board members, investors, colleagues, and other senior executives with whom you are friends. Such referrals are beneficial in two ways, as the banker candidate does not want to disappoint a recommender, and the recommender does not want to disappoint you by sending you a dud. Hiring a banker without some endorsement is not recommended and highly unusual in our hyperconnected world.

Specific industry expertise. You should hire a banker who really knows your industry sector. Not just a "startup" or "technology" banker but, for example, an "enterprise SaaS" banker if that is what your company does. Since your banker will usually be giving the first "elevator pitch" to each potential acquirer, their initial outreach needs to be pitch-perfect and highly credible, which generally involves lots of intense preparatory work around core messaging and company positioning. So, do not be afraid to test a banker's industry knowledge in your very first encounter with her since industry expertise should be a prerequisite to engagement.

Connections to acquirers. Beyond industry knowledge, your banker should have a robust set of personal contacts within the likely buyer universe. These contacts should be fresh and recently used, reflecting current insights into each acquirer's organization chart, so that your M&A process is not delayed by lack of access or false starts. Beware of bankers who simply list CEOs and CFOs as their contacts, as it is highly unlikely that they will have credible relationships at this high level. Moreover, most buyers have dedicated corporate development groups that vet incoming opportunities, and it is important for your banker to have warm, personal relationships with these gatekeepers. It is even better if your banker also has meaningful relationships with operating executives who will likely be responsible for your business post-acquisition.

Deal experience. Your banker should have a track record of getting deals closed. While that may sound obvious, some advisers have deep industry expertise and connections but cannot cite a single example of getting an M&A deal negotiated and closed. There are plenty of inexperienced advisers, who often include recently retired senior executives who are really just beginning their banking career. While the first half of an M&A process is focused on the marketing and courtship leading up to a letter of intent, the second half is all about the hard, often grinding work of negotiating a definitive agreement and completing detailed due diligence. An inexperienced adviser can jeopardize your deal or suboptimize deal terms by simply not knowing what to do, or what the current market terms are.

Personal commitment. When interviewing bankers, always be on guard for the bait and switch around who you will be working with. This is a situation where an impressive, experienced senior banker makes a compelling, eloquent pitch for your business, only to disappear immediately after the engagement letter is signed, leaving you with a junior team. To avoid this, do not be afraid to put the senior banker on the spot during the interview process and extract a personal commitment to remain intimately involved in the engagement, including participation in all status updates, board calls, and important buyer meetings.

Cultural fit. Your banker should be a good representative for your company, understanding your values, vision, mission, and positioning. Your adviser's work style and tools should be compatible with those of your company. Does your company rely heavily on virtual collaboration tools like videoconferencing, chat, and virtual collaboration? If so, you'll want your banker to be conversant with these tools and willing to adapt to your platform. Conversely, if it is important to you to see your banker frequently and face-to-face, you'll want to hire an adviser who is in close physical proximity and who also welcomes a more direct, in-person relationship. There is no right or wrong approach, as the thing that matters is that both you and your banker share a fundamental compatibility.

Negotiating the Engagement Letter

After you've found that perfect banker, you'll need to negotiate terms of engagement that work for both sides. This may sound easier than it actually is, because you will be signing a contract that potentially involves large sums of money and legally obligates your company to specific commitments for a long period of time. Even though bankers refer to these engagement documents as "letters," they are often lengthy, complex contracts full of legalese. But don't feel intimidated. There are a relatively small number of terms that you really need to understand and negotiate. As always, use your lawyer and board extensively when negotiating the following terms:

Scope of work. It sounds really obvious, but make sure that the letter clearly articulates what your board of directors expects of your adviser. Beyond the core sell-side assignment, is the banker offering other services, such as recapitalization advice, valuation analysis, or a fairness opinion? Perhaps the most common additional advisory service is a "dual-track funding and M&A engagement" where your banker simultaneously solicits financial and strategic minority investors in one track and acquirers of the business in the second track, in order to maximize the number of go-forward options for the board to consider. Note that for a dual-track process your banker's placement fee for fundraising will be different from the M&A advisory fee and is usually 5% to 10% of the amount of funds raised. Before authorizing any fundraising activity, make sure that your banker is a licensed broker-dealer and member of FINRA, the governing body of the securities industry.

Success fee. The success fee is the big prize that your banker will be working hard for, as it will generally constitute the vast majority (over 90%) of the compensation they receive from the engagement. Unlike a retainer (which is discussed later), the success fee is payable only upon successful closing of a deal and is typically calculated as a percentage of gross proceeds to shareholders, after debt repayment but before other deal expenses such as legal fees. Higher fee percentages will be quoted for smaller deal sizes, starting at up to 10% of proceeds for deal sizes of less than $5 million, then generally declining to 1% to 2% for deals approaching $100 million. It is also common to see a flat minimum fee that provides downside protection to the banker in the event that the board approves a low-value exit. Often the percentage formula includes a scaled incentive fee that pays out higher percentages for higher exit values, for example, a 2% base fee on proceeds up to $50 million, then a 5% incentive fee on proceeds over $50 million. Be careful, however, with incentive fees as they are easy to concede theoretically but can end up being very expensive and are not always justified by your banker's efforts or abilities. To avoid "fee remorse" at closing, be sure to use a spreadsheet to model your adviser's payouts for all conceivable exit values, to thoroughly understand how those seemingly small fee percentages can add up to large dollar numbers. Finally, make sure that the engagement letter specifically contemplates an acquisition that includes noncash proceeds. Instead of cash, you may receive private company shares or an earn-out based on your company's performance post-acquisition. In most cases you will want your banker to accept the same form of proceeds as your other shareholders and not demand cash payment when little or no cash may be available.

Retainer and expense reimbursement. A banker's engagement almost always requires payment of a nonrefundable monthly fee, called a retainer, in the $5,000 to $15,000 range that extends for at least six months. Think of these payments as "earnest money" that signal your intent to close a deal versus launching a fishing expedition. All retainer amounts paid should be deductible against the success fee, and you should explicitly delineate this in the engagement letter. In addition to the retainer, you will likely reimburse your banker for out-of-pocket expenses incurred on your behalf. Take a close look at this provision to make sure that there are common-sense limits to such reimbursement. Any expenses incurred should be reasonable and conform with your company's practices versus your adviser's. For example, if your company's air travel policy specifies purchase of the lowest-cost coach fare available, your banker should not be submitting a first-class ticket for reimbursement. Travel expenses, in particular, can really add up, so be sure to require pre-approval for any long trips and consider capping overall expenses at a reasonable level like $5,000. Also, beware of reimbursement requests for unidentified expenses that may be labeled as "administrative" or "overhead." You should only be responsible for direct expenses incurred on your behalf.

Term, termination, and tails. Your contractual commitment to your adviser generally extends beyond a year, so it is important to thoroughly understand the extent of your commitment and financial exposure before signing. A one-year term is typical and, while this may seem like a long time, bear in mind that an M&A process typically takes at least six months from a cold start to finish. Because circumstances can change, it is important to negotiate a "termination for convenience" clause in the engagement to provide a clear-cut way to stop the engagement for any reason. Upon expiration or termination of the contract, a "tail" provision will take effect, which protects the banker's success fee in the event that a deal is closed within a fixed period of time, typically between six months and a year. Be sure that this tail applies only to buyers that actually had substantive meetings or time spent with you as part of your banker's solicitation.

Indemnification and dispute resolution. Things can go wrong with any deal, people make mistakes, and the world is filled with honest misunderstandings. Since your banker is working for you during the deal, they will ask for specific risk coverage, called indemnification, in the event that they are sued during or after the engagement for actions taken on your behalf. Be sure to limit your indemnification to banker behavior that is reasonable and professional, and explicitly carve out indemnification for actions that are reckless or grossly negligent. Beyond indemnification relating to third parties, sometimes you may have a serious disagreement with your banker. These disagreements are usually about success fees or the "tail" agreement. It is a good idea to predetermine how such disagreements are going to be worked out, with mediation/arbitration recommended versus litigation, which is much more expensive and time consuming.

Key person(s) provision. Sometimes you want to hire a bank because you value the services of a specific banker who is an industry expert or has specific skills or contacts. In this case it is strongly advised to add a key person provision in the engagement letter that allows you to terminate the engagement and ideally the tail agreement in the event that those individuals leave that bank. You will want the option to transfer the engagement to the new bank that will employ these key persons. Alternatively, these individuals may work out an arrangement with their old employers to split fees and continue under the original engagement.

Fairness opinion. For more complex M&A situations your board may request a fairness opinion from your adviser. A fairness opinion is a formal letter from the banker to the board that confirms the fairness of the transaction being considered. This serves as an additional insurance policy for the board in the event that disgruntled investors, creditors, or suitors subsequently choose to assert their rights to dissent or even sue. Fairness opinions are much more common for a publicly traded company or a private company with a large, diverse investor base. For most technology company sales, a fairness opinion would be overkill and only appropriate for companies with complicated capitalizations and/or potential conflicts of interest among shareholders. By its very nature a fairness opinion increases your banker's risk exposure in the deal, as they often become a target of investor lawsuits or become party to legal proceedings via depositions and testimony. Consequently, fairness opinions are not cheap, and you can expect to pay $1 million or more for such a letter since your banker will be pricing the likelihood of subsequent litigation into the fee for the fairness opinion. In most cases the best protection against shareholder lawsuits is not a fairness opinion but running a broad and transparent M&A process and establishing an auditable record of extensive outreach to all logical buyers of your company.

Helping Your Banker Maximize the Outcome

Negotiating with your banker can be tiresome, but the real work begins after you have signed the engagement letter. If the process was too exhausting, consider how they will look in front of potential acquirers. Given the high stakes involved, it is crucial that all participants in the M&A process know what to expect and are all on the same page. This starts with your board of directors. If you have reached this point your board should be unanimous in seeking a transaction. If this is not the case, pull the emergency brake and schedule another board meeting!

It is equally important to achieve consensus among your senior management team since they will be intimately involved in the M&A process and any dissension or alienation within your team will soon be discerned by prospective buyers. This can be particularly challenging in low-value exits where employees will receive little or no proceeds from their common shares or options. In these cases, the board will often approve a carve-out plan that earmarks a portion of acquisition proceeds to employees, to better align their incentives with those of investors and help retain critical executives during the process.

Finally, all parties need to agree to a common timetable to avoid process drift or mission creep. While the right banker can optimize your exit, it is still up to you and your team to do most of the heavy lifting. It's your business and your vision, and nobody can sell that better than you.

Why Do Term Sheets Even Exist?

One question that we often get is "why does the term sheet even exist?" In fact, why do we need all of this legal paperwork in the first place? Since a careful reader will point out that we have said that it is rare for a VC to sue one of its portfolio companies on reps and warranties, why can't we do all of this with a handshake or a simple document? Given that there are only a few things that really matter, why have all of this ponderous structure and legalese?

It turns out that nothing requires that you use a term sheet. Our favorite negotiations with entrepreneurs have been ones where we've literally shaken hands and agreed on valuation, board structure, and option pool size verbally or over email. From there, we just used our standard forms that we publish on the Foundry Group website (http://foundrygroup.com/resources/) and were done with the deal in a few weeks. We find this spirit of collaboration and trust attractive as it starts the working relationship off on the right foot. The irony that we prefer doing deals without a term sheet is not lost on us.

While this approach works if you are a sophisticated founder, have worked with us before, or are working with attorneys who know us well, this is the exception case. Usually, the term sheet will be the first real negotiated document in a relationship.

Regardless of whether a term sheet is drafted or not, a plethora of legal documents will need to be created. This is just a fact of life. VCs need to answer to their investors, who would not be comfortable if we didn't have legal documents to protect their investment. Our auditors would have nothing to look at to ensure we are getting what we paid for and are valuing our portfolio correctly. Furthermore, there are a few extreme cases out there where these documents were important constraints to bad behavior. Typically, courts will not give VCs any benefit of the doubt in contract negotiations, so if we want a provision, we have to get it clearly and explicitly in writing.

Properly drafted documents should help the parties align incentives so that each desires to act in ways that are beneficial to the other. Following are some general themes of what makes a contract truly useful in a relationship and should be considered as a framework when you consider particular provisions in a contract. Once again, we thank our friend Brad Bernthal (CU Law Professor) for his suggestions.

Constraining Behavior and the Alignment of Incentives

Any good contractual relationship strives to be a win/win situation for both parties, where each party is incentivized to act in each other's best interests. Many things can drive this. It could be that the business relationship is important to both parties, so everyone will be a good actor. There can be reputational constraints involved. However, neither of these have any legal teeth to make sure everyone behaves. Consequently, contracts were developed to make sure that if something went awry, that good behavior, to some extent, would be enforceable.

While it's nice to think that people are generous of spirit, it's a fact of life that most people, especially in a business context, are driven by self-interest. That's not a bad thing, but it's useful to always keep this in mind. If you assume that your VC will do what is best for both of you and it happens that these actions actually make you both better off, then the relationship should be a smooth one. If one day you realize that you are not on the same page, then things can get interesting. For instance, remember a section in a previous chapter around the treatment of stock options in an acquisition. In this situation, there are numerous ways that you, your VCs, and your employees will have meaningfully different self-interests. Decisions that benefit one group will adversely affect the others.

We encourage you to deal with misalignments like this openly and directly. Ultimately, if you can't reach an agreement on how to address them, the situation will be bounded by the contractual terms that you have agreed to beforehand. Because of this, it is critical to think about how term sheets and contracts constrain bad behavior and align incentives.

As we've discussed, the only two things that really matter in a term sheet are economic and control provisions. We could have said that the only two things that matter are making sure incentives were aligned and that potential bad behavior is mitigated, but that would be way too academic for real life. However, keep in mind that the constructs are analogous. Whenever you are trying to figure out if a particular term is good or bad for you, consider how this will either proactively or negatively decrease the ability for people to behave poorly, or whether the term improves the alignment of your incentives with your investor.

If something feels out of whack and you think a particular provision divides your and your investor's incentives, be careful about accepting it. It's in this vein that you have a very powerful negotiating tool. You don't have to say "I don't want this term, it's not market." Instead, try the approach of "Wait a minute, this term starts the relationship by dividing us and resulting in our incentives being misaligned."

Outside of these two considerations, every good contract should deal effectively with transaction costs, agency costs, and information asymmetries, which we'll discuss below.

Transaction Costs

There are different definitions of transaction costs, but for our purposes transaction costs are the cost—in both time and money—associated with creating a relationship between two parties. For instance, in closing a venture deal between an entrepreneur and a VC, transactions costs will include not only the costs of lawyers for both sides but also the costs of meetings, the time involved to complete due diligence, and every step of the process from that first meeting to the signed definitive documents.

If you go back 25 years, it was really difficult to get your startup funded, not just because there were fewer VCs, but there were high transaction costs to deal with. There were no standard forms of documents accepted by the industry, so lawyers spent a lot of time arguing about things. There was no ubiquity of electronic communications other than the telephone and fax machine. This meant more meetings were in-person, time consuming, and hard to schedule. Furthermore, couriers shuffled documents back and forth

(Jason's old law firm had bike, car, and plane couriers staffed full time at the office). Thankfully, technology, transparency, and discussion online and in books like this have dramatically lowered these costs. The dynamics of a financing are no longer a black box controlled by lawyers and a few knowledgeable investors.

When entering a contractual relationship, consider that all good contracts minimize current and future transaction costs. As we discussed earlier, convertible debt became increasingly popular due to the lower legal fees associated with it when compared to equity rounds. Fifteen years ago, an equity financing cost four times that of a convertible debt financing. Today, there isn't much difference at all. When determining which structure to use to raise money for your company, consider what the transaction costs will be to get the deal done.

We find future transaction costs to be even more important to consider. For instance, you should negotiate a detailed merger letter of intent (LOI) before signing it in order to avoid too much negotiation ambiguity while drafting the definitive documents. As you have more negotiating power during the LOI stage, what would take two hours to negotiate now could save you dozens of hours later on. In short, you are defining the relationship up front so that you don't have to run up huge costs, both in time and money, figuring who has which rights and who receives what consideration.

Agency Costs and Information Asymmetry

Agency costs are costs associated with an agent acting on behalf of a principal. Some of these costs are direct. If I hire a stockbroker to buy stocks for me, I must also pay them a fee to complete the trade. Some of these costs are indirect and hard to spot.

Let's use the example of a *walking dead portfolio company*. This is a company that is still in business, but just limping along with no clear path to an outcome. It would probably be in the VC's best interest if the company shut down so the VC could recoup whatever money is left in the bank account and take the tax loss.

Let's consider the VC the principal in the scenario. The CEO, however, has other incentives. He still has a decent salary and gets to walk around town with his CEO business card. His incentive is to keep the company alive as long as possible. The CEO in this case is the agent.

Regardless of the amount of time the VC and the entrepreneur spend together, there is no way either party will know as much about the other's business—and motivation—as they know about their own. This information asymmetry, like agency dynamics, results in a misalignment of incentives.

Consider which contractual provisions could help alleviate this conflict. A contractual right to a board seat for the VC would be helpful. An odd number of board members, with at least one independent board member would be relevant. The VC having redemption rights, while not necessarily palatable to the CEO, provides some additional pressure in the context of making a decision about what to do.

Reputation Constraints

If you are playing a long-term game, *reputation constraints* can be even more important than a specific term in a contract. The venture capital industry is small and reputation matters a lot. Bad behavior gets talked about, even if it's done quietly and not out in the open. The smaller the ecosystem, the more this phenomenon exists, so as you focus on smaller geographies, the importance of reputation increases.

While there are some people who care less about their reputation than others, your reputation will be established over a long period of time. While no contract is airtight, how you deal with ambiguity and conflict will help define your reputation. This impacts both entrepreneurs and investors. Do your homework and find out the real reputation of the other party that you are dealing with. In some regards, this is the most important term of them all.

CHAPTER

19

Legal Things Every Entrepreneur
Should Know

There are a few legal issues that we've seen consistently become hurdles for entrepreneurs and their lawyers. While in some cases they will simply be a hassle to clean up in a financing or an exit, they often have meaningful financial implications for the company, and in the worst case, can seriously damage the value of your business. We aren't your lawyers or giving you legal advice here (our lawyers made us write that), but we encourage you to understand these issues rather than just assume that your lawyer got them right.

If you want to read the best book ever on legal issues that face entrepreneurs, get *The Entrepreneur's Guide to Business Law*, fifth edition, by Constance Bagley and Craig Dauchy (South-Western, 2012). It is written for entrepreneurs, not lawyers, so it's easily digestible and is the best legal resource for entrepreneurs we know. The cost is less than 11 minutes of a typical lawyer's time and the payback is immediate and invaluable.

We also thank our friends at Cooley LLP for helping us with this chapter. And, no, they aren't giving you official legal advice here either.

Intellectual Property

We discussed some intellectual property (IP) issues in Chapter 2 around preparing for fundraising. However, IP issues can kill a start-up before you even really begin. Following is an example.

You and a friend go out and get some beers. You start telling him about your new company that will revolutionize X and make you a lot of money. You spend several hours talking about the business model, what you need to build, and the product requirements. After one beer too many, you both stumble home happy.

Your friend goes back to work at his job at Company X-like. You picked this particular friend to vet your idea because you know that your company is similar to some cutting-edge work he does at X-like. There is even a chance that you'd want to hire this friend one day.

You spend the next six months bootstrapping your company and release a first version of your product. A popular tech blog writes about it and you start getting inbound calls from VCs wanting to fund you. You can't stop smiling and are excited about how glorious life as an entrepreneur is.

The next day your beer buddy calls and says that he's been laid off from Company X-like and wants to join your company. You tell him as soon as you get funding you'd love to hire him. Your friend says, "That's okay. I can start today for no pay since I own 50% of the company." You sit in stunned silence for a few seconds.

As you discuss the issue, your friend tells you that he owns 50% of the IP of your company since you guys went out and basically formed the company over beers. You tell him that you disagree and he doesn't own any of the company. He tells you his uncle is a lawyer.

As strange as this sounds, this is a real example. While we think the claim by your so-called friend is ridiculous, if he takes action (via his uncle, who is likely working for him for free), he can slow down your VC financing. If he keeps after you and you don't give him something, it's possible that he'll end up completely stifling your chance to raise money. If you happen to get lucky and your so-called friend accidentally gets hit by a bus, you still have the outstanding issue that Company X-like may also have a claim on the IP if there is an actual lawsuit filed and X-like happens to stumble upon piecing the story together.

There are endless stories like this in startup land, including the history of the founding of Facebook, popularized (and fictionalized) by the movie *The Social Network*. Our example is one extreme, but there are others, like students starting a company in an MBA class where two go on to actually start the business while the other two don't, but terrorize the company for ownership rights later due to their claimed IP contributions. Or the entrepreneur who hired a contractor to write code for him, paid the contractor, but still ended up in litigation with the contractor, who claimed he owned IP above and beyond what he was paid for. Realize that even if you pay for code written by someone else, you don't own the code unless you get whoever wrote the code to sign a document saying that the code was "work for hire." The exact words are critical.

When things like this come up, even the most battle-hardened VC will pause and make sure that there are no real IP issues involved. Responsible VCs who want to invest in your company will work with you to resolve this stuff, especially when absurd claims like the examples we just gave are being made. In our experience, there's often a straightforward resolution except in extreme circumstances.

The key is being careful, diligent, and reasonably paranoid up front. When friends are involved, you can usually work this stuff out with a simple conversation. However, when talking to random people, be careful of unscrupulous characters, especially those you know nothing about.

Some entrepreneurs, and many lawyers, think the right solution is to carefully guard your idea or have everyone you talk to sign a nondisclosure agreement (NDA). We don't agree with this position. Instead, we encourage entrepreneurs to be very open with their ideas, and we generally believe NDAs aren't worth very much. However, be conscious of whom you are talking to. If there are few reputational constraints to someone acting badly, then think hard before disclosing your IP to them. If you do start heading down the path of actually creating a business, make sure you have competent legal counsel to help you document it.

Patents

One approach to protect against bad actors and create value for you company is to get a patent. A patent provides a company with a 20-year monopoly over making, using, or selling an invention. The vast majority of patents are utility patents, meaning they protect the functional attributes of a device. In order to get a patent, an inventor must file a patent application with the US PTO within the first 12 months of offering the invention for sale or of disclosing an invention to an individual or entity without an accompanying nondisclosure agreement.

It's not easy to determine whether it is worth investing in patent protection. Securing patents is an expensive undertaking with no guarantee regarding the returns. However, for technology startups in particular, patents can be a worthwhile investment that can create an invaluable competitive advantage, be a recurring source of revenues through royalties, and help establish a defensive position in the market.

In considering whether to apply for a patent, founders should weigh the investment required versus the potential upside in securing patent protection. For instance, investing the money required to secure a patent may not have much upside in a fast-developing market where the intellectual property may be obsolete by the time the patent is granted.

To begin the patent application process, a company often files a provisional patent application. This application includes a full and enabling technical disclosure but omits some formal requirements of a utility patent application. The provisional patent application can be converted into a utility patent application within one year of the initial filing date and typically ranges in cost from $2,000 to $10,000. To secure a patent, a startup must finish the full patent application process, which can range in cost from $10,000 to $25,000. This process is lengthier, typically requiring a month or two to complete the entire application. Once a patent application is submitted to the US PTO, it will be pending for several years prior to review and potential approval by the US PTO. Because of the complexities of the patent application process, startups should seek guidance and assistance from patent counsel.

Trademarks

A trademark gives a company a legal mechanism to protect a distinctive name, symbol, or tagline that identifies a company as the owner of a product or service. Trademarks ensure brand owners can prevent others from harming or capitalizing on the goodwill associated with the brand. In the United States, securing a trademark involves a three-step process: clearance, filing a trademark application, and prosecution.

To start the trademark application process, a company must first confirm that their proposed mark is available for registration. This involves counsel performing a search to confirm the mark's availability with the United States Patent and Trademark Office (US PTO), a process that can range in cost from $1,800 to $3,500. This search will compare the company's proposed mark to the names of other companies as well as products or services similar to those the company will provide. It is important for startups to keep in mind that in the United States, unlike in other countries, trademark ownership is not guaranteed by being the first entity to register a mark with the US PTO. Instead, trademark ownership depends on which entity was the first to use a mark. This means that in selecting a trademark, a company should carefully consider both the US PTO's list of registered marks as well as unregistered corporate and product names, taglines, and symbols that competitors have already publicly used.

In the case of a business name, the search with the US PTO must be followed by verification that the corporate name has not already been registered with the secretary of state for the state in which a company is incorporated. No secretary of state will accept the incorporation of a company in its state if the company's proposed name closely resembles a name on its existing company register.

Performing these initial searches and securing a corporate name by filing incorporation documents or registering a domain name does give a company the rights to a trademark. To receive the full protections of a trademark, a startup must file an application with the US PTO. Generally, this application is prepared and filed by a company's counsel, which ranges in cost from $1,500 to $4,000. This application will then be examined and if it meets the US PTO approval, the trademark will proceed to the third step of the application process and be subject to a publication period, also known as prosecution, during which other entities can object to the mark.

Employment Issues

The most common lawsuits entrepreneurs face are ones around employment issues. These are never pleasant, especially in the context of an employee you've recently fired, but they are an unfortunate result of today's work environment.

There are a few things you can do to protect against this. First, make sure that everyone you hire is an at-will employee. Without these specific words in the offer letter, you can end up dealing with state employment laws (which vary from state to state) that determine whether you can fire someone. We've encountered some challenging situations in certain states in the United States that made firing almost as challenging as firing in parts of Europe.

Next, consider whether you want to prebake severance terms into an offer letter. For instance, you might decide that if you let someone go, they will receive additional vesting or cash compensation. If you don't decide this at the outset, you may be left with a situation where you are able to fire someone, but they claim that you owe them something on the way out the door. However, determining up-front severance is about as much fun as negotiating a prenuptial agreement, and the downside to it is that it limits your flexibility, especially if the company is in a difficult financial situation and needs to fire people to lower its burn rate in order to conserve cash to survive.

Every entrepreneur should know at least one good employment lawyer. Dealing with these particular issues can be stressful and unpredictable, especially given the extensive rules around discrimination that again vary from state to state. A knowledgeable employment lawyer can quickly help you get to an appropriate resolution when something comes up. In our opinion it's mandatory to get a lawyer involved when a founder or executive leaves the company. Even if the people involved are on good terms, it's critical that equity and intellectual property issues are clearly settled so that future fundraising and acquisition potential aren't impacted.

Type of Corporate Structure

There are three different corporate structures you can use for your company: a C Corp, an S Corp, or an LLC. If you are going to raise venture capital, you will want to be a C Corp, but it's useful to understand why and when you might benefit from the other corporation structures.

If you are not going to raise any VC or angel money, an S Corp is the best structure as it has all the tax benefits and flexibility of a partnership—specifically a single tax structure versus the potential for the double tax structure of a C Corp—while retaining the liability protection of a C Corp.

Often, an LLC (limited liability company) will substitute for an S Corp as they have similar legal characteristics. However, with an LLC, it is much harder to effectively grant equity to employees. Instead of stock options, LLCs use membership units, which few employees have experience with. In addition, stock options have better and more clearly defined tax dynamics. LLCs work really well for companies with a limited number of owners. They don't work as well when the ownership starts to be spread among multiple people.

If you are going to raise VC or angel money, a C Corp is the best (and often required) structure. In a VC or angel-backed company, you'll almost always end up with multiple classes of stock, which are not permitted in an S Corp. Since this type of company is expected to lose money for a while (in most cases that's the explanation for why you are raising money in the first place), the issue of being taxed at a corporate level on your profits will be deferred. In addition, it's unlikely that you will be distributing money out of a VC-/angel-backed company when you become profitable.

Accredited Investors

Although this isn't a book about securities laws (which, if it were, would make it a dreadfully dull book), much of it is actually about selling securities to investors. There are lots of laws that you need to comply with in order to not get in trouble with the Securities and Exchange Commission (SEC), which is one of the major reasons that you need to have a good lawyer.

When we wrote the prior versions of this book, it was illegal to sell securities to anyone you wanted to. Now, in a crowdfunding/post–JOBS Act world, you have many more options to whom you can sell equities. That being said, the vast majority of entrepreneurs are still sticking with the old regime of selling to accredited investors. This means you should not ask your hairdresser, auto mechanic, and bag boy at the grocery store to buy stock in your company unless they are independently wealthy. There are laws that effectively say that only rich and sophisticated people are *accredited investors* and are allowed to buy stock in private companies. If you try to raise money from people who do not fit this definition, then you're probably committing a securities violation. Normally, the SEC doesn't catch most people who do this, but it does happen sometimes.

If you ignore this advice and sell stock in your private company to people who don't fit the SEC's definition of an accredited investor, then you will have a lifelong problem on your hands. Specifically, these nonaccredited investors can force you to buy back their shares for at least their purchase price anytime they want, despite how your company is doing. This *right of rescission* is a very real thing that we see from time to time. It is particularly embarrassing when the person forcing the buyback is a close family friend or relative who should not have been offered the stock in the first place.

Section 409A Valuations

Another random legal topic is one that often rears its ugly head around an acquisition: Section 409A of the tax code, also known as the 409A valuation. Section 409A says that all stock options given to employees of a company need to be at *fair market value.*

In the old days before the turn of the millennium (pre-409A), the board of a private company could determine what the fair market value of a share of common stock was and this was acceptable to the IRS. It became common practice that the share price for the common stock, which is also the exercise price for the stock options being granted, was typically valued at 10% of the price of the last round of preferred stock. The exception was when a company was within 18 months of an IPO, in which case the price of the common stock converged with the price of the preferred stock as the IPO drew nearer.

For some reason the IRS decided this wasn't the right way to determine fair market value, came up with a new approach in Section 409A of the tax code, and created dramatic penalties for the incorrect valuation of stock options. The penalties included excise taxes on the employee and potential company penalties. In addition, some states, such as California, instituted their own penalties at the state level. When Section 409A was first drafted, it sounded like a nightmare.

However, the IRS gave everyone a way out, also known throughout the legal industry as a *safe harbor.* If a company used a professional valuation firm, the valuation would be assumed to be correct unless the IRS could prove otherwise, which is not an easy thing to do. In contrast, if the company chose not to use a professional valuation firm, then the company would have to prove the valuation was correct, which is also a hard thing to do.

The predictable end result of this was the creation of an entirely new line of business for accountants and a bunch of new valuation firms. Section 409A effectively created new overhead for doing business that helped support the accounting profession. Although we have a bunch of friends who work for 409A valuation firms, we don't believe that any of this is additive in any way to the company or to the value-creation process. Originally, these costs were about $5,000 to $15,000 per year. Recently, Carta announced that they'll do 409A valuations if a company signs up for a $25 per month subscription fee. Either way, money spent here could easily be spent on something more useful to the company, such as beer or search engine marketing.

An unfortunate side effect is that the 10% rule, where common stock was typically valued at 10% of the preferred stock, is no longer valid. We often see 409A valuations in early stage companies valuing common stock at 20% to 30% of the preferred stock. As a result, employees make less money in a liquidity event, as options are more expensive to purchase since their basis (or exercise price) is higher.

Ironically, the IRS also collects fewer taxes, as it receives tax only on the value of the gain (sale price of the stock minus the exercise price). In this case, the accountants are the only financial winners.

(83)b Elections

An 83(b) election is a notification a recipient of a restricted stock grant sends the IRS electing to be taxed on his or her equity on the date the equity was granted rather than on the date the equity vests. 83(b) elections are therefore only applicable to grants of stock that are subject to vesting. Aside from accelerating the individual's ordinary income tax, filing an 83(b) election also starts the individual's long-term capital gains holding period clock earlier.

An 83(b) election must be filed within 30 days of the date of the restricted stock grant. Failure to file within that timeframe cannot be cured. In other words, if you don't file the 83(b) election within 30 days of the stock grant, there is nothing you can do about it in the future. Potential investors will ask whether all service providers have filed timely 83(b) elections and will often require the company to make a representation in the operative purchase agreement that all such elections have been made. Therefore, the company should encourage all recipients of restricted stock to consult their tax advisors and review the 83(b) election before timely filing with the IRS.

We have had multiple firsthand experiences with a missed 83(b) filing, and it's a bummer when you are in the middle of an acquisition and you realize the 83(b) election is unsigned under a pile of papers on a someone's desk. For a firsthand account of this, take a look at the chapter titled "To 83(b) or Not to 83(b)" in Brad and David Cohen's book *Do More Faster* (John Wiley & Sons, 2010).

Founders' Stock

Legally speaking, there is no such thing as founders' stock. Common stock is issued to founders when the company is first formed, while preferred stock is typically sold to investors. Because the company is new and has little value, the common stock can be issued at a very low price, such as $0.0001. At such a low price, a founder can be issued 2,000,000 shares for just $200. When people refer to *founders' stock* they are talking about common stock issued to founders at a very low price at the inception of the company. To ensure that the founders do not need to pay taxes on the difference between the price paid and the fair market value of stock over time, the founding team should ensure that their stock issuances are finalized at or near the time of formation, and, if the stock vests over time immediately file an 83(b) election with the IRS. This means that the company should get all signatures to the purchase documents, receive and cash checks for payment of the stock, and maintain evidence of payment of the purchase documents in the company's records and data site.

When issuing common stock to themselves, the founding team should consider subjecting that stock to vesting, which is often in monthly or quarterly increments over four years and may include a "cliff" which is typically one year. This cliff is the time period that the individual must be with the company before she vests the first increment in the vesting schedule. In the early years of a startup, it is typical that one or more of the founders will leave the company.

By subjecting the stock to vesting, the vesting restriction protects the other founders from having to share a large stake of the company with a departed founder who will not be helping to build the company. In addition, investors often seek some kind of vesting restriction to ensure that the team sticks around following a financing. While the founding team could wait for investors to impose vesting, by implementing vesting at the outset, they may be able to avoid more onerous vesting terms that may be proposed by investors.

Founders' stock vesting provisions can also provide for acceleration of vesting in connection with the sale of the company. Acceleration on a sale of the company (single trigger) or on a sale of the company when the founder is terminated without cause within some time period after the sale (double trigger) protects the founder. These benefits can also be given to employees but are typically reserved for the executive team, outside board directors, and key service providers. There are a number of other rights that founders' stock can have, and the founding team should discuss these options and their implications with corporate counsel.

Consultants versus Employees

While companies can resort to making equity grants to compensate service providers and preserve cash, many legal issues arise when not paying cash compensation to full-time founders and early executives. Regardless of whether service providers are willing to work without cash compensation, state and federal wage and hour laws require that full-time employees be paid minimum wage for their services. Damages for not making such payments include unpaid wages (based on at least minimum wage), additional damages for unpaid overtime, penalties, and misdemeanors charges. Companies should consult employment attorneys to minimize potential liability when they aren't paying wages at market rates.

Companies often classify founders and early executives as consultants or contractors to avoid wage and hour law obligations. It's important when classifying service providers, however, to be sure that the individuals providing services really are contractors. Misclassifying employees as contractors creates potential wage liability when those consultants could later decide that they were actually employees and be entitled to wages. If they were in fact employees, the company would owe them back wages. Thus, if a company has the cash and the individuals providing services are truly employees, the company should classify them as employees and pay wages and taxes accordingly.

If the company does not have the money to pay these early service providers (as is often the case), then the company should enter into contractor agreements with the individuals and do as much as possible to structure those relationships so that the individuals are treated as contractors. Some important ways to structure proper consulting relationships include: (1) engaging the individual for a specific project; (2) compensating the individual by the project rather than by an hourly or monthly fee; (3) not having direction, control, or supervision over the person; (4) not providing equipment or training; (5) permitting the individual to work for other entities because, ideally, these are professionals with real businesses that work with a lot of different clients; and (6) not making arrangements terminable at will.

Compensating Service Providers

Given the cash-strapped nature of startups, companies turn to different forms of compensation. The most typical noncash method of compensating employees, consultants, and advisors (referred to as "service providers") is granting equity. In consulting with your legal advisors, startups often create what is referred to as an equity incentive plan under which they can grant options, restricted stock, and other forms of equity. While grants of equity do not need to be made pursuant to an equity incentive plan or out of the "option pool," companies often do so because it provides a simple and efficient legal and tax framework under which companies can issue stock and options.

By granting equity to service providers, companies can save cash, motivate service providers by giving them a stake in the company, and incent them to stay with the company, since equity typically vests over time. When deciding what type of equity to grant, you need to consider several factors.

Stock is the most common form of equity. The recipient of a stock grant becomes a voting stockholder of the company (assuming that the individual receives a type of stock that has voting rights). When granting common stock to service providers, companies usually subject that stock to vesting, which allows the company to buy back any unvested stock if the service terminates prior to the vesting period ending. Subjecting the stock to vesting incentivizes the service provider to continue working with the company and protects the company in the event that a new hire does not work out well. It also avoids the difficult situation of a former service provider who left on bad terms having a large voting stake.

When the company grants stock to a service provider, that individual recognizes taxable income equal to the fair market value of the stock received in excess of what that individual paid for it. For instance, if an advisor receives a grant of 1,000 shares with a price per share of $1.00 and was granted that stock in exchange for his or her services, then that advisor would recognize taxable income equal to $1,000 the year the grant was made (assuming the advisor files an 83(b) election). It is the taxable income recognized with a stock grant that often leads companies with valuable stock to grant options to purchase common stock rather than outright common stock.

An option is the right to buy stock at a predetermined price (the *exercise price*). Unlike stockholders, option holders do not have the right to vote their shares; they do not own shares, but rather have a *right* to purchase shares. The exercise price of shares subject to an option is the fair market value of a share of the type of stock that is issued if the option is exercised. If the exercise price is at least equal to the fair market value of the stock, the option is not taxable to the recipient at the time of the grant. If the same advisor discussed above was granted an option to purchase 1,000 shares at an exercise price of $1.00, then in order to exercise the option, the advisor would have to pay $1,000 to acquire the stock and therefore become a stockholder. While the advantage of granting options is not having taxable income at the time of the grant, the disadvantage is that the advisor has to pay the value of the exercise price.

Like stock, options typically have vesting periods. Unlike stock, where the vesting works in reverse because the company can buy back the unvested stock, options can typically only be exercised after they vest. For instance, if the option above for 1,000 shares is 25% vested, the advisor could pay $250 to acquire 250 shares. The advisor would become a stockholder able to vote the vested and purchased 250 shares.

Authors' Note

Throughout this book, we have tried to expose you to all of the issues you will face during a venture capital financing along with some issues that you will deal with after raising money. We have covered the nuts and bolts of the term sheet, explored the participants in the process, discussed how to prepare your company for a financing, and explained how the fundraising process works. We have discussed how venture capital firms operate and described some basic negotiating principles. We have also covered a bunch of dos and don'ts around the fundraising process and, as a bonus, added a chapter deconstructing a typical letter of intent you might receive at the beginning of the acquisition process. Finally, in this latest addition, we have covered several new topics, including how to negotiate a venture debt deal, how to prepare your company for a successful financing, and how to work with an investment banker on a sale process.

While we approached the first few editions as early stage investors, we now include later stage financings in the book. We have tried to be balanced between the entrepreneur's view and the VC's view, as we have been both (although we have now been VCs for much longer). We also included an entrepreneur's perspective—from Matt Blumberg, the CEO of Return Path—throughout the book.

We know much of this material is dry, so we tried hard to spice it up with our own special brand of humor. We have reviewed, and read, and proofread, and reread the book over and over again but know there are still mistakes or topics that aren't explained as well as they could be. We learn the most from our mistakes and encourage you to email us at jason@foundrygroup.com or brad@foundrygroup .com with anything you find that is unclear or that you believe is incorrect.

Of course, none of the information in this book should be construed as legal advice from us. We are not your lawyers—just a pair of investors who wrote a book that we hope is helpful to you. If you have legal questions, ask your lawyers. Yes, our lawyers made us write this.

We hope this book has been helpful to you as you work to create, or invest in, an amazing new company. If you have enjoyed it or found it helpful, we always appreciate reviews on Amazon and Goodreads.

Thank you for your support and best of luck to all the entrepreneurs out there creating the next generation of important companies.

—Jason and Brad

Appendix A: Sample Term Sheet

ACME VENTURE CAPITAL 2018, LP

Summary of Terms for Proposed Private Placement of Series A Preferred Stock of NEWCO.COM

_____, 20_____

(Valid for acceptance until_____, 20_____)

Issuer:	NEWCO.COM (the "Company")
Investor(s):	Acme Venture Capital 2018, L.P. and its affiliated partnerships ("Acme") **[and others, if applicable]** ("Investors").
Amount of Financing:	An aggregate of $ million, **[(including $ _____ from the conversion of outstanding bridge notes)]** representing a % ownership position on a fully diluted basis, including shares reserved for any employee option pool. **[The individual investment amounts for each Investor are as follows]:**

Acme $_____

Other investor 1 $_____

Other investor 2 $_____

Total: $ _____]

[If there is to be a second closing, differentiate the Investors and amounts by each closing.]

Price:	$ _____ per share (the "Original Purchase Price"). The Original Purchase Price represents a fully diluted pre-money valuation of $_____ million and a fully diluted post-money valuation of $ _____ million. **[A capitalization table showing the Company's capital structure immediately following the Closing is attached.]** For purposes of the above calculation and any other reference to "fully diluted" in this term sheet, "fully diluted" assumes the conversion of all outstanding preferred stock of the Company, the exercise of all authorized and currently existing stock options and warrants of the Company, and the increase of the Company's existing option pool by [] shares prior to this financing.

276   Appendix A: Sample Term Sheet

POST-CLOSING CAPITILIZATION TABLE

	Shares	Percentage
Common Stock Outstanding		
Employee Stock Options: Reserved Pool		
Series A Preferred Outstanding: Acme		
[Other Investors]		
Fully Diluted Shares		

Type of Security:	Series A Convertible Preferred Stock (the "Series A Preferred"), initially convertible on a 1:1 basis into shares of the Company's Common Stock (the "Common Stock").
Closing:	Sale of the Series A Preferred (the "Closing") is anticipated to take place on _____.

TERMS OF SERIES A PREFERRED STOCK

Dividends:	The holders of the Series A Preferred shall be entitled to receive noncumulative dividends in preference to any dividend on the Common Stock at the rate of **[6–10%]** of the Original Purchase Price per annum **[when and as declared by the Board of Directors]**. The holders of Series A Preferred also shall be entitled to participate pro rata in any dividends paid on the Common Stock on an as-if-converted basis. **[*Adding the second bolded section means discretionary dividends, otherwise automatic.*]**
Liquidation Preference:	In the event of any liquidation or winding up of the Company, the holders of the Series A Preferred shall be entitled to receive in preference to the holders of the Common Stock a per share amount equal to **[2×]** the Original Purchase Price plus any declared but unpaid dividends (the "Liquidation Preference").

[*Choose one of the following three options:*] [*Option 1: Add this paragraph if you want fully participating preferred:* After the payment of the Liquidation Preference to the holders of the Series A Preferred, the remaining assets shall be distributed ratably to the holders of the Common Stock and the Series A Preferred on a common equivalent basis.]

[*Option 2: Add this paragraph if you want participating preferred:* After the payment of the Liquidation Preference to the holders of the Series A Preferred, the remaining assets shall be distributed ratably to the holders of the Common Stock and the Series A Preferred on a common equivalent basis; provided that the holders of Series A Preferred will stop participating once they have received a total liquidation amount per share equal to [two to five] times the Original Purchase Price, plus any declared but unpaid dividends. Thereafter, the remaining assets shall be distributed ratably to the holders of the Common Stock.]

[*Option 3: Add this paragraph if you want nonparticipating preferred:* After the payment of the Liquidation Preference to the holders of the Series A Preferred, the remaining assets shall be distributed ratably to the holders of the Common Stock.]

Don't use if stock we are buying is fully participating. [Upon any liquidation or deemed liquidation, holder of the Series A Preferred shall be entitled to receive the greater of (i) the amount they would have received pursuant to the prior sentence, or (ii) the amount they would have received in the event of conversion of the Series A Preferred to Common Stock, in each case taking into account any carve-outs, escrows, or other delayed or contingent payments.]

A merger, acquisition, sale of voting control, or sale of substantially all of the assets of the Company in which the shareholders of the Company do not own a majority of the outstanding shares of the surviving corporation shall be deemed to be a liquidation.

Conversion: The holders of the Series A Preferred shall have the right to convert the Series A Preferred, at any time, into shares of Common Stock. The initial conversion rate shall be 1:1, subject to adjustment as provided below.

Automatic Conversion: All of the Series A Preferred shall be automatically converted into Common Stock, at the then applicable conversion price, upon the closing of a firmly underwritten public offering of shares of Common Stock of the Company at a per share price not less than **[three to five]** times the Original Purchase Price (as adjusted for stock splits, dividends, and the like) per share and for a total offering of not less than **[$15]** million (before deduction of underwriters' commissions and expenses) (a "Qualified IPO"). All, or a portion of each share, of the Series A Preferred shall be automatically converted into Common Stock, at the then applicable conversion price in the event that the holders of at least a majority of the outstanding Series A Preferred consent to such conversion.

Antidilution Provisions: The conversion price of the Series A Preferred will be subject to a [full ratchet/weighted average] adjustment to reduce dilution in the event that the Company issues additional equity securities (other than shares (i) reserved as employee shares described under "Employee Pool" below; (ii) shares issued for consideration other than cash pursuant to a merger, consolidation, acquisition, or similar business combination approved by the Board; (iii) shares issued pursuant to any equipment loan or leasing arrangement, real property leasing arrangement, or debt financing from a bank or similar financial institution approved by the Board; and (iv) shares with respect to which the holders of a majority of the outstanding Series A Preferred waive their antidilution rights) at a purchase price less than the applicable conversion price. In the event of an issuance of stock involving tranches or other multiple closings, the antidilution adjustment shall be calculated as if all stock was issued at the first closing. The conversion price will [also] be subject to proportional adjustment for stock splits, stock dividends, combinations, recapitalizations, and the like.

[Redemption at Option of Investors: At the election of the holders of at least a majority of the Series A Preferred, the Company shall redeem the outstanding Series A Preferred in three annual installments beginning on the [fifth] anniversary of the Closing. Such redemptions shall be at a purchase price equal to the Original Purchase Price plus declared and unpaid dividends.]

Voting Rights:	The Series A Preferred will vote together with the Common Stock and not as a separate class except as specifically provided herein or as otherwise required by law. The Common Stock may be increased or decreased by the vote of holders of a majority of the Common Stock and Series A Preferred voting together on an as-if-converted basis, and without a separate class vote. Each share of Series A Preferred shall have a number of votes equal to the number of shares of Common Stock then issuable upon conversion of such share of Series A Preferred.
Board of Directors:	The size of the Company's Board of Directors shall be set at [_____]. The Board shall initially be comprised of _____, as the Acme representative**[s]** _____, and_____.

At each meeting for the election of directors, the holders of the Series A Preferred, voting as a separate class, shall be entitled to elect **[one]** member**[s]** of the Company's Board of Directors, which director shall be designated by Acme; the holders of Common Stock, voting as a separate class, shall be entitled to elect **[one]** member**[s]**; and the remaining directors will be

[*Option 1 (if Acme to control more than 50% of the capital stock):* mutually agreed upon by the Common and Preferred, voting together as a single class] [or *Option 2 (if Acme controls less than 50%):* chosen by the mutual consent of the Board of Directors]. *Please note that you may want to make one of the Common seats the person then serving as the CEO*].

[*Add this provision if Acme is to get an observer on the Board:* Acme shall have the right to appoint a representative to observe all meetings of the Board of Directors in a nonvoting capacity.]

The Company shall reimburse expenses of the Series A Preferred directors **[observers]** and advisers for costs incurred in attending meetings of the Board of Directors and other meetings or events attended on behalf of the Company.

Protective Provisions:	For so long as any shares of Series A Preferred remain outstanding, consent of the holders of at least a majority of the Series A Preferred shall be required for any action, whether directly or through any merger, recapitalization, or similar event, that (i) alters or changes the rights, preferences, or privileges of the Series A Preferred; (ii) increases or decreases the authorized number of shares of Common or Preferred Stock; (iii) creates (by reclassification or otherwise) any new class or series of shares having rights, preferences, or privileges senior to or on a parity with the Series A Preferred; (iv) results in the redemption or repurchase of any shares of Common Stock (other than pursuant to equity incentive agreements with service providers giving the Company the right to repurchase shares upon the termination of services); (v) results in any merger, other corporate reorganization, sale of control, or any transaction in which all or substantially all of the assets of the Company are sold; (vi) amends or waives any provision of the Company's Certificate of Incorporation or Bylaws; (vii) increases or decreases the authorized size of the Company's Board of Directors; **[or]** (viii) results in the payment or declaration of any dividend on any shares of Common or Preferred Stock **[or (ix) issuance of debt in excess of ($100,000)]**.

Pay-to-Play:

[*Version 1:* In the event of a Qualified Financing (as defined below), shares of Series A Preferred held by any Investor which is offered the right to participate but does not participate fully in such financing by purchasing at least its pro rata portion as calculated above under "Right of First Refusal" below will be converted into Common Stock.]

[*Version 2:* If any holder of Series A Preferred Stock fails to participate in the next Qualified Financing (as defined below), on a pro rata basis (according to its total equity ownership immediately before such financing) of their Series A Preferred investment, then such holder will have the Series A Preferred Stock it owns converted into Common Stock of the Company. If such holder participates in the next Qualified Financing but not to the full extent of its pro rata share, then only a percentage of its Series A Preferred Stock will be converted into Common Stock (under the same terms as in the preceding sentence), with such percentage being equal to the percentage of its pro rata contribution that it failed to contribute.]

A Qualified Financing is the next round of financing after the Series A financing by the Company that is approved by the Board of Directors who determine in good faith that such portion must be purchased pro rata among the stockholders of the Company subject to this provision. Such determination will be made regardless of whether the price is higher or lower than any series of Preferred Stock.

When determining the number of shares held by an Investor or whether this "Pay-to-Play" provision has been satisfied, all shares held by or purchased in the Qualified Financing by affiliated investment funds shall be aggregated. An Investor shall be entitled to assign its rights to participate in this financing and future financings to its affiliated funds and to investors in the Investor and/or its affiliated funds, including funds that are not current stockholders of the Company.

Information Rights:

So long as an Investor continues to hold shares of Series A Preferred or Common Stock issued upon conversion of the Series A Preferred, the Company shall deliver to the Investor the Company's annual budget, as well as audited annual and unaudited quarterly financial statements. Furthermore, as soon as reasonably possible, the Company shall furnish a report to each Investor comparing each annual budget to such financial statements. Each Investor shall also be entitled to standard inspection and visitation rights. These provisions shall terminate upon a Qualified IPO.

Registration Rights:

Demand Rights: If Investors holding more than 50 percent of the outstanding shares of Series A Preferred, including Common Stock issued on conversion of Series A Preferred ("Registrable Securities"), or a lesser percentage if the anticipated aggregate offering price to the public is not less than $5 million, request that the Company file a Registration Statement, the Company will use its best efforts to cause such shares to be registered; provided, however, that the Company shall not be obligated to effect any such registration prior to the **[third]** anniversary of the Closing. The Company shall have the right to delay such registration under certain circumstances for one period not in excess of ninety (90) days in any twelve (12)-month period.

The Company shall not be obligated to effect more than two (2) registrations under these demand right provisions, and shall not be obligated to effect a registration (i) during the one hundred eighty (180) day period commencing with the date of the Company's initial public offering, or (ii) if it delivers notice to the holders of the Registrable Securities within thirty (30) days of any registration request of its intent to file a registration statement for such initial public offering within ninety (90) days.

Company Registration: The Investors shall be entitled to "piggyback" registration rights on all registrations of the Company or on any demand registrations of any other Investor subject to the right, however, of the Company and its underwriters to reduce the number of shares proposed to be registered pro rata in view of market conditions. If the Investors are so limited, however, no party shall sell shares in such registration other than the Company or the Investor, if any, invoking the demand registration. Unless the registration is with respect to the Company's initial public offering, in no event shall the shares to be sold by the Investors be reduced below 30 percent of the total amount of securities included in the registration. No shareholder of the Company shall be granted piggyback registration rights, which would reduce the number of shares includable by the holders of the Registrable Securities in such registration without the consent of the holders of at least a majority of the Registrable Securities.

S-3 Rights: Investors shall be entitled to unlimited demand registrations on Form S-3 (if available to the Company) so long as such registered offerings are not less than $1 million.

Expenses: The Company shall bear registration expenses (exclusive of underwriting discounts and commissions) of all such demands, piggybacks, and S-3 registrations (including the expense of one special counsel of the selling shareholders not to exceed $25,000).

Transfer of Rights: The registration rights may be transferred to (i) any partner, member, or retired partner or member or affiliated fund of any holder which is a partnership; (ii) any member or former member of any holder which is a limited liability company; (iii) any family member or trust for the benefit of any individual holder; or (iv) any transferee which satisfies the criteria to be a Major Investor (as defined below); provided the Company is given written notice thereof.

Lockup Provision: Each Investor agrees that it will not sell its shares for a period to be specified by the managing underwriter (but not to exceed 180 days) following the effective date of the Company's initial public offering; provided that all officers, directors, and other 1 percent shareholders are similarly bound. Such lockup agreement shall provide that any discretionary waiver or termination of the restrictions of such agreements by the Company or representatives of underwriters shall apply to Major Investors, pro rata, based on the number of shares held.

Other Provisions: Other provisions shall be contained in the Investor Rights Agreement with respect to registration rights as are reasonable, including cross-indemnification, the period of time in which the Registration Statement shall be kept effective, and underwriting arrangements. The Company shall not require the opinion of Investor's counsel before authorizing the transfer of stock or the removal of Rule 144 legends for routine sales under Rule 144 or for distribution to partners or members of Investors.

Right of First Refusal:	Investors who purchase at least ( ) shares of Series A Preferred (a "Major Investor") shall have the right in the event the Company proposes to offer equity securities to any person (other than the shares (i) reserved as employee shares described under "Employee Pool" below; (ii) shares issued for consideration other than cash pursuant to a merger, consolidation, acquisition, or similar business combination approved by the Board; (iii) shares issued pursuant to any equipment loan or leasing arrangement, real property leasing arrangement, or debt financing from a bank or similar financial institution approved by the Board; and (iv) shares with respect to which the holders of a majority of the outstanding Series A Preferred waive their right of first refusal) to purchase **[2 times]** their pro rata portion of such shares. Any securities not subscribed for by an eligible Investor may be reallocated among the other eligible Investors. Such right of first refusal will terminate upon a Qualified IPO. For purposes of this right of first refusal, an Investor's pro rata right shall be equal to the ratio of (a) the number of shares of common stock (including all shares of common stock issuable or issued upon the conversion of convertible securities and assuming the exercise of all outstanding warrants and options) held by such Investor immediately prior to the issuance of such equity securities to (b) the total number of shares of common stock outstanding (including all shares of common stock issuable or issued upon the conversion of convertible securities and assuming the exercise of all outstanding warrants and options) immediately prior to the issuance of such equity securities.
Purchase Agreement:	The investment shall be made pursuant to a Stock Purchase Agreement reasonably acceptable to the Company and the Investors, which agreement shall contain, among other things, appropriate representations and warranties of the Company, covenants of the Company reflecting the provisions set forth herein, and appropriate conditions of closing, including a management rights letter and an opinion of counsel for the Company.

EMPLOYEE MATTERS

Employee Pool:	Prior to the Closing, the Company will reserve shares of its Common Stock so that ____ % of its fully diluted capital stock following the issuance of its Series A Preferred is available for future issuances to directors, officers, employees, and consultants. The term "Employee Pool" shall include both shares reserved for issuance as stated above, as well as current options outstanding, which aggregate amount is approximately ____% of the Company's fully diluted capital stock following the issuance of its Series A Preferred.

Stock Vesting:	All stock and stock equivalents issued after the Closing to employees, directors, consultants, and other service providers will be subject to vesting provisions below unless different vesting is approved by the **[unanimous/majority (including the director designated by Acme) *or* (including at least one director) designated by the Investors)]** consent of the Board of Directors (the "Required Approval"): 25% to vest at the end of the first year following such issuance, with the remaining 75% to vest monthly over the next three years. The repurchase option shall provide that upon termination of the employment of the shareholder, with or without cause, the Company or its assignee (to the extent permissible under applicable securities law qualification) retains the option to repurchase at the lower of cost or the current fair market value any unvested shares held by such shareholder. Any issuance of shares in excess of the Employee Pool not approved by the Required Approval will be a dilutive event requiring adjustment of the conversion price as provided above and will be subject to the Investors' first offer rights.

The outstanding Common Stock currently held by ___ and ___ (the "Founders") will be subject to similar vesting terms **[provided that the Founders shall be credited with (*one year*) of vesting as of the Closing, with their remaining unvested shares to vest monthly over three years]**.

In the event of a merger, consolidation, sale of assets, or other change of control of the Company and should **[a Founder] [or an Employee]** be terminated without cause within one year after such event, such person shall be entitled to **[one year]** of additional vesting. Other than the foregoing, there shall be no accelerated vesting in any event.

Restrictions on Sales:	The Company's Bylaws shall contain a right of first refusal on all transfers of Common Stock, subject to normal exceptions. If the Company elects not to exercise its right, the Company shall assign its right to the Investors.
Proprietary Information and Inventions Agreement:	Each current and former officer, employee, and consultant of the Company shall enter into an acceptable proprietary information and inventions agreement.
[Drag-Along Agreement:	**The holders of the (Founders/Common Stock) Series A Preferred shall enter into a drag-along agreement whereby if a majority of the holders of Series A Preferred agree to a sale or liquidation of the Company, the holders of the remaining Series A Preferred (and Common Stock) shall consent to and raise no objections to such sale.]**
Co-Sale Agreement:	The shares of the Company's securities held by the Founders shall be made subject to a co-sale agreement (with certain reasonable exceptions) with the Investors such that the Founders may not sell, transfer, or exchange their stock unless each Investor has an opportunity to participate in the sale on a pro rata basis. This right of co-sale shall not apply to and shall terminate upon a Qualified IPO.
[Founders' Activities:	**Each of the Founders shall devote 100% of his professional time to the Company. Any other professional activities will require the approval of the Board of Directors. Additionally, when a Founder leaves the Company, such Founder shall agree to vote his Common Stock or Series A Preferred (or Common Stock acquired on conversion of Series A or Former Series A Preferred) in the same proportion as all other shares are voted in any vote.]**

[*Optional Section*] [Key Man Insurance:	The Company shall procure key man life insurance policies for each of the Founders in the amount of ($3 million), naming the Company as beneficiary.]
[*Optional Section*] [Executive Search:	The Company will use its best efforts to hire a (CEO/CFO/CTO) acceptable to the Investors as soon as practicable following the Closing.]

OTHER MATTERS

[Initial Public Offering Shares Purchase:	In the event that the Company shall consummate a Qualified IPO, the Company shall use its best efforts to cause the managing underwriter or underwriters of such IPO to offer to Acme the right to purchase at least (5%) of any shares issued under a "friends and family" or "directed shares" program in connection with such Qualified IPO. Notwithstanding the foregoing, all action taken pursuant to this Section shall be made in accordance with all federal and state securities laws, including, without limitation, Rule 134 of the Securities Act of 1933, as amended, and all applicable rules and regulations promulgated by the National Association of Securities Dealers, Inc. and other such self-regulating organizations.]
No-Shop Agreement:	The Company agrees to work in good faith expeditiously toward a closing. The Company and the Founders agree that they will not, directly or indirectly, (i) take any action to solicit, initiate, encourage, or assist the submission of any proposal, negotiation, or offer from any person or entity other than the Investors relating to the sale or issuance of any of the capital stock of the Company or the acquisition, sale, lease, license, or other disposition of the Company or any material part of the stock or assets of the Company; or (ii) enter into any discussions or negotiations, or execute any agreement related to any of the foregoing, and shall notify the Investors promptly of any inquiries by any third parties in regard to the foregoing. Should both parties agree that definitive documents shall not be executed pursuant to this term sheet, then the Company shall have no further obligations under this section.
Capitalization/Fact Sheet:	The Company shall provide prior to the Closing an updated, post-closing capitalization chart and a list of corporate officers with both business and personal contact information.
Indemnification:	The bylaws and/or other charter documents of the Company shall limit board members' liability and exposure to damages to the broadest extent permitted by applicable law.
[Insurance:	The Company will use its best efforts to obtain directors and officers insurance acceptable to Investors as soon as practicable after the Closing.]
Right to Conduct Activities:	The Company and each Investor hereby acknowledge that some or all of the Investors are professional investment funds, and as such invest in numerous portfolio companies, some of which may be competitive with the Company's business. No Investor shall be liable to the Company or to any other Investor for any claim arising out of, or based upon, (i) the investment by any Investor in any entity competitive to the Company; or (ii) actions taken by any partner, officer, or other representative of any Investor to assist any such competitive company, whether or not such action was taken as a board member of such competitive company, or otherwise, and whether or not such action has a detrimental effect on the Company.

Assignment:	Each of the Investors shall be entitled to transfer all or part of its shares of Series A Preferred purchased by it to one or more affiliated partnerships or funds managed by it or any or their respective directors, officers, or partners, provided such transferee agrees in writing to be subject to the terms of the Stock Purchase Agreement and related agreements as if it were a purchaser thereunder.
Legal Fees and Expenses:	The Company shall bear its own fees and expenses and shall pay at the closing (or in the event the transaction is not consummated, upon notice by Acme that it is terminating negotiations with respect to the consummated transactions) the reasonable fees (not to exceed $___,000) and expenses of **[our counsel]** regardless if any transactions contemplated by this term sheet are actually consummated.
Governing Law:	This summary of terms shall be governed in all respects by the laws of the State of Delaware.
Conditions Precedent to Financing:	Except for the provisions contained herein entitled "Legal Fees and Expenses," "No-Shop Agreement," "Right to Conduct Activities," and "Governing Law," which are explicitly agreed by the Investors and the Company to be binding upon execution of this term sheet, this summary of terms is not intended as a legally binding commitment by the Investors, and any obligation on the part of the Investors is subject to the following conditions precedent:

1. Completion of legal documentation satisfactory to the prospective Investors.

2. Satisfactory completion of due diligence by the prospective Investors.

3. Delivery of a customary management rights letter to Acme.

[4. **Submission of detailed budget for the following twelve (12) months, acceptable to Investors.**]

[5. **The Company shall initiate a rights offering allowing all current "accredited" shareholders the right to participate proratably in the transactions contemplated herein.**]

Finders:	The Company and the Investors shall each indemnify the other for any broker's or finder's fees for which either is responsible.
Acme Counsel:	**TBD**

Acknowledged and agreed:

ACME VENTURE CAPITAL 2018, LP

By: _____

Print Name: _____

Title: _____

NEWCO.COM

By: _____

Print Name: _____

Title: _____

Appendix B: Foundry Group Term Sheet[1]

FOUNDRY VENTURE CAPITAL 2018, L.P.
SUMMARY OF TERMS

Company: X

Total Financing: $X million [(including approximately $X from the conversion of bridge notes)]. Note that if any notes convert at discount or a capped conversion valuation lower than the pre-money valuation listed below the notes shall convert into combination of: (i) Preferred Stock such that holders receive no more than a 1 × nonparticipating liquidation preference equal to the outstanding principal amount of such notes, plus any agreed interest, and (ii) Common Stock representing the balance of the total shares required to be issued pursuant to the notes.

Stock Purchased: Series X Preferred **("Preferred Stock")**

Investors and Amounts: Foundry Venture
Capital 2018, L.P. (**"Foundry"**) $X

[Investor 2] $X

Total (all investors together,
the "**Investors**") $X

Unissued Employee Pool: X%

Pre-Money Valuation: $X

---

[1] In 2016, Jason decided to redo the standard Foundry Group term sheet so that everything that needed to be changed was on the first page. This is the revised term sheet that we use at Foundry Group for a starting point for all financings. In many cases, we don't even use a term sheet anymore and just go straight to draft documents from a set of email bullet points around terms.

285

Voting: A vote of **[at least ___%] [a majority]** of the Preferred Stock (the "**Required Preferred**") will be required for any action by the Preferred Stock.

Founders: X and X

The existing vesting terms of the Founders' restricted stock shall remain in effect

Board of Directors: The Board of Directors ("**Board**") shall be set at **[three]** directors as follows

Director Seat	Investor Designee	Name
Preferred Director	Foundry	•
Common Director	Current CEO	•
[Mutual Director		•]

Legal Fee Cap: **$X**

Major Investor Threshold: **$250,000**

Estimated Closing Date: **X**

This Summary of Terms incorporates by reference all of the Foundry Standard Investment Terms attached here to (the "Standard Investment Terms"). Capitalized terms used herein but not otherwise defined shall have the meanings set forth in the Standard Investment Terms. In the event of any conflict between the terms set forth in this Summary of Terms and the Standard Investment Terms (collectively, the "Terms"), this Summary of Terms shall control. Except for "No Shop Agreement," "Confidentiality," and "Governing Law," which are explicitly agreed by the Investors and the Company to be binding upon execution of this Summary of Terms, the Terms are not a legally binding commitment by the Investors or the Company, and any obligation on the part of the Investors shall be subject to the following conditions precedent: completion and execution definitive satisfactory to the Investors, satisfactory completion of due diligence by the Investors, and delivery of all closing deliverables described in the definitive agreements.

Foundry Venture Capital 2018, L.P.   **Name of Awesome Startup**

By: _____   By: _____

Print Name/Title: _____   Print Name/Title: _____

Date: _____   Date: _____

FOUNDRY STANDARD INVESTMENT TERMS

The following terms and conditions are Foundry's standard investment terms (the "**Standard Investment Terms**"). Capitalized terms used herein but not otherwise defined shall have the meanings set forth in the Summary of Terms to which these Standard Investment Terms are incorporated by reference.

Capitalization:
For purposes of the Terms, any reference to "fully-diluted" shall include the conversion of all outstanding Preferred Stock of the Company, the exercise of all authorized and currently outstanding stock options and warrants of the Company, and the Employee Pool (as defined below).

Purchase Price:
The per share price of the Preferred Stock (the "**Purchase Price**") shall be calculated by dividing the Pre-Money Valuation set forth in the Summary of Terms by the fully-diluted capitalization (including the Employee Pool) as of immediately prior to the closing.

Board Composition:
At the closing the size of the Board shall be set at the number of directors set forth in the Summary of Terms. The Preferred Director(s) set forth in the Summary of Terms shall be elected by the holders of Preferred Stock and shall be designated by the Investors set forth in the Summary of Terms (the "**Preferred Directors**"). The Common Director(s) set forth in the Summary of Terms shall be elected by the holders of Common Stock, one of which shall be the Company's current chief executive officer (the "**Common Director**"). The Mutual Director(s) set forth in the Summary of Terms shall be elected by the holders of Common Stock and Preferred Stock voting together on an as-converted basis and shall be designated by the mutual consent of the other members of the Board (the "**Mutual Directors**"). The Company shall reimburse expenses of the Preferred Director(s) for costs incurred in attending meetings of the Board and other meetings or events attended on behalf of the Company.

Dividends:
Six percent (6%) non-cumulative dividend preference, when and as declared by the Board; pro rata participation in any Common Stock dividends.

Liquidation
Preference:
In the event of any liquidation or winding up of the Company, the holders of the Preferred Stock shall be entitled to receive in preference to the holders of the Common Stock a per share amount equal to the Purchase Price plus any declared but unpaid dividends (the "Liquidation Preference").

After the payment of the Liquidation Preference to the holders of the Preferred Stock, the remaining assets shall be distributed ratably to the holders of the Common Stock.

A merger, acquisition, sale of voting control in which the stockholders of the Company do not own a majority of the outstanding shares of the surviving corporation, or sale of all or substantially all of the assets of the Company (each a "**Change in Control**") shall be deemed to be a liquidation. Any acquisition agreement that provides for escrowed or other contingent consideration will provide that the allocation of such contingent amounts properly accounts for the liquidation preference of the Preferred Stock.

Preferred Stock Conversion:	Convertible into shares of Common Stock at any time at the election of each holder. The initial conversion rate shall be 1:1, subject to adjustment as provided below.
Automatic Conversion:	All of the Preferred Stock shall automatically convert into Common Stock upon the closing of a firmly underwritten public offering of shares of Common Stock of the Company for a total offering of not less than $50 million (before deduction of underwriter's commissions and expenses) (a "**Qualified IPO**"). The Preferred Stock shall convert into Common Stock upon the election of the Required Preferred.
Antidilution Provisions:	The conversion price of the Preferred Stock will be subject to a weighted-average adjustment to reduce dilution in the event that the Company issues additional equity securities, other than (i) shares or options to purchase shares issued to employees, consultants or directors as approved by the Board; (ii) shares issued for consideration other than cash pursuant to a merger, consolidation, acquisition or similar business combination approved by the Board; (iii) shares issued pursuant to any equipment loan or leasing arrangement, real property leasing arrangement, or debt financing from a bank or similar financial institution approved by the Board; and (iv) other issuances approved by the Required Preferred from time to time (collectively, "**Excluded Issuances**"). Approval by the Board for any Excluded Issuance must include approval by at least one of the Preferred Directors (**the "Required Board Approval"**). The conversion price will also be subject to proportional adjustment for stock splits, stock dividends, combinations, recapitalizations, and the like. In addition, in the event that the fully-diluted capital of the Company immediately following the closing is not as set forth in the Company's capitalization representations, the conversion price for the Preferred Stock will be automatically adjusted down based on the Pre-Money Valuation set forth in the Summary of Terms and the Company's actual fully-diluted capital.
Voting Rights:	The Preferred Stock will vote together with the Common Stock on an as-converted basis, and not as a separate class except as specifically provided herein or as otherwise required by law. The Common Stock may be increased or decreased by the vote of holders of a majority of the Common Stock and Preferred Stock voting together on an as-if-converted basis, and without a separate class vote.

Protective
Provisions:

For so long as any shares of Preferred Stock remain outstanding, consent of the Required Preferred shall be required for any action, whether directly or through any merger, recapitalization or similar event, that (i) alters or changes the rights, preferences or privileges of the Preferred Stock; (ii) increases or decreases the authorized number of shares of Common Stock or Preferred Stock; (iii) creates (by reclassification or otherwise) any new class or series of shares having rights, preferences or privileges senior to or on a parity with the Preferred Stock; (iv) results in the redemption or repurchase of any shares of Common Stock (other than pursuant to equity incentive agreements with service providers giving the Company the right to repurchase shares upon the termination of services); (v) results in any Change in Control or other liquidation of the Company; (vi) amends or waives any provision of the Company's Certificate of Incorporation or Bylaws; (vii) increases or decreases the authorized size of the Company's Board; (viii) results in the payment or declaration of any dividend on any shares of Common Stock or Preferred Stock; (ix) issues debt of the Company or any subsidiary in excess of $100,000; (x) makes any voluntary petition for bankruptcy or assignment for the benefit of creditors; (xi) enters into any exclusive license, lease, sale, distribution or other disposition of the Company's products or intellectual property; or (xii) (a) sells, issues or distributes any Company-created digital tokens, coins or cryptocurrency (**"Tokens"**), including through any agreement, pre-sale, initial coin offering, token distribution event or crowdfunding, or (b) develops a computer network either incorporating Tokens or permitting the generation of tokens by network participants.

Major Investor:

Any Investor investing an amount equal to or greater than the Major Investor Threshold amount set forth in the Summary of Terms shall be deemed a **"Major Investor."**

Information Rights:

The Company shall, upon request, deliver customary audited annual, unaudited quarterly and monthly financial statements and budgets to each Major Investor. Each Major Investor shall also be entitled to standard inspection and visitation rights.

Registration Rights:

Registration Rights: Two demand registrations, starting the earlier of three years after the closing or 180 days after the Company's initial public offering, so long as the anticipated aggregate offering price to the public is not less than $15,000,000, and unlimited piggy-back and S-3 registration rights with reasonable and customary terms, including cutback rights to no less than 30% (other than in a Qualified IPO), payment of selling stockholder counsel fees up to $35,000, and no limitations on transfers of registration rights to affiliates and other Major Investors.

Lock-Up Provision: Investors will be subject to a customary 180 day post-IPO lockup provided that all officers, directors, and other 1% stockholders are similarly bound; provided further that any discretionary waiver or termination of lock-up provisions shall also apply pro rata to the Major Investors.

<u>Other Provisions:</u> No stockholder of the Company shall be granted registration rights which would reduce the number of shares includable by the holders of the Registrable Securities in a registration without the consent of the holders of a majority of the Registrable Securities. The Company shall not require the opinion of Investor's counsel before authorizing the transfer of stock or the removal of Rule 144 legends for routine sales under Rule 144 or for distribution to partners or members of Investors.

Right of First Refusal: Prior to a Qualified IPO, Major Investors shall have the right to purchase their pro rata portions (calculated on a fully diluted basis) of any future issuances of equity securities by the Company (with overallotment rights in the event a Major Investor does not purchase its full allocation), other than Excluded Issuances.

EMPLOYEE MATTERS

Employee Pool: Prior to the Closing, in addition to currently outstanding options, the Company shall reserve for future issuance pursuant to a mutually acceptable stock option plan (the **"Stock Option Plan"**) a number of shares of Common Stock equal to the percentage of the post-closing fully-diluted capital stock set forth in the Summary of Terms (the **"Employee Pool"**).

Stock Vesting: All stock and stock equivalents issued after the Closing to employees, directors, consultants and other service providers will be issued pursuant to the Stock Option Plan and will be subject to the vesting provisions below unless otherwise approved by the Required Board Approval: 25% to vest on the one-year anniversary of the applicable vesting commencement date with the remaining 75% to vest monthly over the next three years. The repurchase option shall provide that upon termination of the employment of the stockholder, with or without cause, the Company or its assignee (to the extent permissible under applicable securities law qualification) retains the option to repurchase at the lower of cost or the current fair market value any unvested shares held by such stockholder. Except as set forth in the Summary of Terms there shall be no accelerated vesting except with Required Board Approval.

The outstanding Common Stock currently held by the Founders will be subject to the vesting terms set forth in the Summary of Terms. "**Double Trigger Acceleration**" shall mean full acceleration of all unvested shares in the event that (i) a Change in Control (as defined in the Stock Option Plan documents) occurs and (ii) as of, or within thirteen (13) months after, the effective time of such Change in Control the stockholder's Continuous Service (as defined in the Stock Option Plan documents) with the Company terminates due to an involuntary termination (not including death or disability) without Cause (as defined in the Stock Option Plan documents) or due to a voluntary termination with Good Reason (as defined in the Stock Option Plan documents); *provided that,* as a condition precedent of any accelerated vesting, the stockholder must sign, date and return to the Company a general release of all known and unknown claims in the form satisfactory to the Company (or its successor, if applicable), and must permit the applicable revocation period (if any) to expire unexercised.

Restrictions on Sales:	The Company's Bylaws shall contain a right of first refusal on all transfers of Common Stock, subject to normal exceptions. If the Company elects not to exercise its right, the Company shall assign its right to the Major Investors. The Company's Bylaws shall also contain a provision providing that no shares of capital stock other than those held by Major Investors may be transferred except as approved by the Board in its discretion, which shall include, without limitation, refusal to allow any transfer to the extent such transfer would increase the number of stockholders of the Company or require it to register, or register any class of equity securities, with the Securities and Exchange Commission. If the Company's Bylaws cannot be amended to include such provisions, the Company shall take such other steps as are necessary to impose the rights of first refusal and transfer restrictions set forth above on all outstanding shares of the Company's Common Stock.
Proprietary Information and Inventions Agreement:	Each current and former officer, employee and consultant of the Company shall enter into an acceptable proprietary information and inventions agreement.
Co-Sale Agreement:	The shares of the Company's securities held by the Founders shall be made subject to a co-sale agreement (with certain reasonable exceptions) with the Investors such that the Founders may not sell, transfer or exchange their stock unless each Investor has an opportunity to participate in the sale on a pro-rata basis.
Voting Agreement:	The Investors, the Founders and each current and future holder of stock, warrants or options to purchase stock shall enter a Voting Agreement that provides the following:
	(i) that such stockholders will vote for the election of the members of the Board as provided in the Summary of Terms;
	(ii) that such stockholders will vote all of their shares in favor of a Change in Control or transaction in which 50% or more of the voting power of the Company is transferred, provided such Change in Control or other transaction is approved by (a) the Board, (b) the Required Preferred, and (c) the holders of a majority of the Common Stock held by stockholders then providing services to the Company as an employee or officer; and
	(iii) when a Founder leaves the Company, such Founder will vote all of his or her Common Stock and Preferred Stock (or Common Stock acquired on conversion of Preferred Stock) in the same proportion as all other shares are voted in any vote.
	The Company's Stock Option Plan documents shall require all option holders to execute a counterpart signature page to the Voting Agreement as a condition precedent to the exercise of any option.
Founders Activities:	Each of the Founders and executive officers shall devote 100% of his or her professional time to the Company. Any other professional activities will require the prior approval of the Board.

OTHER MATTERS

Closing Deliverables:	The Company shall provide at or prior to the closing: (i) a post-closing capitalization chart; (ii) a customary management rights letter addressed to Foundry; (iii) a standard opinion of counsel for the Company; and (iv) a QSBS Questionnaire.
Post-Closing Matters:	Within 30 days of Closing, the Company shall (i) obtain D&O insurance in an amount and upon terms acceptable to Foundry and (ii) implement Carta (formerly known as eShares) (http://carta.com) to manage its capitalization table and to issue share certificates, options, warrants and other securities.
Agreements:	The sale of the Preferred Stock shall be made pursuant to a purchase agreement with customary representations and warranties. The purchase agreement, investor rights agreement, co-sale agreement and voting agreement may be amended with the consent of the Company and the Required Preferred, with the co-sale agreement and voting agreement requiring the consent of a majority of the Founders then providing services to the Company as an officer or employee for any change adversely effecting such Founders. Unless otherwise agreed, counsel to the Company will draft the financing documents based on the NVCA form documents. To expedite their preparation, Foundry will provide NVCA forms that implement these Standard Investment Terms.
Legal Fees and Expenses:	The Company shall pay at the closing the reasonable fees (not to exceed the legal fee cap set forth on the Summary of Terms) and expenses of Foundry's counsel in connection with this transaction.
Assignment:	Each of the Investors shall be entitled to transfer all or part of its shares of Preferred Stock to one or more affiliated partnerships or funds managed by it or any of their respective directors, officers or partners, provided such transferee agrees in writing to be subject to the terms of the investor rights agreement, co-sale agreement and voting agreement as if it were an original investor thereunder.
Right to Conduct Activities:	The Company and each Investor hereby acknowledge that Foundry is a group of professional investment funds, and as such invest in numerous portfolio companies, some of which may be competitive with the Company's business. Neither Foundry nor any other Investor shall be liable to the Company or to any other Investor for any claim arising out of, or based upon, (i) the investment by Investor in any entity competitive to the Company; or (ii) actions taken by any partner, officer or other representative of such Investor to assist any such competitive company, whether or not such action was taken as a board member of such competitive company, or otherwise, and whether or not such action has a detrimental effect on the Company; provided, however that nothing herein shall relieve any Investor or any party from liability associated with misuse of the Company's confidential information. The Company's certificate of incorporation shall contain a limited waiver of the corporate opportunity doctrine with respect to matters or transactions presented to the Series A director other than solely in his capacity as a director of the Company.

No Shop Agreement:	The Company agrees to work in good faith expeditiously toward a closing. The Company and the Founders agree that until the 60th day from the date on which the Summary of Terms was signed by both Foundry and the Company they will not, directly or indirectly, (i) take any action to solicit, initiate, encourage or assist the submission of any proposal, negotiation or offer from any person or entity other than the Investors relating to the sale or issuance, of any of the capital stock of the Company or the acquisition, sale, lease, license or other disposition of the Company or any material part of the stock or assets of the Company; or (ii) enter into any discussions, negotiations or execute any agreement related to any of the foregoing, and shall notify the Investors promptly of any inquiries by any third parties in regards to the foregoing. Should both parties agree that definitive documents shall not be executed pursuant to the Terms, then the Company shall have no further obligations under this section.
Confidentiality:	The Terms and any related discussions and correspondence are to be held in strict confidence by the Company and may not be disclosed by the Company to any party (other than counsel to, and the accountants of, the parties to the extent reasonably necessary for such persons to render advice in connection with the proposed transaction and other than to existing stockholders of the Company) without the prior written approval of Foundry.
Governing Law:	The Terms shall be governed in all respects by the laws of the State of Delaware.

Appendix C: Sample Letter of Intent

_____, 20____

[Seller]
[Address]
Re: Proposal to Purchase Stock of the Company
Dear Seller:
This letter is intended to summarize the principal terms of a proposal being considered by _____ (the "Buyer") regarding its possible acquisition of all of the outstanding capital stock of _____ (the "Company") from _____ ("A") and _____ ("B") _____, who are the Company's sole stockholders (the "Sellers"). In this letter, (i) the Buyer and the Sellers are sometimes called the "Parties," (ii) the Company and its subsidiaries are sometimes called the "Target Companies," and (iii) the Buyer's possible acquisition of the stock of the Company is sometimes called the "Possible Acquisition."

The Parties wish to commence negotiating a definitive written acquisition agreement providing for the Possible Acquisition (a "Definitive Agreement"). To facilitate the negotiation of a Definitive Agreement, the Parties request that the Buyer's counsel prepare an initial draft. The execution of any such Definitive Agreement would be subject to the satisfactory completion of the Buyer's ongoing investigation of the Target Companies' business and would also be subject to approval by the Buyer's board of directors.

Part One: Non-Binding Terms

Based on the information currently known to the Buyer, it is proposed that the Definitive Agreement include the following terms:

1. **Basic Transaction**

   The Sellers would sell all of the outstanding capital stock of the Company to the Buyer at the price (the "Purchase Price") set forth in Paragraph 2 below. The closing of this transaction (the "Closing") would occur as soon as possible after the termination of the applicable waiting period under the Hart-Scott-Rodino Antitrust Improvements Act of 1976 (the "HSR Act").

2. **Purchase Price**

   The Purchase Price would be $_____ (subject to adjustment as described below) and would be paid in the following manner:

   (a) At the Closing, the Buyer would pay the Sellers the sum of $_____ in cash;

   (b) at the Closing, the Buyer would deposit with a mutually acceptable escrow agent the sum of $_____, which would be held in escrow for a period of at least ____ years in order to secure the performance of the Sellers' obligations under the Definitive Agreement and related documents; and

   (c) at the Closing, the Buyer would execute and deliver to each Seller an unsecured, nonnegotiable, subordinated promissory note. The promissory notes to be delivered to the Sellers by the Buyer would have a combined principal amount of $_____, would bear interest at the rate of ____% per annum, would mature on the _____ anniversary of the Closing, and would provide for equal [annual] [quarterly] payments of principal along with [annual] [quarterly] payments of accrued interest.

   The Purchase Price assumes that the Target Companies have consolidated stockholders' equity of at least $_____ as of the Closing. The Purchase Price would be adjusted based on changes in the Target Companies' consolidated stockholders' equity as of the Closing, on a dollar-for-dollar basis.

3. **Employment and Noncompetition Agreements**

At the Closing:

(a) the Company and A would enter into a _____ year employment agreement under which A would agree to continue to serve as the Company's [Vice President and Chief Operating Officer] and would be entitled to receive a salary of $_____ per year; and

(b) each Seller would execute a _____ year noncompetition agreement in favor of the Buyer and the Company.

4. **Other Terms**

The Sellers would make comprehensive representations and warranties to the Buyer, and would provide comprehensive covenants, indemnities, and other protections for the benefit of the Buyer. The consummation of the contemplated transactions by the Buyer would be subject to the satisfaction of various conditions, including:

(a) _____

(b) _____

Part Two: Binding Terms

The following paragraphs of this letter (the "Binding Provisions") are the legally binding and enforceable agreements of the Buyer and each Seller.

1. **Access**

During the period from the date this letter is signed by the Sellers (the "Signing Date") until the date on which either Party provides the other Party with written notice that negotiations toward a Definitive Agreement are terminated (the "Termination Date"), the Sellers will afford the Buyer full and free access to each Target Company, its personnel, properties, contracts, books, and records, and all other documents and data.

2. Exclusive Dealing

Until the later of (i) [90] days after the Signing Date or (ii) the Termination Date:

(a) the Sellers will not and will cause the Target Companies not to, directly or indirectly, through any representative or otherwise, solicit or entertain offers from, negotiate with or in any manner encourage, discuss, accept, or consider any proposal of any other person relating to the acquisition of the Shares or the Target Companies, their assets or business, in whole or in part, whether directly or indirectly, through purchase, merger, consolidation, or otherwise (other than sales of inventory in the ordinary course); and

(b) the Sellers will immediately notify the Buyer regarding any contact between the Sellers, any Target Company or their respective representatives, and any other person regarding any such offer or proposal or any related inquiry.

3. Breakup Fee

If (a) the Sellers breach Paragraph 2 or the Sellers provide to the Buyer written notice that negotiations toward a Definitive Agreement are terminated, and (b) within [six] months after the date of such breach or the Termination Date, as the case may be, either Seller or one or more of the Target Companies signs a letter of intent or other agreement relating to the acquisition of a material portion of the Shares or of the Target Companies, their assets, or business, in whole or in part, whether directly or indirectly, through purchase, merger, consolidation, or otherwise (other than sales of inventory or immaterial portions of the Target Companies' assets in the ordinary course) and such transaction is ultimately consummated, then, immediately upon the closing of such transaction, the Sellers will pay, or cause the Target Companies to pay, to the Buyer the sum $_____.

This fee will not serve as the exclusive remedy to the Buyer under this letter in the event of a breach by the Sellers of Paragraph 2 of this Part Two or any other of the Binding Provisions, and the Buyer will be entitled to all other rights and remedies provided by law or in equity.

4. Conduct of Business

During the period from the Signing Date until the Termination Date, the Sellers shall cause the Target Companies to operate their business in the ordinary course and to refrain from any extraordinary transactions.

5. Confidentiality

Except as and to the extent required by law, the Buyer will not disclose or use, and will direct its representatives not to disclose or use to the detriment of the Sellers or the Target Companies, any Confidential Information (as defined below) with respect to the Target Companies furnished, or to be furnished, by either Seller, the Target Companies, or their respective representatives to the Buyer or its representatives at any time or in any manner other than in connection with its evaluation of the transaction proposed in this letter. For purposes of this Paragraph, "Confidential Information" means any information about the Target Companies stamped "confidential" or identified in writing as such to the Buyer by the Sellers promptly following its disclosure, unless (i) such information is already known to the Buyer or its representatives or to others not bound by a duty of confidentiality or such information becomes publicly available through no fault of the Buyer or its representatives, (ii) the use of such information is necessary or appropriate in making any filing or obtaining any consent or approval required for the consummation of the Possible Acquisition, or (iii) the furnishing or use of such information is required by or necessary or appropriate in connection with legal proceedings. Upon the written request of the Sellers, the Buyer will promptly return to the Sellers or the Target Companies or destroy any Confidential Information in its possession and certify in writing to the Sellers that it has done so.

6. Disclosure

Except as and to the extent required by law, without the prior written consent of the other Party, neither the Buyer nor the Seller will make, and each will direct its representatives not to make, directly or indirectly, any public comment, statement, or communication with respect to, or otherwise to disclose or to permit the disclosure of the existence of discussions regarding, a possible transaction between the Parties or any of the terms, conditions, or other aspects of the transaction proposed in this letter. If a Party is required by law to make any such disclosure, it must first provide to the other Party the content of the proposed disclosure, the reasons that such disclosure is required by law, and the time and place that the disclosure will be made.

7. **Costs**

    The Buyer and each Seller will be responsible for and bear all of its own costs and expenses (including any broker's or finder's fees and the expenses of its representatives) incurred at any time in connection with pursuing or con-summating the Possible Acquisition. Notwithstanding the preceding sentence, the Buyer will pay one-half and the Sellers will pay one-half of the HSR Act filing fee.

8. **Consents**

    During the period from the Signing Date until the Termi-nation Date, the Buyer and each Seller will cooperate with each other and proceed, as promptly as is reasonably practi-cal, to prepare and to file the notifications required by the HSR Act.

9. **Entire Agreement**

    The Binding Provisions constitute the entire agreement between the parties, and supersede all prior oral or written agreements, understandings, representations and warran-ties, and courses of conduct and dealing between the parties on the subject matter hereof. Except as otherwise provided herein, the Binding Provisions may be amended or modified only by a writing executed by all of the parties.

10. **Governing Law**

    The Binding Provisions will be governed by and construed under the laws of the State of _____ without regard to conflicts of laws principles.

11. Jurisdiction: Service of Process

Any action or proceeding seeking to enforce any provision of, or based on any right arising out of, this Letter may be brought against any of the parties in the courts of the State of _____, County of _____, or, if it has or can acquire jurisdiction, in the United States District Court for the District of _____, and each of the parties consents to the jurisdiction of such courts (and of the appropriate appellate courts) in any such action or proceeding and waives any objection to venue laid therein. Process in any action or proceeding referred to in the preceding sentence may be served on any party anywhere in the world.

12. Termination

The Binding Provisions will automatically terminate on _____, 20__ and may be terminated earlier upon written notice by either party to the other party unilaterally, for any reason or no reason, with or without cause, at any time; provided, however, that the termination of the Binding Provisions will not affect the liability of a party for breach of any of the Binding Provisions prior to the termination. Upon termination of the Binding Provisions, the parties will have no further obligations hereunder, except as stated in Paragraphs 2, 3, 5, 7, 9, 10, 11, 12, 13, and 14 of this Part Two, which will survive any such termination.

13. Counterparts

This Letter may be executed in one or more counterparts, each of which will be deemed to be an original copy of this Letter and all of which, when taken together, will be deemed to constitute one and the same agreement.

14. No Liability

The paragraphs and provisions of Part One of this letter do not constitute and will not give rise to any legally binding obligation on the part of any of the Parties or any of the Target Companies. Moreover, except as expressly provided in the Binding Provisions (or as expressly provided in any binding written agreement that the Parties may enter into in the future), no past or future action, course of conduct, or failure to act relating to the Possible Acquisition, or relating to the negotiation of the terms of the Possible Acquisition or any Definitive Agreement, will give rise to or serve as a basis for any obligation or other liability on the part of the Parties or any of the Target Companies.

* * *

If you are in agreement with the foregoing, please sign and return one copy of this letter agreement, which thereupon will constitute our agreement with respect to its subject matter.

Very truly yours,
[Buyer]

By: _____
Name: _____
Title: _____

Duly executed and agreed as to the Binding Provisions on:
_____, 20
[Seller]

By: _____
Name: _____
Title: _____

Appendix D: Additional Resources

Since we published the first edition of *Venture Deals* in 2011, there has been a Cambrian explosion of entrepreneurial resources, including many around financing a company. Following are several important ones:

Accelerators: Accelerators modeled after Techstars (www.techstars.com) and Y Combinator(www.ycombinator .com) have emerged all over the world. These programs typically invest a modest amount of money (around $20,000) in companies in exchange for a small amount of equity (typically 6%). In addition, some offer additional financing of $100,000 or more in the form of a convertible note. The companies then go through a 90-day, intensive, full-time program where they accelerate their startup via help from the accelerator, mentors, and the surrounding startup community. Several years ago, Techstars founded the Global Accelerator Network (www.gan.co/) in an effort to link the best accelerators and provide a series of best practices across them.

VentureDeals.com: (www.venturedeals.com) This is the companion website for *Venture Deals* and is maintained by us. On it we have a blog where we answer questions, highlight great blog posts by other VCs, and post new content that eventually finds its way into a future edition of this book. We include the Foundry Group form documents, other forms of financing documents, and sample merger and acquisition (M&A) documents on the site. We also have a list of some of the college courses that use *Venture Deals* along with the syllabus for these courses. The site also has extensive teaching materials that we have created for use with this book.

Equity Crowdfunding: If you are an entrepreneur raising money or are an angel or seed VC looking for seed or early stage investments, there are a number of websites that will help you find each other. The two most popular ones, AngelList (www.angel.co) and Gust (www.gust.com), have become very powerful resources for both entrepreneurs and investors.

Product Crowdfunding: The Internet has given rise to a new form of financing called crowdfunding. Popular sites like Kickstarter (www.kickstarter.com) and Indiegogo (www.indiegogo.com) have popularized the first phase of this, where companies can use crowdfunding to raise money to build their products. In the current model, companies are effectively getting their customers to prepay for their product or service. In April 2012 in the United States, the Jumpstart Our Business Startups (JOBS) Act was passed, which provides for equity crowdfunding.

Databases: A number of private company databases, including Crunchbase (www.crunchbase.com) and Pitchbook (www.pitchbook.com) exist. Keep in mind that with all private company data, accuracy varies a lot, so you'll find plenty of noise in the data, but in general the signal is high. If you don't have a strong VC network, these databases can help you identify the VCs who might be interested in your particular company.

Education: There are an enormous number of entrepreneurship-oriented educational resources on the Web. Several of our favorites include the Kauffman Foundation (www.kauffman.org), Stanford University's Entrepreneurship Corner (http://ecorner.stanford.edu), Khan Academy's venture capital courses (http://bit.ly/2agRJRB), and the Silicon Flatirons Center right here in our hamlet of Boulder, Colorado (www.siliconflatirons.com).

National Venture Capital Association: The NVCA (www.nvca.org) maintains the most widely used set of model documents used in financings (nvca.org/resources/model-legal-documents/).

Other Tech Blogs: There are many tech and VC bloggers who produce significant amounts of excellent content. Several of our good friends, including Fred Wilson (www.avc.com), Mark Suster (www.bothsidesofthetable.com), David Cohen (www.davidgcohen.com), and Seth Levine (www.sethlevine.com), regularly post great stuff. We also read *Pro Rata* by Dan Primack (https://www.axios.com/newsletters/axios-pro-rata/) every day.

Glossary

accelerator   A program intended to mentor founders and accelerate the growth and success of a startup company.

accredited investor   As defined by federal securities laws, a person who is permitted to invest in startups and other high-risk private company securities based on the net worth and income level of the potential investor.

acquisition   A transaction between two companies where one is buying the other.

adverse change redemption   A type of redemption right whereby a shareholder gets the right to redeem his shares if something adverse happens to the company.

advisers   People who advise startup companies. Normally, these people are paid some sort of compensation for their efforts.

affirmative covenants   Action that the company promises to take during the term of the financing contract in a financing.

agency costs   The costs associated in an agency/principal relationship that the principal incurs either directly or indirectly.

alpha   The earliest of early prototypes of a product. This is before the beta, which is still a prototype, but with a lot more polish.

amortization terms   Terms that debt lenders use to better align the debt with the capital strategy of the company.

analyst   A very junior person at a venture capital firm, often a recent college graduate.

angel investor   An individual who provides capital to a startup company. This person is usually independently wealthy and invests her own money in the company.

antidilution   A term that provides price protection for investors. This is accomplished by effectively repricing an investor's shares to a lower price per share in the event that the company completes a financing at a lower valuation than a previous financing round.

as-converted basis   Looking at the equity base of the company assuming that all preferred stock has been converted to common.

assignment   The right of a preferred shareholder to transfer its shares to an affiliated entity without company consent.

associate   A person at a venture capital firm who is involved in deal analysis and management. The seniority of this position varies by firm, but generally associates need a partner to support their activities.

at-will employee   An employee who does not have an employment agreement and can be terminated by the company for any reason.

barter element   The price at which a stock option may be exercised.

basis of stock option   The price at which a stock option may be exercised.

best alternative to negotiated agreement (BATNA)   A backup plan if no agreement is reached between two parties.

beta   A prototype of a product, but more advanced than the alpha. It's not unusual for betas to be released to customers for feedback.

blended preferences   When all classes of preferred stock have equivalent payment rights in a liquidation.

board of directors   A group of people elected by a company's shareholders to represent all the stakeholders of a company. The board is responsible for company oversight including hiring and firing the CEO.

bridge loan   A loan given to a company by investors with the intent that the money will fund the company to the next equity financing.

broad-based antidilution   The denominator in weighted average antidilution calculations that takes into consideration a fully diluted view of the company. The opposite is called a narrow-based antidilution.

burn rate   The amount of money that a company is consuming, usually measured over months, quarters, or a year. This is the net amount of cash that is leaving the bank account over the given time period.

cap   The valuation ceiling that exists in a convertible debt deal.

capital call   The method by which a VC fund asks its investors to contribute their pro rata portion of money being called by a VC fund to make investments, pay expenses, or pay management fees.

capitalization table (cap table)   A spreadsheet that defines the economics of a deal. It contains a detailed description of all the owners of stock of a company.

carry/carried interest   The profits that VCs are entitled to after returning capital committed to their investors. This typically ranges from 20% to 30%.

carve-out (equity)   The concept whereby shareholders agree to give a preferential payment (usually to executives and employees of a company) ahead of the shareholders agreeing to the carve-out. Normally, one would see a carve-out used in the situation where liquidation preferences are such that employees of the company do not have enough financial interests in a liquidation event.

carve-out (merger)   Within the merger context, these are certain representations and warranties that will be indemnified outside of the escrow.

clawback   The provision in the limited partnership agreement that allows investors to take back money from the VC should they overpay themselves with carry.

commitment period   The length of time a venture capital fund has to find and invest in new companies, usually five years.

common stock   The type of stock that has the least amount of rights, privileges, and preferences. Normally employees and founders of a company hold common stock, as the price they pay for the stock can be much less than that of preferred stock.

conditions precedent to financing   A list of items in the term sheet that must be satisfied before an investor will agree to consummate the financing. This can include anything but typically revolves around further due diligence into the company.

control terms   Terms that allow a VC to exert positive or veto control in a deal.

conversion   A process in which preferred stock is converted to common stock.

conversion price adjustment   The mechanism by which an antidilution adjustment takes place. This allows the preferred stock to be converted into more common stock than originally agreed upon and thus allows the preferred to own more stock and voting rights upon converting to common.

convertible debt   A debt or loan instrument that an investor gives to a company with the intent that it will convert later to equity and not be paid back as a standard bank loan would be.

corporate venture capital   A venture firm that is sponsored and backed by a corporation, often but not always part of a publicly traded company.

co-sale   The right of a shareholder (typically a VC) to sell shares alongside another shareholder that is selling some or all of its equity to a buyer.

cross-fund investment   When a venture capital firm operates more than one fund and more than one fund invests in the same company.

crowdfunding   When a group of individuals fund a company either through equity purchase, debt purchase, pre-sale ordering of a product, or gifting of money.

director   A junior deal partner at a venture capital firm.

discount   A standard mechanism in a convertible note agreement that allows noteholders the right to convert the amount of the loan, plus interest, at a reduced price (in percentage terms) to the purchase price paid by equity investors who later consummate a financing.

dividends   An amount of money or shares of stock that is paid out to investors based on their holdings of stock in a company.

double-trigger acceleration   A term that describes the situation in which a person would receive accelerated vesting. In a double-trigger situation, two events would trigger accelerated vesting, such as a merger of the company followed by a termination of a person's employment.

down round   A financing round that is at a lower valuation than the previous round.

drag-along   A term that sets up a proxy on one's stock ownership to vote the same way as others do on a particular issue.

draw period   The time during which cash advances may be requested under a loan (also called the availability period).

due diligence   The process by which investors explore a company that they are thinking of investing in.

early stage funds   VC funds that invest in Seed and Series A financings.

earn-out   An amount agreed upon by an acquirer and a target company that the former shareholders of the target company will get if certain performance milestones are met post-merger.

economic terms   Terms that impact the returns of a VC's investment in a company.

elevator pitch   A short synopsis of what your company does and why it's compelling.

employee option pool   The shares set aside by a company to provide stock options to employees.

enterprise value   The post-money valuation plus debt minus cash.

entrepreneur   Someone who creates a new company, also known as a founder.

entrepreneur in residence (EIR)   A person at a venture firm that is usually a former entrepreneur who is helping out the venture firm by finding deals to invest in, or working on his next company that the venture firm will one day fund.

equity   Ownership in a company.

equity crowdfunding   A financing process made legal by the JOBS Act in 2012 and popularized by AngelList.

escrow   The amount of consideration that an acquiring company holds back following a merger to make sure that representations and warranties made by the purchased company are true.

escrow cap   The amount of money in a merger that is set aside to remedy breaches of the merger agreement.

executive managing director   A senior partner in a venture capital firm who is superior to a managing director or general partner.

executive summary   A short summary document, normally one to three pages, that describes material facts and strategies of a company.

exercise   The act of purchasing stock pursuant to a stock option or warrant.

exercise period   The amount of time an employee can exercise her stock after she leaves a company.

exercise price   The price at which a stock option can be exercised (and subsequently the price per share the employee pays for the stock option).

fair market value   The price that a third party would pay for something in the open market.

fiduciary duties   A legal and ethical duty that an individual has to an entity.

final payments   A loan fee that is paid at the end of the loan.

first right of refusal   A right that allows an investor to have the first ability to either make another investment in the company or acquire the company.

flat round   A financing round done at the same post-money valuation as that of the previous round.

founder   Someone who creates a new company, also known as an entrepreneur.

founders' activities   A provision in the term sheet that mandates that founders spend all of their business time working for the company.

founders' stock   Common stock issued to founders at a very low price at the formation of the company.

founding general partner   A senior partner in a venture capital firm who founded the firm.

full-stack venture capital firms   A venture capital firm that employs many people beyond deal professionals, such as marketing, operations, public relations, engineering, and financial executives, to attempt to help companies more than traditional venture capital firms.

fully diluted   A term explicitly defining that all rights to purchase equity should be in the valuation calculation.

fundamental rep   A representation made by the seller in an acquisition that survives longer than the escrow period.

game theory   The concept that one's actions depend on what actions other persons may or may not take and the inherent incentives behind these actions.

general partner (GP)   A senior partner in a venture capital firm.

general partnership (GP)   The entity that manages the limited partnership.

general solicitation   Fundraising to potential investors without a "substantial preexisting relationship." Some also consider this to be when a startup advertises for funding.

GP commitment   The amount of money, usually between 1% and 5% of the fund, that the general partners invest in their own fund.

growth investors   VC funds that invest in Series B and later financings.

holdback   The amount of consideration that an acquiring company holds back following a merger to make sure that representations and warranties made by the purchased company are true.

indemnification   The promise by one party to protect another party should something go wrong.

information rights   The minimum amount of information the company must give its investors on a regular basis.

initial coin offering   A fundraising mechanism where a company sells crypto tokens instead of equity.

initial public offering shares purchase   A term sheet provision that allows the preferred stockholders to buy shares of the company in an initial public offering.

interest-only (I/O) period   A length of time where only interest (and no principal) is paid on a term loan.

interest rate   One of the key pricing mechanisms in a loan.

investment term   The length of time that a venture capital fund can remain active, typically 10 years with two 1-year extensions.

IRS   Internet Revenue Service (in the United States).

JOBS Act   Formally known as the Jumpstart Our Business Startups Act, enacted in 2012. It created rules around crowdfunding, changed some dynamics around IPOs, and gave Congress a way to say they were helping startups.

key person clause   Contractual provision within the limited partnership agreement that describes what will happen if certain partners leave the venture capital fund.

KISS   An acronym for Keep It Simple Security, which can be an alternative for either a debt or equity financing. See http://500.co/kiss/.

late stage funds   Entities, including VC funds and hedge funds, who invest in the last financing before an IPO.

lead investor   The investor in a startup company who takes on the leadership position in a VC financing.

Lean Startup methodology   A business methodology that posits business-es can reduce product develop cycles by combining iterative releases and experimentations of their product. Popularized by Eric Ries.

letter of intent (LOI)   A term sheet for a merger or acquisition.

light preferred   A version of a preferred stock financing that has very simple and watered-down terms.

limited partners (LPs)   The investors in a VC fund.

limited partnership (LP)   The entity used by the limited partners to invest in a venture capital fund.

limited partnership agreement (LPA)   The contract between a venture capital fund and its investors.

liquidation event/liquidity event   When a company is sold and ceases to exist as a stand-alone company.

liquidation preference   A right given to a class of preferred stock allow-ing that stock to receive proceeds in a liquidation in advance of other classes of stock.

liquidation preference overhang   The cumulative amount of liquidation preferences that a company has agreed to during their existence. The amount of money owed to investors before common stock will receive proceeds.

loan fees   A part of a loan agreement that charges a fixed fee for getting the deal done.

major investor   A concept used in venture capital financings that allows a company to distinguish between shareholders who purchase more stock than others.

management carve-out   An agreement between a company and its preferred shareholders to divert part of the proceeds that would normally flow (pursuant to liquidation preferences) to the preferred shareholders to management and employees upon an acquisition.

management company   The entity that services each fund that a VC raises.

management fee   The fee that the venture capital funds have a right to receive from their LPs as money to manage their business operations regardless of the performance of the fund.

managing director (MD)   A senior partner in a venture capital firm.

materiality qualifiers Inserting the word "material" in front of things, such as protective provisions. Lawyers love to argue about this word.

mentors People who advise startup companies or their executives. Normally, these people are not paid.

micro VC fund A super angel who raises a small fund made up of professional investors.

mid stage funds Another name for growth investors who are VC funds that invest in Series B and later financings.

minimum viable product (MVP) The product with the least number of features necessarily to make it useful to ship and learn more about the users. This concept was made popular by Eric Ries as part of the lean startup methodology.

most favored nation (MFN) The right to get the equivalent terms to anyone who gets better terms than you in the future.

multiplay game A term in game theory that deals with a game or situation where there is a continuing relationship after the game is played, like a venture capital financing whereby after the transaction is completed the VC and the entrepreneur will join forces to work together.

negative covenants Behaviors and actions that the company may not engage in without the lender's consent as a condition of the loan in a debt deal.

nondisclosure agreement (NDA) An agreement whereby one party promises not to share information of another party.

nonparticipating preferred A simple preferred stock that does not have a participation feature.

no-shop agreement One of the few binding terms in a term sheet, this provision prohibits a company from seeking other investors (unless approved by the term sheet–issuing VC) once a term sheet has been signed.

operating partner A position at a venture capital firm that is normally under managing director, but above principal.

option budget The amount of options a company plans to allocate to employees over a finite time period.

option pool The shares set aside by a company to provide stock options to employees.

outside director   A member of a company's board of directors who is not an executive or major investor of the company.

pari passu   When all classes of preferred stock have equivalent payment rights in a liquidation.

partners   An investment professional at a venture firm that may or may not be an actual "partner" but has some level of deal-evaluation and deal-making authority.

party round   A financing round with many participants, usually at small dollar amounts.

pay-to-play   A term that forces VCs to continue to invest in future company financings or suffer adverse consequences to their ownership positions.

perfected lien   A document that has been filed with the appropriate agency allowing for a legal claim to seize assets if a loan borrower defaults on the loan.

performance warrant   A warrant that is exercisable if certain performance metrics are met by the holder of the warrant.

post-money   The value of a company after an investor has put money into the company.

PowerPoint   Throughout this book, we use PowerPoint to describe presentation software that was originally made famous by Microsoft. Many of the presentations we now see are in Google Docs or Apple Keynote, both competitive products to Microsoft PowerPoint. Oh, and we actually prefer PDF files.

preferred stock   A type of stock that has preferential terms, rights, and privileges compared to common stock.

pre-money   The value ascribed to a company by an investor before investing in the company.

prepayments   The arrangement whereby a borrower can or cannot prepay a loan down before the maturity date. In venture debt, prepayments are generally allowed but may have some additional costs depending on when the prepayment is made.

pre-seed round   The round before a seed round. This term is now used to refer to the very first financing round in a company.

price per share   The dollar amount assigned to purchase one share of stock.

prime rate   A specific reference index that a floating, or variable rate loan, is based on. Most venture loans are indexed to the prime rate, either the prime rate of the bank providing the loan or the published benchmark, such as the prime rate published by the *Wall Street Journal.*

principal   A junior deal partner at a venture capital firm.

private placement memorandum (PPM)   A legal document that is prepared by the company, its bankers, and its lawyers that is a long-form business plan created to solicit investors.

product crowdfunding   An approach to funding product development by using customers to preorder products that was popularized by Kickstarter.

proprietary information and inventions agreement   (also called proprietary rights agreement) This is a contract that should be signed by anyone who works for a company that specifically states that all intellectual property developed by the person is the property of the company. It also will have the person guarantee that they are not using anyone else's intellectual property while working at the company.

pro rata   The right of a shareholder to purchase shares in a future financing equal to the percentage the shareholder currently holds at the time of such financing.

protective provisions   Contractual rights that allow the holders of preferred stock to vote on certain important matters pertaining to a company.

ratchet-based antidilution   A style of antidilution that reprices an investor's shares in previous rounds, usually through a conversion price adjustment, to the price paid in the current round.

redemption rights   The ability of a shareholder to force the company to purchase his or her shares at a previously agreed-upon price.

registration rights   The contractual rights allotted to investors pursuant to a financing that detail the ability of shareholders to force the company to register their shares on a public stock market.

representations and warranties   Provisions in a financing purchase agreement or merger agreement whereby the company makes certain assurances about itself.

reputation constraints   The impact that reputation has on one's behavior.

reserves   The amount of money that a venture capital firm allocates for future investments in a particular portfolio company.

restricted stock units (RSUs)   A substitution for traditional stock options that provides different tax accounting for the company that issues them.

restrictions on sales   A right but not an obligation to purchase shares of another shareholder who wishes to sell.

reverse dilution   The situation in which stock is returned to a company by departed employees whose stock has not vested, thus increasing the effective ownership of all shareholders in a company.

right of first refusal (ROFR)   A right but not an obligation for an investor to participate in future rounds of financing.

right of rescission   The right of shareholders to force the company to buy back their stock, usually given to people who were not supposed to buy the stock in the first place under federal securities law.

runway   The number of months of cash remaining, based on the projected monthly cash burn.

safe   Acronym for "simple agreement for future equity," which is an alternative to the issuance of convertible debt. See www.ycombinator.com/documents/#safe.

safe harbor   A legally defined way of escaping liability under a law if a party performs certain acts as defined by such law.

schedule of exceptions   A list of exceptions to representations and warranties in a venture financing or acquisition agreement.

schmuck insurance   Preferences, including ones that guarantee a return for an investor, especially in a situation where an investor has concerns about overpaying at a particular point in time.

secondary sale   The sale by a VC of stock in a portfolio company or its entire portfolio to an outside party in a private transaction.

security   A financial instrument that represents an ownership right in a company.

seed preferred   Same as a light preferred: A simple watered-down version of a preferred stock financing.

seed rounds   What Series Seed financings used to be called in the old days of venture capital.

seed stage   A startup that is in its infancy.

seed stage funds   VC funds typically focused on being the first institutional money in a company.

Series A financing   The first or early round of financing that a company raises.

Series Seed financing   A small financing that occurs before the Series A financing and is often the very first financing of a company.

simple preferred   A very lightweight preferred stock, usually with only a liquidation preference and minimal rights.

single-play game   A term in game theory that deals with a game or situation in which there is no continuing relationship after the game is played.

single-trigger acceleration   A term used to describe the situation in which a person would receive accelerated vesting.

stacked preference   When different classes of preferred stock have senior rights to payment over other classes of preferred stock.

stock option   A right to purchase shares of stock in a company.

straight line amortization   The principal balance of a loan is divided up equally among the number of payments.

strike price   The price at which a stock option may be exercised.

structure   Multiple liquidation preference or participation in a preferred stock. This is often found in late stage deals.

super angel   A very active and experienced angel investor.

super pro rata rights   The right of shareholders to purchase shares in a future financing equal to some multiple of the percentage they currently hold at the time of such financing.

syndicate   The group of investors who invest in a startup.

term sheet   A summary document of key terms in contemplation of a financing.

transactions costs   The direct and indirect costs (time and money) associated with the creation of a business relationship.

unicorn   A mythical beast that rides on a silver moonbeam and shoots rainbows out of its ass. Also, a private company that has achieved a $1 billion valuation.

valuation   The value ascribed to a company by an investor.

valuation cap   A term in a convertible note deal that sets the maximum conversion price of the debt into equity.

venture capital fund (VC fund)   The entities that make up the investment family of a VC.

venture capitalist (VC)   A person who invests in startup companies.

venture debt   Debt for an equity-backed company that doesn't have the cash flows to support traditional debt.

venture debt fund   A provider of venture debt that is not a bank.

venture partner   A position at a venture capital firm that is normally under managing director, but above principal.

vesting   The notion that a stock award is not earned until some period of time or milestone is reach.

vesting cliff   The length of time required for an employee to be at a company before any of her stock or options vest. This is typically a year.

voting rights   The specific rights of how preferred stock and common stock vote.

walking dead portfolio company   A company that has no growth, no exit opportunities, no financing options, but just enough revenue, cash, or cash flow to stay in business.

warrant   A right to purchase shares of stock in a company.

weighted average antidilution   A style of antidilution that reprices an investor's investment, usually through a conversion price adjustment, to a lower price per share, but considers the relative effect of the number of shares sold in the current round.

zone of insolvency   When a company is nearly insolvent and doesn't have the assets to pay off its liabilities.

About the Authors

Brad Feld (brad@foundrygroup.com, @bfeld, www.feld.com) is a cofounder and managing director of Foundry Group (www.foundrygroup.com), a Boulder, Colorado–based venture capital fund. Foundry Group invests in technology companies all over the United States and Canada. It also invests in the next generation of venture fund managers.

Prior to cofounding Foundry Group, Brad cofounded Mobius Venture Capital and, prior to that, founded Intensity Ventures, a company that helped launch and operate software companies.

Brad is also a cofounder of Techstars and has coauthored several books, including *Do More Faster, Startup Communities, Startup Life, Startup Boards*, and *Startup Opportunities*.

In addition to his investing efforts, Brad and his wife, Amy Batchelor, run the Anchor Point Foundation (www.anchorpointfoundation .org), which helps nonprofit organizations and leaders creatively solve problems in their communities around the world. Brad is a nationally recognized speaker on the topics of venture capital investing and entrepreneurship and writes blogs at www.feld.com, www.venturedeals.com, and www.startuprev.com.

Brad holds bachelor of science and master of science degrees in management science from the Massachusetts Institute of Technology. He is also an avid art collector and long-distance runner, having completed 25 marathons as part of his mission to run a marathon in each of the 50 states in America.

* * *

Jason Mendelson (jason@foundrygroup.com, @jasonmendelson) is also a cofounder and managing director of Foundry Group.

Prior to cofounding Foundry Group, Jason was a cofounder of SRS Acquiom, the leading platform to manage escrows, payments, risk documents, and claims on M&A transactions. Jason was also a managing director and general counsel for Mobius Venture Capital, where he acted as its chief administrative partner, overseeing all operations of the firm.

Prior to his involvement with Mobius Venture Capital, Jason was an attorney with Cooley LLP, where he practiced corporate and securities law with an emphasis on representing emerging companies in private and public financings, mergers, and acquisitions. As an attorney, Jason has consummated over $2 billion of venture capital investments, $5 billion in mergers, and had extensive experience in fund formation, employment law, and general litigation, serving as an expert witness in these related fields.

Before his legal career, Jason was a senior consultant and software engineer at Accenture.

As one of the first full-time, in-house general counsels at a venture capital firm, Jason has been at the forefront of thought leadership around venture capital. He has co-chaired the National Venture Capital Association's (NVCA) General Counsel group and has been an active participant on the NVCA's Chief Financial Officer group. He was one of the key draftspersons for the NVCA model document task force, which created the venture capital industry's first set of standardized financing documents, which greatly aided efficiency of completing venture capital deals. He previously sat on the executive board of the NVCA.

Jason holds a bachelor of arts degree in economics, and a juris doctorate from the University of Michigan. He is an active musician, playing drums and bass guitar in several bands, most recently Legitimate Front (www.legitimatefront.com). He enjoys home remodeling, food, and travel. Jason used to blog about his experiences in the venture capital industry on his blog at www.jasonmendelson.com but got tired of it several years ago and stopped. Hit him up on Twitter @jasonmendelson.

Brad and Jason have worked together for 20 years and intend to be business partners for the duration of their working lives.

Index

EXCERPT FROM

STARTUP COMMUNITIES

CHAPTER THREE

PRINCIPLES OF A VIBRANT STARTUP COMMUNITY

Now that you've had an introduction to Boulder and its history from my point of view, I'd like to describe the principles that drive the Boulder startup community, which I'll call the Boulder Thesis. First, however, I'll discuss the three historical frameworks that have been used to describe why some cities become vibrant startup communities.

Historical Frameworks

The investigation into startup communities is among the most important inquiries of our time. Why do some places flourish with innovation while others wither? What are the determinants that help a startup community achieve critical startup mass? Once under way, how does a startup community sustain and expand entrepreneurship? Why do startup communities persist, despite often having higher real estate costs and wages than other areas? At stake is nothing less than the continued economic vitality, and even the very existence of towns, cities, and regions.

Studies show that the geography of innovation is neither democratic nor flat. This may be surprising since you might think that location should matter less than ever in today's society. Information can be quickly sent and received by anyone from almost anywhere. In theory, expanding access to resources and information from anywhere might decouple the relationship between place and innovation.

Economic geographers, however, observe the opposite effect. Evidence suggests that location, rather than being irrelevant, is more important than ever. Innovation tilts heavily toward certain locations and, as scholar Richard Florida (professor at Rotman School of Management, at the University of Toronto and author of *The Rise of the Creative Class* [2002]) says, is "spiky" with great concentration of creative, innovative people in tightly clustered geographies. Location clearly matters.

Three prominent frameworks explain why some locales are hotbeds of entrepreneurship whereas others are the innovation equivalent of a twenty-first century economic mirage. Each explanation of regional entrepreneurial advantage comes from a different discipline—one from economics, another from sociology, and a third from geography. These explanations are, for the most part, nonexclusive and complementary.

The first explanation, *external or agglomeration economies,* comes from economics. This line of analysis reaches back to the research of economist Alfred Marshall, and, in recent decades, Michael Porter, Paul Krugman, and Paul Romer have deepened this account. External economies focus on the benefits of startup concentration in an area. This explanation focuses on economic concepts as they apply to location. One is that companies co-located in an area benefitting from "external economies of scale." Emerging companies need certain common inputs—for example, infrastructure, specialized legal and accounting services, suppliers, labor pools with a specialized knowledge base—that reside outside the company. Companies in a common geographic area share the fixed costs of these resources external to the company. As more and more startups in an area can share the costs of specialized inputs, the average cost per startup drops for the specialized inputs. This provides direct economic benefit to companies located within a startup community.

Another economic concept, *network effects,* explains why geographic concentration yields further advantage. Network effects operate in systems where the addition of a member to a network enhances value for existing users. The Internet, Facebook, and Twitter are examples in which network effects operate powerfully. These services may have some value to you if there are just 100 other users. However, these networks are immensely more useful if there are 100 million other users that you can connect with. Startup communities similarly feature strong network effects. For example, an area with 10 great programmers provides a valuable pool of labor talent for a startup. However, an additional 1,000 amazing programmers in the same area is vastly more valuable to startups, especially if programmers share best practices with other programmers, inspire one another, or start new companies. External economies of scale lower certain costs; meanwhile, network effects make co-location more valuable.

The second explanation of startup communities, *horizontal networks,* comes from sociology. In her PhD work at MIT, AnnaLee Saxenian (currently Dean of the UC Berkeley School of Information) noticed that external economies do not fully explain the development and adaptation of startup communities. In particular, in her seminal book *Regional Advantage: Culture and Competition in Silicon Valley and Route 128* (1994), Saxenian noted that two hotbeds for high-tech activity—Silicon Valley and Boston's Route 128—looked very similar in the mid-1980s. Each area enjoyed agglomeration economies associated with the nations' two high-tech regions. Yet just a decade later, Silicon Valley gained a dominant advantage over Route 128. External economies alone did not provide an answer. Saxenian set out to resolve the puzzle of why Silicon Valley far outpaced Route 128 from the mid-1980s to mid-1990s.

Saxenian persuasively argues that a culture of openness and information exchange fueled Silicon Valley's ascent over Route 128. This argument is tied to network effects, which are better leveraged by a community with a culture of information sharing across companies and industries. Saxenian observed that the porous boundaries between Silicon Valley companies, such as Sun Microsystems and HP, stood in stark contrast to the closed-loop and autarkic companies of Route 128, such as DEC and Apollo. More broadly, Silicon Valley's culture embraced a horizontal exchange of information across and between companies. Rapid technological disruption played perfectly to Silicon Valley's culture of open information exchange and labor mobility. As technology quickly changed, the Silicon Valley companies were better positioned to share information, adopt new trends, leverage innovation, and nimbly respond to new conditions. Meanwhile, vertical integration and closed systems disadvantaged many Route 128 companies during periods of technological upheaval. Saxenian highlights the role of a densely networked culture in explaining Silicon Valley's successful industrial adaptation as compared to Route 128.

Finally, the third explanation of startup communities, the notion of the *creative class,* comes from geography. Richard Florida describes the tie between innovation and creative-class individuals. The creative class is composed of individuals such as entrepreneurs, engineers, professors, and artists who create "meaningful new forms." Creative-class individuals, Florida argues, want to live in nice places, enjoy a culture with a tolerance for new ideas and weirdness, and—most of all—want to be around other creative-class individuals. This is another example of network effects, because a virtuous cycle exists where the existence of a creative class in an area attracts more creative-class individuals to the area, which in turn makes the area even more valuable and attractive. A location that hits critical mass enjoys a competitive geographic advantage over places that have yet to attract a significant number of creative-class individuals.

Each of the three explanations just outlined provides a useful lens to understand why the entrepreneurial world has concentrations of startup communities in specific geographies. They are incomplete, however, concerning how to put a startup community into motion. There is a serious chicken and egg problem; although it is not difficult to see why innovation havens have an advantage, it is more challenging to explain how to get a startup community up and running.

The Boulder Thesis

I suggest a fourth framework based on our experience in Boulder. Let's call it the Boulder Thesis. This framework has four key components:

1. Entrepreneurs must lead the startup community.
2. The leaders must have a long-term commitment.
3. The startup community must be inclusive of anyone who wants to participate in it.
4. The startup community must have continual activities that engage the entire entrepreneurial stack.

Led by Entrepreneurs

The most critical principle of a startup community is that entrepreneurs must lead it. Lots of different people are involved in the startup community and many nonentrepreneurs play key roles. Unless the entrepreneurs lead, the startup community will not be sustainable over time.

In virtually every major city, there are long lists of different types of people and organizations who are involved in the startup community including government, universities, investors, mentors, and service providers. Historically, many of these organizations try to play a leadership role in the development of their local startup community. Although their involvement is important, they can't be the leaders. The entrepreneurs have to be leaders.

I define an entrepreneur as someone who has cofounded a company. I differentiate between "high-growth entrepreneurial companies" and "small businesses." Both are important, but they are different things. Entrepreneurial companies have the potential to be or are high-growth businesses whereas small businesses tend to be local, profitable, but slow-growth organizations. Small-business people are often "pillars of their community" as their businesses have a tight codependency with their community. By contrast, founders of high-growth entrepreneurial companies generally are involved in the local community as employers and indirect contributors to small businesses and the local economy, but they rarely are involved in the broad business community because they are extraordinarily focused on their companies.

Because of this intense focus, it's unrealistic to think that all entrepreneurs in a community will be leaders. All that is needed is a critical mass of entrepreneurs, often fewer than a dozen, who will provide leadership.

Long-Term Commitment

These leaders have to make a long-term commitment to their start-up community. I like to say this has to be at least 20 years from today to reinforce the sense that this has to be meaningful in length. Optimally, the commitment resets daily; it should be a forward-looking 20-year commitment.

It's well understood that economies run in cycles. Economies grow, peak, decline, bottom out, grow again, peak again, decline again, and bottom out again. Some of these cycles are modest. Some are severe. The lengths vary dramatically.

Startup communities have to take a very long-term view. A great startup community such as Silicon Valley (1950–today) has a long trajectory. Although they have their booms and busts, they continued to grow, develop, and expand throughout this period of time.

Most cities and their leaders get excited about entrepreneurship after a major economic decline. They focus on it for a few years through a peak. When the subsequent decline ultimately happens, they focus on other things during the downturn. When things bottom out, most of the progress gained during the upswing was lost. I've seen this several times—first in the early 1990s and again around the time of the dot-com bubble. All you have to do is think back to the nickname of your city during the Internet bubble (Silicon Alley, Silicon Swamp, Silicon Slopes, Silicon Prairie, Silicon Gulch, and Silicon Mountain) to remember what it was like before and after the peak.

This is why the leaders have to first be entrepreneurs and then have a long-term view. These leaders must be committed to the continuous development of their startup community, regardless of the economic cycle their city, state, or country is in. Great entrepreneurial companies, such as Apple, Genentech, Microsoft, and Intel, were started during down economic cycles. It takes such a long time to create something powerful that, almost by definition, you'll go through several economic cycles on the path to glory.

If you aspire to be a leader of your startup community, but you aren't willing to live where you are for the next 20 years and work hard at leading the startup community for that period of time, ask yourself what your real motivation for being a leader is. Although you can have impact for a shorter period of time, it'll take at least this level of commitment from some leaders to sustain a vibrant startup community.

Foster a Philosophy of Inclusiveness

A startup community must be extremely inclusive. Anyone who wants to engage should be able to, whether they are changing careers, moving to your city, graduating from college, or just want to do something different. This applies to entrepreneurs, people who want to work for startups, people who want to work with startups, or people who are simply intellectually interested in startups.

This philosophy of inclusiveness applies at all levels of the startup community. The leaders have to be open to having more leaders involved, recognizing that leaders need to be entrepreneurs who have a long-term view of building their startup community. Entrepreneurs in the community need to welcome other entrepreneurs, viewing the growth of the startup community as a positive force for all, rather than a zero-sum game in which new entrepreneurs compete locally for resources and status. Employees of startups need to recruit their friends and open their homes and city to other people who have moved into the community.

Everyone in the startup community should have a perspective that having more people engaged in the startup community is good for the startup community. Building a startup community is not a zero-sum game in which there are winners and losers; if everyone engages, they and the entire community can all be winners.

Engage the Entire Entrepreneurial Stack

Startup communities must have regular activities that engage the entire entrepreneurial stack. This includes first-time entrepreneurs, experienced entrepreneurs, aspiring entrepreneurs, investors, mentors, employees of startups, service providers to startups, and anyone else who wants to be involved.

Over the years, I've been to many entrepreneurial award events, periodic cocktail parties, monthly networking events, panel discussions, and open houses. Although these types of activities have a role, typically in shining a bright light on the people doing good things within the startup community, they don't really engage anyone in any real entrepreneurial activity.